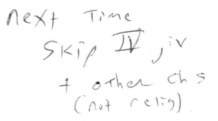

Jean-Jacques Rousseau

On the Social Contract

WITH **Geneva Manuscript**
AND **Political Economy**

next Time
skip IV, iv
+ other ch s
(not relig).

On The Social Contract

WITH **Geneva Manuscript**
AND **Political Economy**

Jean-Jacques Rousseau

Edited by Roger D. Masters
Translated by Judith R. Masters

Bedford/St. Martin's   Boston 🖙 New York

Cover design: Deborah Prymas

Library of Congress Catalog Card Number:
Copyright © 1978 by St. Martin's Press, Inc.
All Rights Reserved.
Manufactured in the United States of
America.
2 1 0 9
n m l k
For information, write: Bedford/St. Martin's,
75 Arlington Street, Boston MA   02116
(617-426-7440)

Paper ISBN: 0–312–69446–6
Cloth ISBN: 0–312–69445–8

EDITOR'S PREFACE

This volume brings together three major statements of the political thought of Jean-Jacques Rousseau. *Political Economy*, an article published in 1755 (in Volume V of the *Encyclopédie* edited by Diderot and d'Alembert), contains Rousseau's first explicit use of the concept of the "general will." The *Geneva Manuscript*, or first draft of the *Social Contract* (whose date is uncertain, but in its extant form must be after January 1756), includes important material deleted from the definitive version of the *Social Contract* (which was published in 1762).

The book attempts to meet three goals. First, to provide an exact translation of Rousseau's *Social Contract;* second, to make available the first complete English translation of the *Geneva Manuscript* as well as a version of the *Political Economy;* third, to offer in the Introduction and editorial footnotes useful background information and an explanation of references that might otherwise be unclear. In short, the book is designed as a critical edition which combines a reliable new translation with material not hitherto available in English.

Several editorial practices follow from these objectives. So that the reader will be as close as possible to Rousseau's original, the translations are literal—like those in our edition of the *First and Second Discourses* (St. Martin's Press, 1964); terms are rendered to produce as much consistency between editions as possible. While seeking to provide a readable English version, we have tried to avoid editorial interpretations that would mask Rousseau's meaning. No attempt has been made to follow Rousseau's punctuation, however, since such a practice would substitute pedantry for common sense.

Wherever a passage of the *Geneva Manuscript* appears in either *Political Economy* or the final version of the *Social Contract,* material has been translated in exactly the same way insofar as the French texts are identical. Every effort has been made to modify *only* those words or phrases which Rousseau himself changed in revising his manuscripts. Since editorial notes indicate the location of all repeated sections, interested readers can compare texts and judge for themselves the importance of Rousseau's revisions.

It has been said that Rousseau's ideas evolved and changed from one of these works to another. Although Rousseau's own statements contradict such an interpretation, the evidence should be judged impartially. As a result, this edition provides an all-too-rare possibility to follow, in English, the elaboration of one of the great classics of Western political thought.

To this end, the original text of the *Political Economy* is used, with changes in later editions indicated in the editorial notes. In the texts included here, therefore, the *Political Economy* represents Rousseau's position in 1755; the *Geneva Manuscript* is clearly a little later; and the *Social Contract* incorporates Rousseau's final corrections, first published in the posthumous edition of 1782.

This edition thus makes possible historical analysis based on an English translation. It is, however, my own opinion that the *Political Economy, Geneva Manuscript,* and *Social Contract* reflect changes of expression rather than substantive differences or inconsistencies. For this reason, the detailed history of these works' composition is discussed only in editorial notes (see *Political Economy,* editorial note 1; *Social Contract,* editorial note 4; and Introduction, note 47).

In any event, many readers will be primarily interested in the *Social Contract,* since it represents the definitive statement of Rousseau's political teaching. For this reason, the Introduction will focus on Rousseau's most famous work of political thought, while indicating how it relates to both the *Geneva Manuscript* and *Political Economy.* This general concern also explains why the texts are presented in reverse chronological order: *Social Contract, Geneva Manuscript,* and *Political Economy.*

The Introduction and editorial notes owe an enormous debt to other scholars who have edited Rousseau's political writings. In particular, this edition would have been either simply impossible or greatly impoverished had it not been possible to consult and profit from the following editions of the French text:

JEAN-JACQUES ROUSSEAU, *Oeuvres Complètes* (4 vols. to date: Éditions de la Pléiade; Paris: Gallimard, 1959–1969)—cited as "Pléiade" followed by volume and page.

This critical edition, which is generally taken as a definitive text, has been the basis for our translation. The editor of the two versions of the *Social Contract* and *Political Economy,* which appear in Vol.

III, is Robert Derathé; his extensive editorial notes are a mine of valuable information and have been frequently utilized.

JEAN-JACQUES ROUSSEAU, *Political Writings*, ed. C. E. Vaughan (2 vols.: Oxford: Blackwell, 1915)—cited as "Vaughan" followed by volume and page.

Prior to the publication of Vol. III of the Pléiade edition, Vaughan's text was authoritative; his edition—reprinted in 1962—remains extremely useful. Our translation was, therefore, thoroughly collated with Vaughan's text as well as with that of Derathé in the Pléiade.

JEAN-JACQUES ROUSSEAU, *Oeuvres Complètes*, ed. Michel Launay (2 vols. to date, Collection "l'Intégrale"; Paris: Seuil, 1967–1971)—cited as "Launay" followed by volume and page.

The most recent French edition of Rousseau's complete works. In addition to a number of texts that are not generally available (such as the first draft of *Political Economy* and contemporary criticisms of Rousseau's *Discourses*), Launay's edition is graced by numerous eighteenth-century illustrations.

JEAN-JACQUES ROUSSEAU, *Du Contrat Social*, ed. Ronald Grimsley (Oxford: Clarendon Press, 1972)—cited as "ed. Grimsley."

An excellent recent edition, with a thoughtful introduction and many notes.

JEAN-JACQUES ROUSSEAU, *Du Contrat Social*, ed. Bertrand de Jouvenel (Éditions du Cheval Ailé; Geneva: Constant Bourquin, 1947)—cited as "ed. de Jouvenel."

An excellent edition, with notes that include Voltaire's marginalia on his copy of the *Social Contract;* de Jouvenel's Introductory "Essai sur la Politique de Rousseau" is valuable.

JEAN-JACQUES ROUSSEAU, *Du Contrat Social*, ed. Maurice Halbwachs (Paris: Éditions Montaigne, 1943)—cited as "ed. Halbwachs."

A careful edition with excellent notes and commentaries on each chapter.

JEAN-JACQUES ROUSSEAU, *Du Contrat Social*, ed. C. E. Vaughan (Modern Language Texts; Manchester: University Press, 1918)—cited as "ed. Vaughan."

Vaughan's own text of the *Social Contract*, republished from vol. II of *Political Writings*, with the addition of extensive critical notes in English.

In addition, we have sometimes consulted the English translations of the *Social Contract* or *Political Economy* edited by Frederick Watkins (*Rousseau—Political Writings*, London: Nelson, 1953); Maurice Cranston (Harmondsworth, Eng.: Penguin Books, 1968); Charles Frankel (New York:

Hafner, 1947); G. D. H. Cole (Everyman's Library; New York: E. P. Dutton, 1950); the revision of Cole's edition by J. H. Brumfitt and John C. Hall (Everyman's Library; New York: E. P. Dutton, 1973); Charles M. Sherover (Meridian Books; New York: New American Library, 1974); Lester B. Crocker (New York: Washington Square Press, 1967). References to the foregoing—and to Watkin's translations of *Considerations on the Government of Poland* and *Constitutional Project for Corsica*—follow the format "ed. Watkins" and page. In the same way, reference is made to the excellent translations of Rousseau's *Letter to d'Alembert* by Allan Bloom (*Politics and the Arts*, Glencoe, Ill.: Free Press, 1960), and of Rousseau's *Essay on the Origin of Languages* by John Moran (in *On the Origin of Language, ed.* John Moran and Alexander Gode, New York: Frederick Ungar, 1966).

No attempt has been made to provide a bibliography of critical works on Rousseau's political thought. Instead, examples of recent interpretations are cited in the notes to the Introduction. On a number of occasions, I have taken the liberty of citing my own commentary, *The Political Philosophy of Rousseau* (Princeton, N.J.: Princeton University Press, 1968), which contains an annotated bibliography of secondary works to that date (pp. 445–457).

Thanks are due to Dartmouth College for a Humanities Development Grant which helped finance the leave during which final editorial work was undertaken. Need it be added that it has been a continuous pleasure for the editor to work with the translator? While I take full responsibility for all errors that remain, this edition would never have been started, let alone completed, without her many labors.

Roger D. Masters

CONTENTS

INTRODUCTION

The *Social Contract* by Jean-Jacques Rousseau, like Plato's *Republic* and Machiavelli's *Prince*, is one of a small shelf of books that form the tradition of Western political thought. Such works are often called "classics." There is a presumption that anyone with a liberal education will have studied them—or at least will be familiar with the ideas and arguments that they contain. Since such books are so famous, each generation should reexamine them with an open mind.

Before reading this book, therefore, three questions should be raised. First, why is the *Social Contract* a "classic" in the history of political theory? Second, what are its main contributions to our understanding of politics? And third, how do the time and place of its composition, as well as the personality of its author, illuminate the text? The answers should help situate the *Social Contract*, especially for those who have never studied it, and explain the importance of Rousseau's first draft—the so-called *Geneva Manuscript*—which has never before been completely translated into English.

WHY IS THE SOCIAL CONTRACT A CLASSIC?

Why read the *Social Contract*? What has made this book, first published in 1762, one of the "great books" of our tradition? The answer depends on the ways any work of art, literature, or philosophy can become famous in its genre. Let us therefore survey the possible reasons for calling something a "classic" and consider how they apply to Rousseau's analysis of what he calls "The Principles of Political Right."

Educational Tradition

The word "classic" once meant the books that were used in *classes* in schools. Since the curriculum in the West was for centuries based on Greek and Roman antiquity, by extension the "classics" were the writings of ancient authors like Homer, Plato, Aristotle, Cicero, and Horace. After the Renaissance, the term was applied to conscious imitations of the style or subject matter of ancient literature and art. More recently, any work that is somehow "great" has been considered a "classic."

Although the *Social Contract* was obviously not written in antiquity, the example of Greece and Rome was—as we shall see—of profound importance for Rousseau's political thought.[1] In the narrow sense of having been inspired by ancient models, therefore, the *Social Contract* might be called a "classic" work. But since we no longer read many works by ancient Greeks and Romans, not to mention more modern authors imitating them, the influence of classical antiquity on Rousseau is not enough to explain the fame of his book or the reasons for studying it.

Perhaps it is enough to return to the first meaning of the word: Isn't Rousseau a "classic" author precisely because he is studied in so many "classes"? While this reasoning is not entirely foolish, a moment's reflection will indicate that it is insufficient. Either this justification is completely circular, or it implies that what is important to study is merely the result of chance and fashion.

Without denying that accident plays a role in the process by which some become famous and others forgotten, this can hardly account for the perennial interest in that small shelf of books forming the Western tradition. To be sure, there are fads in education. But these changing methods and concepts do not seem to explain why authors like Plato, Machiavelli, and Rousseau have been assigned, year in and year out, to generations of students. There must be something special about the works of art, philosophy, and literature that we call "classics" because of their lasting importance.

Historical Impact

Some novels, poems, plays, paintings, and musical compositions are famous because of their historical effects, either in the development of an art form or on political events in society as a whole. The *Social Contract* can lay claim to historical importance in both respects. Not only did it have considerable political impact in the late eighteenth century (especially as one of the texts inspiring many French revolutionaries), but also it has continued to influence political thinkers to our own day.

Although the *Social Contract* was one of the least-read works of Rousseau until 1788 (the year before the Bastille was stormed), its fame was insured by revolutionaries like Robespierre who quoted "the divine Jean-Jacques" to justify their actions, as well as by conservatives who blamed him for the revolution's excesses.[2] However one measures historical influence, Rousseau's *Social Contract* would have to be included in any list of the epoch-making books about politics that were written in the last three centuries.

Similarly, Rousseau's place as a major figure in the field of political philosophy is beyond question. References to the *Social Contract* and to its leading concepts (notably the "general will") are so frequent that, without knowing Rousseau, it would be difficult to claim a profound understanding of such diverse theorists as Kant, Hegel, Marx, or Durkheim—not to mention more recent writers like John Rawls. Hence Rousseau's importance as a figure in European history could readily justify including the *Social Contract* among those books which one "ought" to have read.

Style and Organization

The word "classic" can also refer to a model exemplifying the best way of practicing an art. Rousseau's writing is of such clarity and beauty that he is regularly included in the study of French literature. For evidence that this appreciation is well founded, one need go no further than the beginning of Book I, chapter i of the *Social Contract: "L'homme est né libre, et partout il est dans les fers"*—"Man is born free, and everywhere he is in chains." This sentence, famous as a ringing assertion of human freedom, is also an impressive example of stylistic power.

Experience teaches how difficult it is to master the art of writing. Not only does each sentence have to be properly formed, but it must fit into a coherent structure of the work as a whole. Rousseau gave careful thought to such matters, as we can see from the first draft or *Geneva Manuscript.*

For example, the famous sentence just quoted was originally: *"L'homme est né libre, et cependant partout il est dans les fers."*—"Man is born free, and nevertheless everywhere he is in chains."[3] In revising his manuscript for publication, Rousseau deleted *"cependant"* ("yet" or "nevertheless"). Although seemingly insignificant, note how this change increases the impact of the sentence: by removing a superfluous word, Rousseau heightens the contradiction between man's natural freedom and his current slavery. At the same time, the deletion improves the rhythm and melody of the phrase. Great writing is based on attention to such details.

In addition to providing a model of concise style, the *Social Contract* has impressive breadth and coherent organization. Here too, the effectiveness of the final version was enhanced by Rousseau's revisions of the *Geneva Manuscript.* Would the sentence we have discussed be as powerful if it had remained in the third chapter of Book I, as in the earlier draft? By removing the long discussion of Diderot's conception of natural right, which originally comprised Book I, chapter ii, Rousseau was able to use his explosive statement of principle as an introduction, thereby capturing the reader's attention from the outset.[4]

Comparison of the original and published versions of the *Social Contract* thus confirms the traditional view of Rousseau as one of the greatest writers of the eighteenth century. But even those who only read the final text will be amply rewarded. Everyone can benefit from knowing how to express thoughts clearly and incisively, and there is no better encouragement for so doing than the example of the best writers of the past. Both in style and in organization, therefore, the *Social Contract* can legitimately claim to be a "classic."

Ideas and Concepts

Educational tradition, historical importance, and literary excellence can explain why a book is called great and may even justify our reading it. But it would be strange indeed if these were the only—or even the most important—reasons for studying a philosophic text. If it contains no ideas of intrinsic merit, other considerations are not likely to motivate us.

At this level, Rousseau's *Social Contract* contains several of the most vigorous—and vigorously debated—ideas in modern times. Most notable, of course, is the "general will" (*volonté générale*) which for many is almost synonymous with Rousseau. But he also transformed the meaning of such terms as "right," "freedom," "government," "sovereign," "law," and "citizen"—not to mention the concept used as the title of his book.

These ideas will be defined and explained when summarizing Rousseau's contribution to political thought later in this Introduction. For the moment, it is enough to say that we would learn a great deal from Rousseau's concepts even if he had not so profoundly influenced modern political thought. Since the *Social Contract* compels us to rethink the fundamental ideas which are conventionally used to justify political action (or inaction), in this sense too it could be called a "classic."

Originality of Conceptual System

A final category of "classics," at least in philosophical matters, consists of works which present the most significant and memorable answers to perennial questions. Most discussions focus on one or two presumably basic problems, studied in isolation. For some, the issue is individualism versus collectivism; for others, the rights of property versus the needs of the poor. Thinkers can be classified as democrats or monarchists, as materialists or idealists, as revolutionaries or traditionalists. Since the French Revolution the "left-right" dichotomy has been used to separate liberals or radicals from conservatives.

These conventional categories fail to do justice to the complexity of different viewpoints. For example, the word "liberal," which today refers to the *left* in the United States, usually designates a position on the *right* or *center* in Europe. But far from proving that there are no perennial issues, such difficulties illustrate the need to identify more carefully the basic dimensions along which political ideas differ.

Attitudes toward human nature and history are especially important. Every political theorist must consider at least two fundamental issues: "What is human nature?" and "What is history?" The answers to these two questions tend to determine one's general approach to politics. It could be argued, therefore, that a "classic" thinker is one who represents—with exceptional clarity—a particular combination of views concerning human nature and history.

Some thinkers describe human nature as essentially selfish or individualistic. Others assert that cooperation and social life are natural to our species. On the one hand, society is merely a conventional or customary means to satisfy the private interests of individuals. On the other, since society itself is primary or natural, the common good is a standard for judging individual interests or rights. Although such attitudes toward human nature are sometimes described as "pessimism" versus "optimism," clearly they should be distinguished from the expectation that historical change will improve political life. Regardless of one's view of human nature, the second issue can also be answered with "optimism" (progress is possible or likely) or with "pessimism" (change is often if not always for the worse).

Answers to these two questions can thus be combined in at least four different ways. For some thinkers, like Machiavelli and Hobbes, men are "wretched" or selfish (i.e., human nature is essentially egoistic and unreliable), but with the proper leadership one can improve political institutions here on earth; indeed, Hobbes goes so far as to assert that, using his science, one can construct virtually eternal political institutions.[5] Other political philosophers shared the view that human beings are naturally selfish, but deny that historical progress is likely. To cite the most important example, this combination of principles is clearly articulated by the pre-Socratic thinkers generally known as the Sophists and forcefully represented by Thrasymachus in Plato's *Republic*.

Alternatively, one can assert that human cooperation is at least as naturally (or historically) fundamental as conflict and selfishness. This view is combined with a basic optimism toward the possibility of social improvement by Karl Marx, whereas it coincides with a tendency to question historical "progress" in the great tradition of Plato and Aristotle.

This characterization of Western political philosophy is very sketchy, and its adequacy can only be judged in a fuller exposition.[6] But these brief remarks should be enough to suggest that political thought can be studied in terms of a finite number of basic options. And if political theorists address the same questions about human nature and history, does Rousseau present a significant and unique combination of positions on the fundamental issues? I believe that the answer is yes—and that, more than any other single factor, this explains why the *Social Contract* is a "classic." Since the evidence for this interpretation lies in Rousseau's contribution to our understanding of politics, let us turn to the second main question of this Introduction.

WHAT DOES THE SOCIAL CONTRACT TEACH US?

It has been suggested that all political thought must answer a number of basic questions, among which are a definition of human nature and an attitude toward historical progress. When considered on these two dimensions, Rousseau's *Social Contract* articulates a distinct and important position in political philosophy. From this perspective, it will be easier to define his main concepts and explain the numerous controversies that have divided Rousseau's critics over the years.

Human Nature and Social Convention

Attitudes toward this dimension of political thought have been described in terms of a simple dichotomy. To some, like Machiavelli, Hobbes, or Thrasymachus (sometimes called "pessimistic" observers of human nature), men are selfish. To others, like Plato, Aristotle, or Marx, social life and cooperation are natural. Rousseau was perfectly aware of the importance of this issue. As he puts it in the *Discourse on the Origin of Inequality* (usually called the *Second Discourse*), a scientific approach to "the nature of man" is "the only means we have left to remove a multitude of difficulties that hide from us knowledge of the real foundations of human society."[7]

Published in 1755, the *Second Discourse* contains an evolutionary approach to human history which is all the more remarkable in that it was written fully a century before Darwin. According to Rousseau, humans originally lived in an animal condition not unlike that of the chimpanzees and baboons described by early European travelers to Africa. He therefore insists that the perennial issue of human nature be approached with the best scientific evidence of human evolution, and not merely be treated as a subject of armchair speculation or religious dogma.

In the *Second Discourse*, Rousseau concludes that civilization could not possibly be "natural" to our species. Since the "primitive" tribes or "savage societies" encountered by Europeans when they discovered Africa and America did not have highly developed governments, written laws, and extensive wealth, civilized life must have resulted from historical evolution. We take this observation to be self-evident, but it was not always so. Indeed, Rousseau's contribution to evolutionary thought was so great that he has been called a founder of modern anthropology and sociology.[8]

But the *Second Discourse* goes further. If civilized societies are not natural, our original condition must have been that of an animal. And if society itself resulted from evolution, this animal could not have been endowed with language. Rousseau therefore concludes that the "state of nature"—the condition of men before the foundation of civil societies—was that of a dumb animal who did not recognize legal or moral obligations to others: "wandering in the forests, without industry, without speech, without domicile, without war and without liaisons, with no need of his fellow-men, likewise with no desire to harm them."⁹

This celebrated image of the state of nature rejects both definitions of human nature that had dominated the Western tradition. Machiavelli, Hobbes, and Thrasymachus were wrong to describe humans as naturally evil or aggressive; for Rousseau, man is by nature "good." But Plato, Aristotle, and the natural law tradition were also wrong to say that human society, cooperation, and the obligation to help others are natural to the species; for Rousseau, men are by nature isolated and solitary. As Rousseau later put it, all of his works are based on the "great principle that nature made man happy and good, but that society depraves him and makes him miserable."¹⁰

Rousseau's conception of human nature and social cooperation is thus a well-thought-out attempt to resolve an issue that had divided Western philosophers for centuries. Since men were originally isolated, he agrees with Hobbes that men are basically selfish—but adds that their stupidity and independence prevented this selfishness from taking the form of vanity or wickedness. And since man is naturally good, Rousseau agrees with Plato and Aristotle that there is a natural standard for judging human behavior—only this standard is a minimal one of refraining from uselessly harming others. Because all society is the result of an evolutionary process, the natural definition of "goodness" must be based on instinct or feeling, not reason, and must suit a solitary animal lacking speech and forethought.

This approach to human nature can be restated in terms of two basic concepts: natural freedom and the social contract. First, men are by nature free. Indeed, the absence of any moral, rational, or political laws governing human behavior is a definition of the state of nature; as Rousseau puts it in both the *Second Discourse* and the *Social Contract*, freedom is the "quality of being a man."¹¹ Second, it follows that all social obligations must result from an agreement between individuals who were originally—and who remain in principle—free agents. The technical term for the act which creates a civil society with morally binding laws and duties is the "social contract." Hence the title of Rousseau's most famous work of political philosophy can be read as a shorthand reference to his definition of human nature.

Human History and Political Change

It has been argued that optimism or pessimism toward improvement in the human condition is a dimension of political thought which is distinct from assumptions about human nature. One could put this question as follows: is it possible for human beings to establish a better form of government on earth, or are all changes of regime simply transfers of power from one group to another? As Thrasymachus puts it, is all government merely the "advantage of the stronger" (so that every government benefits some individuals or groups at the expense of others)? Or was Hobbes correct when he asserted that he had discovered a science of government which could solve the political problem in a way that "opposeth no man's profit, nor pleasure"?[12]

More precisely, this issue concerns the extent to which humans can develop a science that "conquers" or "masters" natural scarcity so that the conflicts between rich and poor, powerful and weak, can be overcome to the satisfaction of all. Unlike the first dimension of political thought, which was fully explored by ancient Greek thinkers as well as by the moderns, this second dimension appears to have a historical character in a double sense. That is, whereas there were both "optimists" and "pessimists" about human nature in classical antiquity, attitudes toward human history seem to coincide with the distinction between the ancients and moderns.

By and large, the philosophers of pagan antiquity taught that there were inescapable limits to human "progress." In contrast, modern thinkers from Bacon to Marx viewed the prospects of historical improvement with great optimism, believing that natural science permits a conquest or mastery of nature. Whereas the ancients treated scientific knowledge primarily as a way of understanding or contemplating the world, the moderns foresaw progressive scientific advance making possible a better life on earth. Evidence for this difference between the ancients and moderns is hardly limited to philosophical texts. Whereas there was a fundamental distinction between the arts (*techne*) and theory (*theoria*) or wisdom (*sophia*) in antiquity, the modern combination of science and technology has produced a kind of industrial society unknown in the past.

What Rousseau himself called his "system" of thought was directly addressed to this issue. Late in his life, as noted, Rousseau claimed that all his writings were essentially devoted to the "principle that nature made man happy and good, but that society depraves him and makes him miserable." Nor was this "principle" invented after the fact in order to bring unity to his ideas. In January 1762, shortly before the *Social Contract* was published, Rousseau explained the inspiration for his philosophic career in a now famous letter to Malesherbes:

> I was going to see Diderot, then prisoner at Vincennes; I had in my pocket a *Mercure de France* that I leafed through on the way. I fell on the question of the Academy of Dijon, which gave rise to my first writing. If ever something was like a sudden inspiration, it is the movement which occurred to me at that reading; suddenly I felt my mind dazzled by a thousand lights. . . . Oh Monsieur, if I had ever been able to write a quarter of what I saw and felt under that tree, with what clarity would I have shown all the contradictions of the social system; with what force would I have exposed all the abuses of our institutions, with what simplicity would I have demonstrated that man is naturally good, and that it is by these institutions that men become wicked.[13]

From the outset of his career, therefore, Rousseau was extraordinarily critical of the concept of irreversible "progress."

This view of time is explicit throughout the *Second Discourse*. At most, Rousseau is willing to admit that the historical evolution leading to preliterate or "primitive" society was beneficial; beyond this point, however, history is essentially a process of decline. Speaking of "savage" or uncivilized societies, Rousseau asserts:

> The more one thinks about it, the more one finds that this state was the least subject to revolutions, the best for man, and that he must have come out of it only by some fatal accident, which for the common good ought never to have happened. The example of savages, who have almost all been found at this point, seems to confirm that the human race was made to remain in it always; that this state is the veritable prime of the world; and that all subsequent progress has been in appearance so many steps toward the perfection of the individual, and in fact toward the decrepitude of the species.[14]

Although the contradiction between the individual and the species which concludes this passage deserves further attention, the central point should be clear enough for present purposes.

Rousseau's pessimistic view of history rests on a denial that science could conquer natural scarcity and thereby overcome the conflicts within human societies. Indeed, Rousseau's *Discourse on the Sciences and Arts*—the *First Discourse*, which was composed after the "Illumination of Vincennes" described in the letter to Malesherbes—explicitly attacks the enlightenment project of linking science and technology as a way of improving the human condition. For Rousseau, "advancement in the sciences and arts" has destroyed "virtue" and strengthened "slavery" in "all times and in all places."[15]

In this regard, Rousseau's political thought directly addresses the controversy between the ancients and the moderns—and resolves it by siding with the ancients. This preference is apparently stated in ethical terms:

> I know that our philosophy, always rich in peculiar maxims, holds contrary to the experience of all centuries that luxury produces the splendor of States. . . . What will become of virtue when one must get rich at any price? Ancient political thinkers incessantly talked about morals and virtue, those of our time talk only of business and money.[16]

Behind this concern for "virtue and morals" however, the *First Discourse* presents Rousseau's powerful denunciation of the sciences and arts as instruments for strengthening "thrones" and destroying the "original liberty for which [men] seemed to have been born."[17]

Rousseau's basic concepts of "natural goodness" and "freedom" as the "quality of manhood" thus have two functions. On the one hand, they resolve the perennial question of human nature: society is the result of an agreement or "social compact" between naturally free individuals. On the other hand, Rousseau's notions of "natural goodness" and "freedom" are based on the presumed "state of nature" which existed before civil society corrupted the human species. As a result, he saw history as decay rather than progress. On the second fundamental dimension surveyed here, Rousseau sides with the classics of antiquity against the moderns.

In so doing, however, Rousseau does not simply go back to the position of antiquity. Just as he sought to resolve the age-old debates concerning human egoism versus altruism, suggesting the natural goodness of an isolated but stupid animal as a third alternative, so Rousseau approaches human history by trying to transcend the conflict between traditionalists and partisans of change. Although Rousseau has been accused of contradicting himself, the complexity of his position arises in part because he tries to reconcile the two attitudes toward history that dominated prior political thought.

In this light, the famous opening of Book I, chapter i, of the *Social Contract* is not only a model of stylistic force and concision, but also the summary of Rousseau's political teaching. This is even more evident in the French text, which is—in an important respect—impossible to translate. Rousseau says; *"L'homme est né libre, et partout il est dans les fers."* This could be (and has been) translated into English in two different ways: "Man *is* born free, and everywhere he is in chains" or "Man *was* born free, and everywhere he is in chains."[18]

"Man *was* born free" . . . that is, there were no civil societies, no laws, no obligations binding the first men. And "Man *is* born free" . . . that is, every human being is born with a natural freedom to choose whether or not to obey others. Since "Man *was* born free" in the state of nature, the origin of civilized governments must have been a "social contract" that was freely accepted by every individual. And since "Man *is* born free," no existing government is legitimate without the free consent of the governed.[19]

The revolutionary implications of this conception of human liberty are clear in the second phrase of the sentence: although man was and is by nature free, *"everywhere* he *is* in *chains."* No government on earth is legitimate. Every existing society can be rejected in the name of human nature and freedom. Little wonder that the French revolutionaries revered the author and placed his body in the Pantheon with other national heroes. As one commentator recently put it, the *Social Contract* "is the work of a revolutionary condemning all existing institutions."[20]

It is, however, very misleading to leave an analysis at that. As another scholar has said:

"Over and over again, from his earliest political writings, [Rousseau] shows himself to be a traditionalist, with all the typical traditionalist's belief in the value of habits and institutions tested by time. . . . In the first chapter of the *Social Contract*, he lays down that "social order is a sacred right, the basis of all others," and puts the meaning of the phrase beyond all doubt by presenting it as a refutation of the justification of revolution which he might have offered if he had considered only "force and the effects of force."[21]

Was Rousseau full of contradictions—as has often been claimed? Since he repeatedly denied this charge, it would be unfair to condemn Rousseau's logic before we have understood his text.

Reconsider the famous sentence we have taken as the summary of Rousseau's conception of human nature and history. "Man was/is born free, and everywhere he is in chains." If we use the present tense—and Rousseau does so elsewhere in the *Social Contract*—the phrase is clearly revolutionary, because all humans now living are naturally free and have no reason to continue to bear the "chains" of the governments existing "everywhere." But if we use the past tense—and Rousseau's *Second Discourse* tries to prove that this reading is absolutely essential to an understanding of human nature and society—there has been an irreversible evolution *from* the natural freedom of the state of nature *to* the slavery of civilized society. The first reading is "revolutionary" if not optimistic, the second pessimistic or "traditionalist" with regard to the possibility of historical progress.

In this way, Rousseau responds to the battle of the ancients (who denied that a science of politics could definitively "solve" the perennial tensions of civic life) and moderns (who proclaimed the discovery of just such a science). "Man *was born* free, and *everywhere* he *is* in chains": human evolution reflects an irreversible loss of the innocence, freedom, and goodness of the state of nature. The ancients were, therefore, essentially correct in their view of science as limited in its ability to conquer or master natural necessity. By and large, the trend of history is toward corruption and despotism (as the *First* and *Second Discourses* make clear). "Man *is* born *free, and every*where he is *in chains*": all human beings are, by nature, free. Not only are all existing governments "chains," but in principle these chains can be transformed into "legitimate" institutions.

This double reading is perfectly clear if we now look at the entire first paragraph of Book I, chapter i:

> Man was/is born free, and everywhere he is in chains. One who believes himself the master of others is nonetheless a greater slave than they. How did this change occur? I do not know. What can make it legitimate? I believe I can answer this question.[22]

Even tyrants, kings, and the wealthy—who seem to have power over others—are merely "slaves"; because no one in existing civilized society is free, human history reveals a general trend toward despotism. But since the transition from freedom to slavery had been the explicit theme of the *First* and *Second Discourses*, the *Social Contract* focuses on the very different question: "What can make it [this change] legitimate?" Despite his pessimism with regard to the overall direction of historical evolution,

Rousseau thinks he has an answer which could, at least in principle, combine "justice and utility."[23]

In short, Rousseau's attitude toward historical progress based on scientific knowledge is fundamentally negative over the long run, but is qualified by radical optimism—at least with respect to a few societies—in the short run. This interpretation readily explains the apparent "contradictions" or tensions between evolutionary "pessimism" and revolutionary republicanism which have so often been found in the *Social Contract*.[24] Whereas what Rousseau elsewhere calls his "system" emphasizes the loss of freedom resulting from civilization, the *Social Contract* elaborates the principles which can sometimes provide at least a provisional respite. Although Rousseau's *Émile* and the two *Discourses* were based on the "principle that nature made man happy and good, but society depraves him and makes him miserable," Rousseau's political thought admits that "the social order is a sacred right that serves as a basis for all the others."[25]

Rousseau's attitude toward history, like his conception of human nature, thus goes beyond the simple dichotomy of revolutionary versus conservative. True, he sometimes argues like a traditionalist:

> Most peoples, like men, are docile only in their youth. They become incorrigible as they grow older. Once customs are established and prejudices have taken root, it is a dangerous and foolhardy undertaking to want to reform them.[26]

But Rousseau also emphasizes the "exceptions" in which a people "liberates itself" by revolting against tyranny and setting up a republic:

> There sometimes occur during the lifetime of States violent periods when revolutions have the same effect on peoples as do certain crises on individuals: when horror of the past is equivalent to amnesia, and when the State, set afire by civil war, is reborn so to speak from its ashes and resumes the vigor of youth by escaping from death's clutches. Sparta in the time of Lycurgus and Rome after the Tarquins were like this, and among us so were Holland and Switzerland after the expulsion of the tyrants.[27]

The ancient republics of Sparta and Rome are models which can be used to criticize modern politics—but some modern republics can approximate freedom and legitimacy under conditions that are "rare" and "hard to find all together."[28]

Rousseau's "Principles of Political Right"

Given this outline of Rousseau's novel approach to the perennial questions of human nature and history, the ideas which have helped make him famous may be more readily intelligible. To explain in detail his contributions to our understanding of politics, it is appropriate to begin with the term Rousseau chose for his title.[29]

The "Social Contract"

As has already been remarked, the idea of a "social contract" summarizes the view that civil society results from a voluntary agreement between naturally free and equal individuals. For Rousseau, such a "social contract" has a logic which is as universal as the law of gravity:

> The clauses of this contract are so completely determined by the nature of the act that the slightest modification would render them null and void. So that although they may never have been formally pronounced, they are everywhere the same, everywhere tacitly accepted and recognized, until the social compact is violated, at which point each man recovers his original rights and resumes his natural freedom, thereby losing the conventional freedom for which he renounced it.[30]

Like the law of gravity, these "clauses determined by the nature of the act" of forming a civil society operate fully whether or not men have "formally pronounced them"; like Newton, Rousseau hopes to provide a scientific statement of regularities "that are everywhere the same, everywhere tacitly accepted and recognized."

Rousseau's definition of the social contract is thus based on "principles of political right." By "principles" Rousseau means universally valid "rules" discovered by human reason, explaining why naturally free individuals behave as they do. By "political right" he means standards of obligation or duty, which make it reasonable for one man to obey another. As we will see, Rousseau distinguishes such "principles of political right" from the study of "conveniences" or the "art of politics." In contemporary terms, the idea of the social contract is concerned with theory as distinct from practice.

For Rousseau, "political right"—that is, a legitimate reason for obeying a government and laws, defined in theoretical terms—does not come from "nature." While this was clearly a main conclusion of the *Second Discourse*, Rousseau reviews the grounds for denying that natural rights create social obligations in Book I, chapters i through v of the *Social Contract*. Parental authority, and especially the rights of the father, cannot be used to justify political institutions because the "natural bond" between parents and their children "dissolves" when the young grow up and become "independent" (I, ii). The "right of the strongest" may truly exist in the state of nature, especially when it has degenerated into a state of war, but such a right cannot produce legitimate obedience; "yielding to force is an act of necessity" or "prudence," rather than a "duty," whereas a "right" in the precise sense must create an "obligation" that is rationally binding "by conscience." Hence "might does not make right" (I, iii). By the same logic, slavery cannot be natural—nor can it be a legitimate convention or agreement, since no one could rationally surrender his freedom to anyone else. "To renounce one's freedom is to renounce one's status as a man, the rights of humanity, and even its duties" (I, iv).

Rousseau's redefinition of the "social compact" thus rests on the radical assertion of individual freedom as a basic "natural right." But his conception of society seems at first sight extremely odd, for the social contract is stated in terms of the community rather than the individual:

> Properly understood, all of these clauses [in the social contract] come down to a single one, namely the total alienation of each associate, with all his rights, to the whole community (I, vi).

How could Rousseau, having developed the theory that man is by nature an isolated individual, conclude that the only legitimate society is based on a "total alienation of each associate, with all his rights, to the whole community"? In contrast to the "inalienable" rights claimed in the American Declaration of Independence, doesn't Rousseau's formulation lead to the supremacy of the community over the individual, and therewith to totalitarianism?

Before we condemn Rousseau, on this point as on others, we have to read him carefully and try to follow his thought. It is, after all, possible that he has stated a position which is superior to the views held by his critics. And, although the Declaration of Independence speaks of "inalienable rights," did Rousseau find a flaw in such a concept when he asserted that "if some rights were left to private individuals, . . . the association would necessarily become tyrannical or ineffectual" (I, vi)? In short, the essence of Rousseau's political teaching requires us to reconsider the proper relationship between the "individual" and the "community."

For Rousseau himself, the answer lies in the concept of the general will *(volonté générale)*. In the published version of the text, the first use of the term occurs in Rousseau's definition of the contractual basis of social obligation:

> If, then, everything that is not of the essence of the social compact is set aside, one will find that it can be reduced to the following terms: *Each of us puts his person and all his power in common under the supreme direction of the general will; and in a body we receive each member as an indivisible part of the whole* (I, vi).

But what does this mean? If the "alienation" to the community is "total," how can Rousseau assert that under the general will each individual "obeys only himself and remains as free as before" (I, vi)?

While a full answer presupposes detailed study of the entire *Social Contract*, two crucial points should be stressed here. First, Rousseau was an exponent of popular sovereignty who hated tyranny perhaps more than any other political theorist. Whereas the general will may not be the true basis of political obligation, Rousseau's purpose should not be lost from sight when analyzing his concept. And second, Rousseau seeks "principles of political right" which—to use a phrase from his first draft—define "the idea of the civil state" (*Geneva Manuscript*, I, v). There is somehow a kinship between what Plato called the Ideas or Forms and Rousseau's conception of the "general will." Each of these qualifications deserves emphasis.

The "General Will" and Popular Sovereignty

While the *Social Contract* is often treated as the first book to speak of the "general will," others had used this term before. In the *Second Discourse*, Rousseau describes the "fundamental compact of all government" as an act of "will" in which "the people" has united "all their wills into a single one"— and calls this a "common opinion" (*Second Discourse*, Part 2; ed. Masters, p. 169). One previous discussion of the "general will"—Diderot's article on *Natural Right* in the *Encyclopédie*—is explicitly mentioned by Rousseau in both the *Political Economy* and *Geneva Manuscript*. By tracing Rousseau's disagreement with Diderot through successive texts, therefore, we can gain a more precise understanding of this famous concept.

Diderot's *Natural Right* includes an indirect criticism of Rousseau's *Second Discourse*. For Rousseau, there can be no rational morality in the primitive state of nature. Since man "is obliged to give himself preference" when his preservation is "concerned" (*Second Discourse*, Preface; ed. Masters, p. 96), each individual is the only judge of how to preserve himself. When men begin to reason and acquire wealth, the result is a horrible war of all against all which is only ended by the social contract (*Second Discourse*, Part 2; pp. 156–159).

In reply, Diderot denies that natural right can be defined by an individual in the state of nature; instead, the only legitimate judge of right and wrong is the "entire human species":

> The human species alone ought to decide, because the good of all is the only passion that it has. Individual wills are suspect, they could be good or wicked; but the general will [*volonté générale*] is always good; it has never been mistaken, and it never will be.[31]

For Diderot, the "general will of the human species" is essentially what had been called the *ius gentium* or "law of nations" by the natural law tradition. In this view, any rational man can discover the basis of moral principles by "a pure act of the understanding" (*Natural right*, § ix).

Diderot's article on *Natural Right* was published in Volume V of the *Encyclopédie* (1775). Rousseau's *Political Economy*, which appeared in the same volume, treats Diderot's article as the "source" of the "great and luminous principle" that the "body politic" is a "moral being" guided by the "general will." While not stressing the difference between Diderot's use of the concept and his own, Rousseau thus made it clear that he was taking an existing notion of a "general will of the human species," and transforming it into the "single" or united "will" animating each human society's social contract.[32]

In the *Geneva Manuscript* Rousseau began with an explicit criticism of Diderot's *Natural Right*. The *Second Discourse* had already rejected the traditional view of a "natural law" based on what Diderot calls "a pure act of the understanding"; for Rousseau, such a conception makes it "impossible to understand the law of nature and consequently to obey it without being a great reasoner and a profound metaphysician" (*Second Discourse*, Preface; ed. Masters, p. 94). In Book I, chapter ii of the *Geneva Manuscript,* Rousseau goes further by showing that our species necessarily lives in distinct political societies. The abstract conception of humanity is a philosophic generalization based on prior social experience—and only exists "in the systems of philosophers."

In rejecting Diderot's notion of a "general will of the human species," Rousseau quotes him indirectly:

> The philosopher will send me back to the human race itself, which alone ought to decide because the greatest good of all is the only passion it has. He will tell me that the individual should address himself to the general will in order to find out to what extent he should be man, citizen, subject, father, child, and when it is suitable for him to live and to die (*Geneva Manuscript*, I, ii).

Rousseau replies that this foundation of ethics must answer a basic question: "Doesn't it still remain to be seen how [a rational man's] personal interest requires his submission to the general will?" In other words, the first version of the *Social Contract* began with a careful discussion of Diderot's "general will of the human species," which Rousseau found inadequate because "healthy ideas of natural right and the brotherhood of all men were disseminated rather late" in human history—and hence could not explain the origin of governments and laws (*Geneva Manuscript*, I, ii).

Rousseau was probably wise to delete this chapter from the final version since it presupposed familiarity with Diderot's article on *Natural Right*. But in revising the *Social Contract* for publication, Rousseau obscured the extent to which his concept of the "general will" was linked to the existence of many "sovereign" political communities, each based on a separate "social contract." Instead of seeking universal ethical principles derived from a nonexistent "general society of the human species," Rousseau's political thought is an attempt to make "legitimate" and just the kind of civilized society which is observed in reality.

Before reconsidering Rousseau's use of the concept of a "general will," therefore, it is essential to explain what he meant by a "community." This is all the more imperative because, as noted, Rousseau defines the social contract as follows: "*Each of us puts his person and all his power in common*

*under the supreme direction of the general will, and in a body we receive
each member as an indivisible part of the whole"* (*Social Contract*, I, vi).
What then is this "whole" or "community" to which "each associate" gives
"all his rights"?

The answer is given immediately after Rousseau formulates the social
contract:

> Instantly, in place of the private person of each contracting party, this
> act of association produces a moral and collective body, composed of as
> many members as there are voices in the assembly, which receives from
> this same act its unity, its common *self*, its life, and its will. This public
> person, formed thus by the union of all the others, formerly took the
> name City, and now takes that of *Republic* or *body politic*, which its
> members call *State*, when it is passive, *Sovereign*, when active, and
> *Power*, when comparing it to similar bodies (I, vi).

For Rousseau, a "community" is not any collection of human beings, but
rather a "Republic" governed by an "assembly" in which "each contracting
party" or citizen has a vote. Rousseau thus seems to have in mind something
like the traditional New England town meeting as the only basis of legitimate
social obligation.

Of the terms used by Rousseau to explain the logic of such a political
community, only one can be discussed here: "sovereignty." In the eighteenth
century, especially in French, the term "sovereign" generally meant the King
or absolute monarch. One of Rousseau's most original and most revolutionary ideas was the definition of sovereignty as an attribute of the entire
body politic which could never be "represented" nor delegated to any individual or group. This usage, which amounts to a radical assertion of popular
sovereignty, leads to a further terminological innovation—the distinction
between the "government" and the "sovereign."

Although many political thinkers blur these two concepts, Rousseau
emphatically insisted that the exercise of political power by individual leaders
must be subordinate to the freely expressed will of the people as sovereign.

> Those who claim that the act by which a people subjects itself to leaders
> is not a contract are entirely right. It is absolutely nothing but a com-
> mission, an employment in which, as simple officers of the sovereign,
> they exercise in its name the power that has been entrusted to them by
> the sovereign, and that the sovereign can limit, modify, and take back
> whenever it pleases, since the alienation of such a right is incompatible
> with the nature of the social body and contrary to the goal of the associa-
> tion (III, i).

In stating what the social contract is, one cannot forget what it is not—
namely a contract to obey individual rulers or what we, following Rousseau,
call the "government."[33]

Rousseau thus used the "general will" to describe the logic by which a popular assembly could make decisions that bind each individual member. More simply, he tries to explain why it is usually said that the principle of "majority rule" is legitimate or fair. Rousseau's answer lies in the concept of transforming private interests into general rules or laws, which obligate each individual equally. "Since the condition is equal for everyone, no one has an interest in making it burdensome for the others" (I, vi).

Rousseau's concept of an act of the "general will" thus presupposes an egalitarian community in which each citizen has a vote, and in which the actions of the whole assembly have an equal effect on every individual. Hence Rousseau defines a "law" as an instance "when the entire people enacts something concerning the entire people" so that "the subject of the enactment is general like the will that enacts" (II, vi). In other words, for a decision to be legitimate, it must meet two distinct criteria: first, every citizen must vote on it; second, it must affect every citizen equally. The "general will" can create socially binding duties if and only if it is general both in its source and in its object.

Each reader must decide whether Rousseau succeeded in discovering the logic behind all collective decisions worth obeying. For the purpose of introducing his thought, it is enough to emphasize how Rousseau's "general will" converts the traditional concept of the common good into a requirement of popular sovereignty. When Rousseau flatly asserts that "every legitimate government is republican" (II, vi), he condemns all forms of absolute government as "slavery" based on little more than brute force and necessity. In this sense, the *Social Contract* remains as revolutionary today as when it could be read as an attack on hereditary monarchy and the *ancien régime* in France.

Nonetheless, Rousseau himself does not speak of his political principles as requiring an immediate revolution. On the contrary—as has been noted— his thought has a side that can be called "traditionalist." How can this be? What is the status of Rousseau's definition of the "nature of the social body"? Once again, reference to the first draft of the *Social Contract* helps to resolve an issue which has puzzled many readers of the final version.

The "General Will" as a Platonic "Idea"

While Rousseau sought to be realistic, in the *Social Contract* he formulates an abstract or general logic of political obedience. These "principles of political right" are, however, distinguished from their practical application to concrete circumstances (for example, III, xviii). In this regard Rousseau's "general will" can be compared to what Plato calls the "Forms" or "Ideas." Such a Platonic inspiration was especially evident in Rousseau's first draft, which originally had as its subtitle: "Essay about the Form of the Republic."[34]

For Plato, political philosophy had the task of describing the "best regime." Rousseau replies that this question is, in principle, impossible to answer:

People have always argued a great deal over the best form of government, without considering that each of them is the best in certain cases, and the worst in others (III, iii). . . . Therefore when the question is asked which is absolutely the best government, one poses a question that is insoluble because it is indeterminate. Or, if you prefer, it has as many correct answers as there are possible combinations in the absolute and relative situations of peoples (III, ix).

Since the quest for a best regime, symbolized by Plato's *Republic*, must be abandoned, Rousseau transforms this traditional issue into the question: "What is law?"[35] Having done so, Rousseau proposes the "general will" as what he explicitly calls the "idea of the civil state" (*Geneva Manuscript*, I, iv), thus reminding us that his principles are a modern equivalent of the Platonic "Ideas" or "Forms."

This intention, which was clearest in the first draft, helps to answer one of the most frequently asked questions about the *Social Contract*. How do we know whether a given decision is indeed the result of the general will? Since rulers so often hide their private interests in the garb of the "common good," does Rousseau's concept really tell us anything?

As is often the case with a great book, the question most often asked by critics is already asked by the author himself:

Only those who are forming the association have the right to regulate the conditions of the society. But how will they regulate them? . . . How will a blind multitude, which often does not know what it wants because it rarely knows what is good for it, carry out by itself an undertaking as vast and as difficult as a system of legislation (II, vi)?

How can the general will be "inalienable" (II, i), "indivisible" (II, ii), and "indestructible" (IV, i) if the sovereign people do not know what it is?

Precisely because Rousseau is aware of the problem, his concept has seemed especially frustrating:

The general will is always right, and always tends to the public utility. But it does not follow that the people's deliberations always have the same rectitude (II, iii).

Rousseau even provides us with a specific concept designating a public decision which fails to satisfy the criterion of the general will; he calls such an act "the will of all":

There is often a great difference between the will of all and the general will. The latter considers only the common interest; the former considers private interest, and is only a sum of private wills (II, iii).

How then can one tell the difference between the general will (which is legitimate) and the will of all (which is not)?

In the first draft, it had been even clearer that the "general will" was a modern version of a Platonic "Idea" or "Form." Not only did Rousseau use these terms, but he stressed the impossibility of achieving the general will by using a mechanical analogy consistent with Newtonian physics:

> The general will is rarely the will of all, and the public force is always less than the sum of the private forces, so that in the mechanism of the State there is an equivalent of friction in machines, which one must know how to reduce to the least possible amount and which must at least be calculated and subtracted in advance from the total force, so that the means used will be exactly proportionate to the effect desired. But without going into this difficult research which constitutes the science of the legislator, let us finish determining the idea of the civil state (*Geneva Manuscript*, I, iv).

That Rousseau conceived of the "general will" as a frictionless surface—that is, as an "ideal" model which is difficult if not impossible to realize in practical circumstances, though it can be minimized by applied engineering—is confirmed by an unpublished reference to the "friction" in the "machine" of State, not to mention other mechanistic analogies in the *Social Contract*.[36]

Rousseau knew better than his critics that the concept of the "general will" was an abstraction and that, in practice, it would often be subverted by private interests ("the will of all") falsely parading under the banner of the common good. But he distinguishes between the formal presentation of his "principles of political right"—the logic of the general will—and the "science of the legislator" (which studies the actual friction between the general will and the wills of the citizens in each concrete situation). It is not the least of Rousseau's claims to greatness that he combined what we today call an empirical science of politics with an examination of the principles of legitimacy.

Rousseau's "Science of the Legislator": Maxims of Politics

In the first draft of the *Social Contract*, Rousseau makes a sharp distinction between "the idea of the civil state" and the "science of the legislator"; the latter deals with the practical questions of applying concepts like the "general will," popular "sovereignty," and the "law" to specific circumstances (*Geneva Manuscript*, I, iv). In the final version, this distinction is stated in somewhat different terms:

> The established government must never be touched until it becomes incompatible with the public good. But this circumspection is a maxim of politics and not a rule of right, and the State is no more compelled to leave civil authority to its leaders than military authority to its generals (III, xviii).

Whether called "the science of the legislator" (as in the first draft) or the "maxims of politics" (as in the final version), one of the striking contributions of the *Social Contract* is Rousseau's analysis of the varied circumstances in actual political life.

Although most commentators have stressed Rousseau's "principles" or "rules of right," the concrete examination of what is today called "empirical political science" actually takes up the largest part of the *Social Contract*. After introducing the ways that circumstances determine which laws are appropriate for a "People" (II, viii–x), Rousseau surveys the kinds of legislation and laws (II, xi–xii) as a prelude to discussing different forms of government in Book III. And having devoted the third book—whose eighteen chapters make it the longest of the work—to "the various forms of government," Rousseau spends most of Book IV discussing the constitution of Republican Rome (IV, iv–vii). Indeed, in the final version, the exposition of Rousseau's "principles of political right" is essentially contained in Book I, chapters vi–ix; Book II, chapters i–vii; Book III, chapters xvi–xvii; and Book IV, chapters i–ii.

It is not possible to set forth Rousseau's practical science of politics in detail here.[37] The reader interested in this side of the *Social Contract* is invited to pay especial attention to those propositions that Rousseau calls "maxims" of politics. Three aspects of this political science are, however, of general importance: first, Rousseau's "maxims" reinforce his preference for the republican regimes of pagan antiquity; second, they reveal the causes which generally lead political institutions to decline into corruption and tyranny; third, they help explain the role of the "legislator" and "civil religion" in Rousseau's political thought.

Rousseau's preference for the ancient republican *polis* or city-state is clear enough from his explicit praise of Sparta and early Rome. But behind this choice is a practical understanding of the way the tension between the general will and private interest produces "friction" in every political community. When turning to a comparison of "different forms of government" in Book III, Rousseau develops a very subtle theory of the relation between the individual politican, the government as a collective group, and the entire society:

> We can distinguish three essentially different wills in the person of the magistrate. First, the individual's own will, which tends only toward his private advantage. Second, the common will of the magistrates, . . . which may be called the corporate will, and is general in relation to the government and private in relation to the State, of which the government is a part. Third, the will of the people or the sovereign will, which is general both in relation to the State considered as a whole and in relation to the government considered as part of that whole (III, ii).

In a remarkable way, Rousseau here transforms the logic of the general will from a theory of obligation into a sociological insight, used simultaneously to describe the "common will of the magistrates" and the "will of the people."

Since any corporate group, including a government, has a set of common interests, the general will of an entire society can be opposed not only by the private will of an individual, but by the corporate will of a group whose members share an interest dividing them from the other citizens. While Rousseau spells out this group theory of politics in the *Political Economy*,[38] it has several implications that are particularly striking in the *Social Contract*.

First of all, it stands to reason that the smaller the number of individuals and the more similar their situation, the less the "friction" or contradiction between private interests and their common interest. As Rousseau puts one of his basic "maxims": "The more the social bond stretches, the looser it becomes" (II, ix). This relationship between size and harmony operates on the level of civil society as a whole, reinforcing Rousseau's preference for a small community: "In general, a small state is proportionally stronger than a large one" (II, ix); "the larger the State grows, the less freedom there is"(III, i). But the same relationship operates within the government itself: "the more numerous the magistrates, the weaker the government" (III, ii).

It follows, therefore, that the natural tendency of human behavior is the reverse of the logic of Rousseau's "principles of political right":

> In the perfect legislation, the private or individual will should be null; the corporate will of the government very subordinate; and consequently the general or sovereign will always dominant and the unique rule of all the others.
>
> According to the natural order, on the contrary, these different wills become more active as they are more concentrated. Thus the general will is always the weakest, the corporate will has second place, and the private will is first of all (III, ii).[39]

Although this explains why the "perfect" realization of the general will is as unlikely as the construction of a perfectly frictionless machine, it also reinforces Rousseau's basic attitude toward human history.

From his "maxims," Rousseau goes on to deduce "that the government becomes slack in proportion as the magistrates multiply" and "that the more numerous the people, the greater the increase in repressive force should be." As a result, "the more the State grows, the more the government should shrink" (III, ii).

> If the number of supreme magistrates in different States ought to be in inverse proportion to the number of citizens, it follows that in general democratic government is suited to small states, aristocratic to medium-sized ones, and monarchical to large ones (III, iii).

The scientific study of social behavior points to the impossibility of justice in a large, monarchical society—and therewith to the superiority of ancient political practice in the republican *polis*.

On the one hand, modern secular political theorists, following Machiavelli, Hobbes, and Locke, tend to favor an expansionist commercial society which inevitably increases the size of the State and strengthens the attachment to private interests. For Rousseau, a society which must "cultivate commerce and navigation" will "have a brilliant and brief existence" (II, xi). On the other hand, however, modern Christianity has tremendously complicated the political problem. As Rousseau puts it:

> Communion and excommunication are the social compact of the clergy, a compact by means of which it will always be master of peoples and kings. . . . The pagan priests had nothing that resembles it, and therefore they never constituted a body of clergymen (IV, viii, note).

The city-states of pagan antiquity were thus superior to large monarchies like eighteenth-century France both because they were small enough for citizens to share common interests, and because they were not burdened by a church which constituted a State within the State. Rousseau's extensive discussion of the Roman Republic (IV, iii–vii) thus gives concrete expression to a well-thought-out critique of the political practice of all modern societies.

But Rousseau's maxims of politics do more than provide additional reasons for admiring pagan republics in ancient times. These sociological regularities also explain why even the best government is bound to decline into despotism and slavery:

> Just as the private will acts incessantly against the general will, so the government makes a continual effort against sovereignty. The greater this effort becomes, the more the constitution changes, and as there is no corporate will which, by resisting the will of the prince, would balance it, sooner or later the prince will finally oppress the sovereign and break the social treaty. That is the inherent and inevitable vice which, from the emergence of the body politic, tends without respite to destroy it (III, x).[40]

Rousseau's pessimistic view of human history, which had been set forth at length in the two *Discourses,* operates within the maxims comprising the "science of the legislator." As Bertrand de Jouvenel puts it: "Rousseau the social scientist predicts the destruction of what Rousseau the moralist recommends."[41]

These comments hardly do justice to Rousseau's analysis of the political effects of climate, geography, history, size, and economic structure. But they do suggest why Rousseau's scientific "maxims of politics" predict the failure of his "principles of right." Indeed, Rousseau's political thought stresses the inevitable contradiction between democracy and science. By right, the laws are legitimate only if enacted by free popular vote; in practice, legislation will fail unless it satisfies numerous "matters of expediency" (*convenances*),which can only be discovered by the few who have mastered a complex science of politics. But since the science necessary for successful legislation is exceedingly difficult, Rousseau saw that the populace could hardly be expected to understand it.

This tension, which is illustrated by the dilemmas of public policy in all modern regimes, explains two important features of Rousseau's *Social Contract*: the "legislator" (II, vii) and the "civil religion" (IV, viii). The "genius" discovering the laws best suited for a particular community is personified as an individual—the "legislator" who is somehow above the level of ordinary men. And since a successful policy cannot be based on popular understanding of the "science of the legislator," the patriotic opinions needed to support good laws are transformed into dogmas—the "civil religion" which converts selfish private individuals into virtuous citizens. While we do not usually think of politics in these terms, Rousseau's conceptions of the legislator and civil religion are worth study, for they concern contradictions between democracy and science that remain very much with us.

Rousseau's Originality

To use contemporary terms, Rousseau's principles are "democratic" and "revolutionary." But whereas democrats or revolutionaries often imply that historical progress will inevitably result if corrupt regimes are swept away, Rousseau rejects such an optimistic view of history—and yet still favors a republican or egalitarian form of government. In other words, the revolutionary side of Rousseau's thought takes on added power precisely because he accepts the view of history usually adopted by traditionalists; the argument that many societies will inevitably be ruled by despots and tyrants only makes the assertion of political freedom all the more striking. Perhaps these paradoxical features of Rousseau's position help to explain the fame of the *Social Contract*.

Rousseau's originality thus lies in his attempt to combine a view of human nature derived from moderns like Hobbes and Locke with a view of history derived from ancients like Plato and Aristotle. At the same time, however, Rousseau replaces the aggressive or rational egoism of Hobbes and Locke with the more passive and instinctive self-preservation of isolated animals. And while sharing the ancient's skepticism toward radical historical progress, Rousseau modifies it by presenting scientific principles which show how to construct a legitimate and free government, at least in some instances.

If Rousseau is considered in terms of his conceptions of human nature and of history, which are fundamental to all political thought, the reasons for treating the *Social Contract* as one of the "great books" become clearer. Unlike most writers, he not only saw the basic issues which had divided prior political philosophers, but he also tried to resolve them by transforming the terms of the debate. In short, Jean-Jacques Rousseau is one of the few political theorists who goes to the root of most of the perennial questions, and who thereby contributed new concepts if not a new frame of reference to our understanding of politics.

WHEN AND WHY DID ROUSSEAU WRITE THE SOCIAL CONTRACT?

The historical circumstances surrounding the composition of the *Social Contract* as well as the personality of its author have been largely ignored to this point. Do we not learn much about a book by understanding the historical epoch in which it was written as well as the character and experience of the author? Of course, the answer is yes. But there was a reason for postponing a survey of Rousseau's life and times.

Unless a book is worth reading, the conditions in which it was written—not to mention the character of the writer—are of no particular interest to the political theorist as distinct from the historian or biographer. Thus the questions one asks about the life and times of Jean-Jacques Rousseau depend to some extent on the philosophical importance attached to his books. Having argued that the *Social Contract* is a classic, it is well to ask how its teaching is clarified by the eighteenth-century historical background and the personality of its author.

Eighteenth-Century Europe: the Enlightenment Attack on Tradition

The two most influential political events of the eighteenth century probably were the successful revolutions of 1776 in North America and of 1789 in France. The American revolution (which was, ironically, supported by the French monarchy) marked the first major step in the collapse of the colonial empires established by European states after Columbus discovered the "New World." The French Revolution, whether or not it was inspired by the principles of the American Declaration of Independence, signaled the first major step in the collapse of the hereditary monarchies which had ruled in Europe since the Middle Ages.

By 1800, therefore, the traditional basis of political life in the West had been subject to massive attack. Broadly speaking, this crisis of civilization can be seen as a challenge to established authority in the name of the "rights of man"; privilege and age-old customs were swept away as a new form of society developed into the industrial civilizations we know today. And though Napoleon's attempted conquest of Europe failed, his armies effectively spread the doctrines of the French Revolution throughout the continent, while the United States served as an example (and an ally) for revolt and independence throughout Latin America.

The eighteenth century was thus a period of transition from the early modern state of the seventeenth century to the nation-state and industrial economy of the nineteenth and twentieth centuries. Between 1700 and 1800, however, political change was to some extent foreshadowed and prepared by intellectual ferment. The sciences developed rapidly as Newtonian physics spread throughout Europe. The bases of modern scientific method were still being contested in 1700, but by 1800 the fundamentals of modern chemistry and applied science were well on the way to acceptance, bringing with them the possibility of technological innovations in commerce and industry. Similarly, new attitudes and approaches in philosophy, literature, and the arts were hallmarks of the period.

Rousseau's historical epoch, therefore, was a time when established traditions were under question in all areas from theology to natural science. Yet the so-called *ancien régime*—while soon to fall—was still very much in power from Rousseau's birth in 1712 until his death in 1778. Indeed, his major works were all completed by 1762, when the publication of the *Émile* and *Social Contract* gave rise to legal actions against Rousseau (first in France, where the *Émile* was burned on orders of the Parlement of Paris; then in Geneva, where both the *Émile* and *Social Contract* were condemned).

Rousseau thus represents the generation which rejected the principles of the old order without being able to overthrow it, thereby preparing the way for the coming revolution. This general movement is often called the "Enlightenment." Faced with traditional beliefs that were being questioned in every field, men of letters, scientists, and even theologians sought to bring new *light* to bear on old problems. And France was the center of this "*siècle des lumières*" (century of lights) thanks to the indefatigable efforts of a group known as the "*philosophes*."

Among these intellectuals and scientists, the best known are Montesquieu, Buffon, Voltaire, Diderot and d'Alembert (cofounders of the great *Encyclopédie*), d'Holbach, Grimm, and Helvétius—all Rousseau's contemporaries and, with the exception of Montesquieu, all acquaintances if not friends. Rousseau worked with the leading minds of his day in France, contributing to the *Encyclopédie* and participating in the cultural life of Parisian salons. After his persecution, he left France and for a while lived with David Hume, perhaps the greatest English-speaking philosopher of the century. Rousseau also knew and worked with leading musicians (from Rameau to Gluck), hereditary nobles (like the Duke and Duchess of Luxembourg), and young men like Bernardin de Saint-Pierre, who was to become one of the important romantic writers of the early nineteenth century.

Rousseau not only lived in a period when European traditions were challenged by the "Enlightenment"; he was a key participant in this movement. But does this tell us anything important about the *Social Contract*? What is the particular relevance of the historical background to Rousseau's classic statement of the "principles of political right"?

The answer is twofold. Rousseau was the most audacious of the critics of the old regime. But he also was the first to challenge the Enlightenment on its own terms, attacking modern principles on secular grounds rather than in the name of revealed religion, the divine right of kings, or scholastic dogma. Precisely because Rousseau saw the impending revolution which was to sweep away the *ancien régime*, he denounced the irrationality of the existing order with intransigent passion. Yet Rousseau also saw the defects of the modern principles with which the *philosophes* attacked the tradition. Rousseau thus sought to go beyond the immediate problem—and in so doing, broke with his friend Diderot as well as with Grimm, Voltaire, and Hume.

The historical circumstances of Rousseau's time were especially propitious for a radical critique of all prior political principles. As a period of changing attitudes, the eighteenth century was ripe for a thoroughgoing application of modern philosophy and science to the problems of political theory. But as a period before the revolution, the eighteenth century also permitted a perspective on antiquity which was to become difficult when, in the flush of revolutionary optimism, classical history, architecture, and even clothing became symbols of a new regime. Rousseau's historical situation was thus well suited to an attempt to synthesize modern and ancient thought. In much the same way, the private life of Jean-Jacques symbolized the conflict between individual and society which serves as the other leitmotiv of Rousseau's writings.

Jean-Jacques, the Solitary Wanderer

Rousseau's life is probably better known than that of any other famous philosopher. This is no accident, since he wrote three well-known autobiographical works: the *Confessions* (a detailed account of his youth and maturity), *Rousseau Juge de Jean-Jacques* or the *Dialogues* (a somewhat schizophrenic book, in which "Rousseau" and a "Frenchman" discuss "Jean-Jacques"), and the *Rêveries d'un Promeneur Solitaire* (perhaps his most beautiful and haunting writing, both revealing his character and introducing stream-of-consciousness style into Western literature). Even without the publication of his massive correspondence and extensive biographical scholarship, we would be entitled to ask how the life of Jean-Jacques influenced the philosophic writing of Rousseau. After all, is any other great philosopher familiarly known by his first name?

The *Confessions* begin with a striking assertion of individuality:

> I conceive of an enterprise for which there is no prior example and of which there will be no imitation. I want to show my fellows a man in all the truth of nature; and that man will be myself.
> Myself alone. I feel my heart and I know other men. I am not made like any of them I have seen; I dare believe not like any of them who

exist. If I am not better, at least I am different. Whether nature did well or ill to break the mould in which she formed me, that is something one can only judge after reading me.[42]

The *Rêveries,* identifying the author as a *promeneur solitaire* (a man who goes walking alone), has an equally striking and individualistic beginning:

I am therefore alone on earth, no longer having any brother, neighbor, friend, or society except myself. The most sociable and the most loving of human beings has been proscribed by unanimous agreement.[43]

Who then was this author who felt himself to be unique and, at the end of his life, "alone on earth" due to "unanimous agreement"?

Jean-Jacques Rousseau was born in the Protestant city-state of Geneva on June 28, 1712, and died on July 2, 1778, at the country estate of the Marquis de Girardin in Ermenonville, north of Paris. His life can conveniently be divided into five periods: his youth in Geneva to the age of sixteen (1712–1728); his travels and self-education (1728–1742); his early career in Paris (1742–1749); the writing of his major philosophical and political works (1749–1762); and the years of persecution, flight, and self-justification until his death (1762–1778). Each of these periods had an impact on Rousseau's written corpus.

Youth in Geneva (1712–1728)

Jean-Jacques's parents, Isaac Rousseau (a watchmaker) and Suzanne Bernard, were both citizens of Geneva. As is made clear in the *Social Contract,* to be a male citizen in Geneva had a different meaning from being a citizen elsewhere (I, vi, note): at least in principle, all male citizens had the right to vote in the *Conseil Général.* When Jean-Jacques Rousseau signed his works as a "*Citoyen de Genève,*" he thus pointed to an inheritance that was political as well as familial.

Recent research on the Rousseau family indicates that they lived in the quarter of artisans which had been the center of popular agitation in Genevan politics: Issac Rousseau's neighbors included the ringleaders of an uprising against the upper classes who dominated Geneva.[44] Suzanne Rousseau died from complications of Jean-Jacques's birth, and he was brought up by his father Isaac. In 1722, however, Isaac Rousseau left Geneva after getting into a fight with a retired captain well connected in the ruling circles. Young Jean-Jacques spent two years in pension with a Protestant minister just outside of Geneva, then served as an apprentice in several trades—none of which he found pleasing. Always somewhat rebellious, he returned from a walk in the countryside on March 14, 1728, to find the gates of the city already closed. Rather than return to his master, who had beaten him previously for a similar fault, Jean-Jacques Rousseau left.

Jean-Jacques's upbringing was thus unusual in several respects. His attitude toward women seemed to reflect a latent sense of guilt, as if he had been responsible for his mother's death. His early education was marked not only by the impetuous and freedom-loving character of Isaac Rousseau, but also by the mixture of popular republican sentiments and readings of Plutarch's *Lives*. Above all, the young Jean-Jacques was a highly independent child of Geneva's artisan class. His friends, seeing him walk off rather than face a whipping on that March day in 1728, could hardly have expected that this Rousseau was to become a famous political philosopher.

Travels and Self-Education (1728–1742)

Alone. While late in life Rousseau described himself as the *promeneur solitaire*, in 1728 Jean-Jacques actually did set out, on foot and alone, on an odyssey that carried him across Europe, into peasants' barnyards, royal courts, and philosophic salons. He first went to Annecy, where he had been directed to Mme de Warens, a convert to Catholicism who in turn directed him to a hospice in Turin. To make his way, Jean-Jacques abjured his native Protestantism and, after being baptized a Catholic, became a lackey. Dismissed from one household, he became secretary to an abbot; dismissed again, he returned to Mme de Warens. Then followed several months at a seminary, experiences under an assumed name as a music teacher, interpreter for an imposter posing as a Greek archimandrite, travels to Fribourg, Neuchâtel, Paris, Lyon, Chambéry, and Montpellier; tutor to a nobleman's son; and most significant of all, several prolonged periods with Mme de Warens ("*Maman*"), who became his mistress.

Throughout this period—but especially at Les Charmettes, Mme de Warens's house in the country outside of Chambéry—Jean-Jacques educated himself. By the time he set out for Paris again in 1742, having invented a new system of musical notation, Jean-Jacques had learned enough to become not only a composer, but also a poet, dramatist, essayist, philosopher, political scientist, novelist, chemist, and botanist.

This period left its marks in Jean-Jacques's breadth of experience, his radical sense of independence, and his profound taste for the countryside. Jean-Jacques's love of music was transformed into a skill, providing the basis of his entry into Parisian society. Simultaneously, and more important, his love of ideas was transformed into a trained mind, providing the basis for his subsequent fame as a writer and thinker. Rousseau was, in a very real sense, a self-made man.

Early Career in Paris (1742–1749)

Alone once again, Jean-Jacques arrived in Paris during the summer of 1742 with some letters of recommendation and his new system for writing music. Although this was not his first trip to the French capital, it marked the beginning of his direct contacts with the cultural, scientific, and philosophic leaders of the century. After presenting his scheme of musical notation at the Academy of Sciences—with little effect—Jean-Jacques published his *Dissertation sur la Musique Moderne*. Then followed almost a year as secretary to the Comte de Montaigu, French ambassador in Venice; a violent quarrel with the ambassador ended this introduction to high politics, and Jean-Jacques returned to Paris in 1744.

In the following year, Rousseau completed an opera, *Les Muses Galantes*, became friendly with Diderot and Condillac, and revised the musical score of *Les Fêtes de Ramire* (originally written by Rameau in collaboration with Voltaire). By 1745, Jean-Jacques was no longer alone; he now was living with Thérèse Levasseur (a young laundress who was to be his lifelong companion and ultimately his wife), and had friends and contacts in the Parisian world. Attached to the household of the Dupin family, Jean-Jacques stayed at their castle of Chenonceaux on several occasions, composing poetry and plays. By 1749, when he was asked to write the articles on music for the *Encyclopédie*, Jean-Jacques was already familiar with the intellectual *salons* of Paris and the *philosophes* who animated them.

This period left Rousseau with a rich experience of politics as well as of philosophic discussion. Although by nature shy, Jean-Jacques met and mingled with the great names of the day and began to interact as an equal with the leading *philosophes*. Diderot and d'Alembert had launched the *Encyclopédie* as a massive enterprise, destined to spread the latest technical know-how and skeptical ideas throughout France and Europe; Jean-Jacques was their collaborator and their friend. To be sure, he was generally unknown. But that was not to last for long.

The Composition of Rousseau's "System" (1749–1762)

In 1749, Diderot was imprisoned in Vincennes for the unorthodox views expressed in his writing; Jean-Jacques went to visit him. Rousseau's description of the "Illumination of Vincennes," which resulted in the *First Discourse*, has already been quoted. Having received the Prize of the Academy of Dijon for this essay, Rousseau became known. Having criticized the prevailing opinions of most men of letters, Rousseau was attacked in print—and his spirited replies made him even better known.

Meanwhile, in 1751, Jean-Jacques went through a personal "reform": ceasing to work as a secretary to the wealthy Francueil, he adopted a simple mode of life and supported himself by copying music. The following year, he completed the *Devin du Village*, an opera which was successfully performed before the King—and then refused a royal pension for fear of compromising his independence. In 1753, he published the *Lettre sur la musique française*, which so outraged the orchestra of the Paris Opera that they hung Rousseau in effigy and refused to honor his lifetime pass. The same year, he set to work on the *Discourse on Inequality*, which was completed in 1754 and published in 1755 along with the article on *Political Economy* in Volume V of the *Encyclopédie*.

In the years that followed, important works flowed from Jean-Jacques's pen with astonishing fluency. Having moved to a house outside of Paris, he completed a summary and commentary on the political writings of the Abbé de Saint-Pierre, *Lettre à d'Alembert sur les Spectacles, Julie ou la Nouvelle Héloïse* (which became a best-selling novel after its publication in late 1760), and above all the *Social Contract* and the *Émile* (both completed in 1761 and published the next year). While undergoing a bitter break with his close friend Diderot, not to mention stormy personal affairs with both intellectuals and members of the nobility, Jean-Jacques composed the major philosophic works that earned him enduring fame, a novel that greatly contributed to the emergence of romanticism, and lesser works which another writer might view as major contributions.

Looking back, Rousseau says of the "effervescence" that "burst into flame" in him during this period:

> I was really transformed, my friends and acquaintances no longer recognized me. I was no longer that timid man, more ashamed than modest, who did not dare to stand up or speak, who was disconcerted by a jesting word, who blushed at the glance of a woman. Bold, proud, intrepid, I brought self-assurance everywhere. . . . All Paris repeated the sharp and biting sarcasms of the same man who two years before and ten years later never knew how to find the right thing to say, nor the word to use. If you looked for the condition that is the most opposed to my nature, that would be it.[45]

This passage of the *Confessions* is particularly interesting because it suggests that Rousseau felt himself carried along "in another intellectual world"; only when this period had passed did he become "the same Jean-Jacques I had been before."[46]

Some scholars have argued that there are few important differences between the *Political Economy, Geneva Manuscript*, and *Social Contract*. Others claim that there are major shifts of emphasis. One difficulty with the latter interpretation concerns the composition of the *Geneva Manuscript*. This manuscript has been dated as early as 1752 and as late as 1761. In all probability, it includes material first drafted around 1755, although the existing manuscript is usually said to have been written out in 1760 or 1761—or at the earliest 1759. Since the historical details are in doubt, hypotheses concerning changes in Rousseau's point of view are risky. As one editor wisely said, "the exact truth on this point is now beyond our reach."[47]

There have also been many attempts to interpret Rousseau's philosophy in terms of the personality of Jean-Jacques. Assuredly there is some truth in the best of such analyses.[48] But the account in the *Confessions* indicates that the epoch of Rousseau's greatest philosophic productivity was unique: kindled by the "Illumination of Vincennes," he poured forth his creative works in the seclusion of the countryside. Whatever the relationship between the character of Jean-Jacques and the "system" of Rousseau, the latter must stand on its own as a profound exploration of the human condition.

Persecution, Flight, and Self-Justification (1762–1778)

On May 27, 1762, Rousseau's *Émile* was put on sale in Paris, apparently with tacit permission from the censors. On June 3 the police confiscated the book. On June 7 it was attacked at the Sorbonne. On June 9 the Parlement of Paris (a court, not a legislature) condemned the *Émile* and ordered the arrest of its author. That afternoon, warned of these actions, Jean-Jacques fled the French capital. Two days later, the *Émile* was burned in Paris, while in Geneva both the *Émile* and the *Social Contract* were confiscated. On June 19 the authorities of Rousseau's native city burned both books and ordered his arrest.

The *promeneur solitaire* again set out, crisscrossing Europe. But this time, not voluntarily. No sooner did Jean-Jacques get to Yverdun, in the canton of Bern, than the government ordered his expulsion. Another move led to Môtiers, in territory controlled by Frederick the Great of Prussia (who granted Jean-Jacques's petition for asylum). By the end of 1762, Rousseau had already completed the *Lettre à Christophe de Beaumont*, replying to an attack on the *Émile* by the archbishop of Paris. The pattern of persecution, flight, and self-justification—which was to characterize the last sixteen years of his life—was already established.

The details of these final years are of interest mainly to the biographer. In calm moments, Rousseau wrote not only trenchant replies to critics and his three great autobiographical works, but also lucid proposals for constitutional reform in Corsica and Poland. Overt persecution struck again: in 1765, his *Lettres Écrites de la Montagne*—a defense of the *Émile* and *Social Contract* which carefully analyzed the constitution of Geneva and violently attacked the injustice of its government—was burned both in the Hague and in Paris. The same year, Rousseau fled Môtiers after a nearby pastor preached a sermon attacking him and his house was stoned; a brief stay on the Isle of Saint-Pierre, immortalized in the *Fifth Promenade*, was abruptly ended by an order of expulsion.

To be sure, these years had moments of public recognition, even in Paris (where, although the order for Rousseau's arrest remained in force, he stayed briefly in 1765 and at length from 1770 to 1778). Invited to England by David Hume, Jean-Jacques was even granted a pension by King George III. But these years were also a time of deep psychological depression: fears of persecution, only too well founded, combined with natural sensitivity and physical illness to produce intermittent paranoia. The conviction that there was a universal plot against him, which marks the opening of the *Rêveries*, on occasion carried Jean-Jacques to the depths of madness—as in April 1776, when he wrote out a message "To Every Frenchman Who Still Loves Justice and Truth," and distributed it in the streets.

Some critics have engaged in psychological interpretation by using the moments of insanity in Jean-Jacques's last years as a supposed key to Rousseau's philosophy. That this is unfair should be evident: not only was he subject to repeated and all-too-real persecution, but also the *philosophes* clearly did engage in a literary campaign against Jean-Jacques. To be sure, one can argue that the persecution complex of his old age was merely an exaggeration of Jean-Jacques's extreme sensitivity and social rebelliousness, which can be traced from his flight from Geneva to his arguments with the Comte de Montaigu in Venice, Diderot and other *philosophes* in Paris, Mme d'Épinay at l'Ermitage, and Hume in England. Before the publication of the *Émile,* Rousseau was tormented by the idea that the Jesuits had gotten hold of the manuscript and were transforming it.

Jean-Jacques was decidedly a difficult and tortured soul. In his last years, this psychological fragility often plunged him into despair. But it is a question of the chicken and the egg to ask whether his sensitivity was heightened by his theories of the unnatural and corrupt character of modern times, or whether these ideas were exaggerated by his personality. In any event, the causes which led Rousseau to write as he did were not merely psychological, since he was also greatly influenced by the times and places in which he lived. And whatever these causes, the result was Rousseau's unique combination of answers to the perennial issues of political thought.

Rousseau as Political Philosopher

Whatever one's judgment of Jean-Jacques, he was a genius. Not merely one of the best prose stylists who ever wrote in the French language. Not merely one of the most important educational theorists in history. And not merely an accomplished composer and musical theorist whose influence on Gluck, and thereby on the development of the opera, is greater than generally suspected.

The word "genius" should probably be used very sparingly. Names like Newton, Aristotle, and Einstein come to mind. At most, once or twice in a century there is a person who combines the native intelligence, the experience, and the good fortune to bring together the most fundamental knowledge available, synthesize it, and go beyond the limits of time and place to pose crucial issues whose existence is not even suspected by lesser intellects. By this definition, Jean-Jacques Rousseau was a genius.

It is appropriate to conclude on this note because Rousseau's status in the history of Western civilization has some relevance to the way we read his works. I have argued that the *Social Contract* is a genuine "classic," one of the "great books" that educated men and women should study with care. And I have asserted that Rousseau himself was a "genius," a man whose mind was simply better than that of most human beings. But classifying a book or an author in these terms is not a popularity contest. Rather, it concerns our obligations toward the texts in this special category.

If a scientist or philosopher is truly a genius, or a single work truly a classic, as readers we have a duty. It is likely that, in such cases, the author had good reasons for writing as he did—and probably even thought of our questions or objections in advance. Hence we ought to study the great works with a special care and seek to understand what they mean, word by word if need be, *before* we start to criticize them. This deference to the "great books" does not require that we be servile. It only obliges us to admit that those few authors who are read century after century were probably smarter than we are—and hence that hasty or superficial criticism reflects on us not them.

These general remarks are obviously relevant to the work at hand. Rousseau said of his own books that they "are not . . . groups of separate thoughts on each of which the reader's mind can rest"; hence "they demand continued attention . . . when one insists on wanting to follow their thread well, it is necessary to come back to them with effort and more than once." This advice is especially appropriate before reading the *Social Contract*, which Rousseau described as containing "difficult material, fit for few readers."[49] Lest we quite literally make fools of ourselves, it is therefore necessary to read this book carefully.

To conclude, one does well to start the *Social Contract* with the premise that it may indeed by true, simply *true*. Then, after it has been studied with care, understood, and digested, make time for further dialogue with Rousseau's ideas. Contrast this book to other classics. Confront its concepts with your own experience. The *Social Contract* by Jean-Jacques Rousseau, like Plato's *Republic* and Machiavelli's *Prince*, is one of the small shelf of books that form the tradition of Western political thought.

EDITOR'S NOTES

[1] See especially *Social Contract*, III, xi (below, p. 98); III, xii (p. 99); and IV, iii–viii (pp. 111–132).

[2] The French revolutionary leader Robespierre wrote of Rousseau: "Divine man! you taught me to know myself; very young, you made me appreciate the dignity of my nature and reflect on the great principles of the social order. The old edifice has crumbled; the portals of a new edifice have been built on the debris and, thanks to you, I have contributed my share . . . " *Dédicace de Maximilien Robespierre aux manes de Jean-Jacques Rousseau,* quoted in Hippolyte Buffenoire, *Le Prestige de Jean-Jacques Rousseau* (Paris; Émile-Paul, 1909), pp. 433–434. On the relative lack of attention to the *Social Contract* before 1788, see William Pickles, "The Notion of Time in Rousseau's Political Thought," in *Hobbes and Rousseau,* ed. Maurice Cranston and Richard S. Peters (Garden City, N.Y.: Anchor Books, 1972), pp. 369–370. Since this

volume provides an excellent sample of the enormous secondary literature on Rousseau, it will be cited frequently.

³For the original texts, compare *Geneva Manuscript*, I, iii, and *Social Contract*, I, i (Pléiade, III, 289 and 351; or Vaughan, I, 454 and II, 23). For full references to these and other editions of Rousseau cited in this volume, see the Editor's Preface.

⁴As J. McManners has remarked, Rousseau often "advances a shattering proposition, then explains it"—a stylistic device which Michel Launay aptly called "a blow, followed by a caress." "The Social Contract and Rousseau's Revolt against Society," in *Hobbes and Rousseau*, ed. Cranston and Peters, p. 295. On the clarity which resulted from Rousseau's reorganization of Book I, compare Vaughan, I, 435–445; *Geneva Manuscript*, editorial note 18; and Roger D. Masters, *The Political Philosophy of Rousseau* (Princeton, N.J.: Princeton University Press, 1968), p. 323, n. 83.

⁵Thomas Hobbes, *Leviathan*, Part II, chap. 30, ed. Michael Oakeshott (Oxford: Blackwell, 1960), p. 220—cited below in editorial note 101 to the *Social Contract*.

⁶Roger D. Masters, *The Nature of Political Thought* (New York: St. Martin's Press, forthcoming). For a shorter statement, see Roger D. Masters, "Human Nature, Nature, and Political Thought," in *Nomos XVII: Human Nature and Politics*, ed. Roland Pennock and John Chapman (New York: Lieber-Atherton, 1976), chap. 3.

⁷*Second Discourse*, Preface, in *Rousseau's First and Second Discourses*, ed. Roger D. Masters (New York: St. Martin's Press, 1964), p. 93. All translations from the two *Discourses* are taken, with permission, from this edition.

⁸See, for example, Émile Durkheim, *Montesquieu and Rousseau* (Ann Arbor: University of Michigan Press, 1960); and Claude Lévi-Strauss, *Tristes Tropiques* (New York: Atheneum, 1974). In the mid-eighteenth century, criticism of the Biblical account of God's creation of Adam and Eve was not merely unpopular but dangerous to the life and limb of the author. Rousseau knew this perfectly well, since his friend Diderot had been imprisoned in 1749 for the "subversive" implications of his writing. Although Rousseau wrote with circumspection, he was himself subjected to persecution on theological grounds (pp. 32–33.)

⁹*Second Discourse*, Part 1 (ed. Masters p. 137). For the original text, see Pléiade, III, 159–160.

¹⁰*Rousseau Juge de Jean-Jacques*, Dialogue III (Pléiade, I, 934), quoted in Masters, *The Political Philosophy of Rousseau*, p. xiii.

¹¹The phrase in French is "*qualité d'hommes*" in the *Second Discourse*, Part 2 (Pléiade, III, 184) and "*qualité d'homme*" in the *Social Contract*, I, iv (Pléiade, III, 356). Some critics have claimed that Rousseau's political thought changed radically over time (for example, see note 47 below). But careful study shows that the basic concepts in his major works are consistent, forming what Rousseau himself called his "system" (see Masters, *Political Philosophy of Rousseau*, pp. x–xiii, 206–207). There are, however, differences of emphasis in Rousseau's various works. The *Second Discourse* distinguishes between freedom in the sense of *free will* ("Man . . . realizes that he is free to acquiesce or resist" physical causes or impulses) and freedom in the sense of *perfectibility* ("The faculty of self-perfection . . . which, with the aid of circumstances, successively develops all the others, and resides among us as much in the species as in the individual"). Although Rousseau claims that he bases the distinction between "man and animal" on the latter notion of freedom, it is the former—according to which humans are "free agents" whereas every other animal "chooses or rejects by instinct"—which is an "essential gift of nature" establishing politically relevant "rights." *Second Discourse*, Part 1 (ed. Masters, pp. 113–115), Part 2 (p. 168), note j (p. 208). This notion of human beings as "free agents" is presumed in the *Social Contract* (e.g.,

III, i), although Rousseau further distinguishes between *natural freedom* (the liberty of the state of nature, where each individual has "an unlimited right to all that tempts him and that he can get" and is free of any social obligation), *civil freedom* (the liberty of freely consenting to obey the laws of a legitimate society), and *moral freedom* (the liberty of "obedience to the law one has prescribed for oneself"). See *Social Contract*, I, viii (p. 56).

[12]Compare Plato, *Republic*, I.338e–339a, ed. Allan Bloom (New York: Basic Books, 1968), p. 16; and Hobbes, *Leviathan*, "A Review and Conclusion" (ed. Oakeshott, p. 468).

[13]Letter to M. de Malesherbes, January 12, 1762 (Pléiade, I, 1135–1136). Compare *Confessions*, VIII (Pléiade, I, 351). Jean-Jacques himself thus describes all his mature writings as based on a single "principle" resulting from the "Illumination of Vincennes." For further evidence that the main outlines of Rousseau's position did not change over time, see the *Préface d'une Seconde Lettre à Bordes*, written in 1753–1754 (Pléiade, III, 106) and *Confessions*, VIII (Pléiade, I, 388), both cited in Masters, *Political Philosophy of Rousseau*, pp. 206–207.

[14]*Second Discourse*, Part 2 (ed. Masters, p. 151; Pléiade, III, 171).

[15]*First Discourse*, Part 1 (ed. Masters, pp. 36–40; Pléiade, III, 7–10).

[16]Ibid., Part 2 (ed. Masters, pp. 50–51; Pléiade, III, 19).

[17]Ibid., Part 1 (ed. Masters, p. 36; Pléiade, III, 7). On the grounds of Rousseau's rejection of modern natural science, especially as it was conceived by Bacon, see editorial note 66 to the *Social Contract*.

[18]The ambiguity arises because the verb *"est né"* is the past tense of *"naître"* (to be born), whereas *"est"* (is) *"né"* (born) is an equally possible reading. For example, the present tense is used in the translations of the *Social Contract* by Watkins, Cole, Frankel, and Sherover; the past tense by Cranston and Crocker. (Compare ed. Brumfitt and Hall, p. 317). Moreover, the ambiguity was evidently *chosen* by Rousseau. He could, after all, simply have used the present tense, as did a book he elsewhere quotes: *"selon le Droit Naturel, tous les hommes naissent libres"* (Barbeyrac's translation of Pufendorf, *Droit de la Nature et des gens*, cited in Pléiade, III, 1433, note 5). In fact, later Rousseau uses the present tense himself in exactly this fashion; see *Social Contract*, I, iv: all children *"naissent [are born] hommes et libres"* (Pléiade, III, 356).

[19]Note that the past tense roughly corresponds with the definition of freedom as "perfectibility," whereas the present tense emphasizes each individual's status as a "free agent." Compare note 11.

[20]J. McManners, "The Social Contract and Rousseau's Revolt against Society," in *Hobbes and Rousseau* (ed. Cranston and Peters, p. 305).

[21]William Pickles, "The Notion of Time in Rousseau's Political Thought," in *Hobbes and Rousseau* (ed. Cranston and Peters, pp. 372–373). As Rousseau once advised: "When in doubt, stop every innovation, large or small." *Lettres Écrites de la Montagne*, IX (Pléiade, III, 873).

[22]*Social Contract*, I, i (p. 46; Pléiade, III, 351). Note that, at the risk of appearing awkward, the play on words of the French *"L'homme est né libre"* will be translated by "Man was/is born free . . ."

[23]*Social Contract*, I, Proemium (p. 46; Pléiade, III, 351). For a commentary on this passage, see Masters, *The Political Philosophy of Rousseau*, pp. 301–306. The same ambivalence is evident in the *Émile*: although the "science" of "political right" is "useless," it is the "yardstick" for measuring all existing laws (Book V; Pléiade, IV, 836–

837). For a thoughtful statement on the tension between Rousseau's cautious attitude toward change and his revolutionary principles, see Hilail Gildin, "Revolution and the Formation of Political Society in the *Social Contract*," *Interpretation*, 5 (Spring 1976), 247–265.

24See Vaughan, I, 77 as well as the essays by McManners, Pickles, and de Jouvenel in *Hobbes and Rousseau*, ed. Cranston and Peters, chaps. 12, 15, 19. Among recent studies of Rousseau's political thought, compare Judith N. Shklar, *Men and Citizens: A Study of Rousseau's Social Theory* (London: Cambridge University Press, 1969); Raymond Polin, *La Politique de la Solitude* (Paris, Sirey, 1971); Victor Goldschmidt, *Anthropologie et Politique: Les Principes du Système de Rousseau* (Paris: Vrin, 1974); Stephen Ellenburg, *Rousseau's Political Philosophy: An Interpretation from Within* (Ithaca, N.Y.: Cornell University Press, 1976); and Merle L. Perkins, *Jean-Jacques Rousseau on the Individual and Society* (Lexington, Ky.: University Press of Kentucky, 1974). For an example of the interpretation that Rousseau is "ultimately incoherent," see John Charvet, *The Social Problem in the Philosophy of Rousseau* (London: Cambridge University Press, 1974).

25 This assertion in the *Social Contract* (I, i) does not, however, contradict Rousseau's earlier writings. For example, compare the Preface to the *Second Discourse*: "human establishments appear at first glance to be founded on piles of quicksand. It is only by examining them closely, it is only after removing the dust and sand that surround the edifice, that one perceives the unshakable base upon which it is built, and that one learns to respect its foundations" (ed. Masters, p. 97; Pléiade, III, 126–127). Indeed, Rousseau later asserted that "The foundations of the State are the same in all Governments, and these foundations are better established in my Book than in any other." (*Lettres Écrites de la Montagne*, VI [Pléiade, III, 811]). Rousseau's distinction between long-range pessimism and short-range optimism, at least in some cases, is perfectly logical albeit unconventional. At the deepest level, the main question one must ask of Rousseau's political philosophy is not whether he contradicts himself, but whether his image of political society as a man-made "edifice" or "machine" is correct. Compare Aristotle, *Politics*, I.ii.1252a–1253a.

26*Social Contract*, II, viii (p. 70; Pléiade, III, 385).

27Ibid. Rousseau's attitude to the regime of his native Geneva was thus ambivalent. It is in principle a republic, and hence a model for Europeans living under monarchies (*Second Discourse*, Dedication, and *Lettres Écrites de la Montagne*, VI; Pléiade, III, 111–121, 809–810). But in practice the government has usurped sovereignty and is unjust (*Lettres Écrites de la Montagne*, VII–VIII, IX; Pléiade, III, 813–868, 877–897).

28*Social Contract*, II, x (p. 75; Pléiade, III, 391). Hence, although Rousseau generally condemned the corruption of European societies in his own time, he argues that "in Europe there is still one country capable of legislation; it is the island of Corsica" (Ibid.) See the *Constitutional Project for Corsica* (ed. Watkins, pp. 277–330; Pléiade, III, 901–950).

29In the original manuscript, Rousseau started to title his work *Du Contrat Social*. He then changed it to *De la Société Civile* (*Of Civil Society*), only to return to his original title (Pléiade, III, 1410). One can therefore say that Rousseau carefully *chose* his title.

30*Social Contract*, I, vi (p. 53). For simplicity, references to the final version will hereafter be made by citing book and chapter in the text.

31Diderot, *Droit Naturel*, § vi (Vaughan, I, 431), partly cited in *Geneva Manuscript*, I, ii (p. 161 and editorial note 10 thereto). It is clear, not only from Diderot's text but from the way Rousseau cites it in the *Geneva Manuscript*, that the article on *Droit Naturel* (*Natural Right*) is directed against Rousseau's *Second Discourse*. According to

Rousseau, "nascent man" has "the life of an animal limited at first to pure sensations" (*Second Discourse*, Part 2; ed. Masters, p. 142). Hence Rousseau treats reason as unnatural: "If nature destined us to be healthy, I almost dare affirm that the state of reflection is a state contrary to nature and that the man who meditates is a depraved animal" (*Second Discourse*, Part 1; ed. Masters, p. 110). Diderot replies that "man is not only an animal, but an animal who reasons" (*Droit Naturel*, §iv; Vaughan, I, 431).

[32]For Rousseau's citation of Diderot's *Droit Naturel* as the "source" of his principle of the general will, see *Political Economy*, p. 212 and editorial note 9 thereto. One cannot infer from this passage that Rousseau shared Diderot's conception of a "general will of the human species" when he wrote the *Political Economy* in 1755. To be more precise, one need not assume that Rousseau ever shared Diderot's conviction that such a "general will of the human species" was the effective basis of human morality. In both the *Second Discourse* (Part 1; ed. Masters, p. 133) and final version of the *Social Contract* (II, vi; p. 65), Rousseau admits that once civilization has developed, some individuals can discover the "sublime maxim of reasoned justice" or golden rule, which can be called "a universal justice emanating from reason alone"; essentially the same point is made in *Geneva Manuscript*, I, ii. But while Rousseau agrees with Diderot that a perfectly rational man can discover such a rule of justice, he denies Diderot's argument that the resulting natural law generates binding social obligations. As Rousseau puts it in the first draft of the *Social Contract:* "concepts of natural law, which should rather be called the law of reason, begin to develop only when the prior development of the passions renders all its precepts impotent" (*Geneva Manuscript*, I, ii; p. 159). In *Political Economy*, written for Diderot's *Encyclopédie*, Rousseau obviously tries to minimize the differences between his concept of the "general will" and that of Diderot, who was at that time his best friend. Later, Rousseau and Diderot broke with each other; in subsequent editions of *Political Economy*, Rousseau therefore deleted the reference to Diderot's *Natural Right*. Still, there is no reason to presume that Rousseau did not actually derive his concept of the "general will" from ideas of the man who was—at the time—his closest friend. Compare ed. Halbwachs, pp. 125–134.

[33]In *Lettres Écrites de la Montagne*, Rousseau insists that his distinction between sovereign and government is "very important": "In Monarchies where the executive power is joined to the exercise of sovereignty, the Government is nothing but the Sovereign himself, acting by his Ministers, his Council, or by Bodies that depend absolutely on his will. In Republics, above all in Democracies, where the Sovereign never acts immediately by itself, it is something else. Then the Government is only the executive power, and it is absolutely distinct from sovereignty" Letter V (Pléiade, III, 770–771). Rousseau's position on this point was already clear in the *Second Discourse*, Part 2 (ed. Masters, pp. 161–171; Pléiade, III, 179–186).

[34]*Geneva Manuscript*, title page (p. 157; Pléiade, III, 279). It may seem forced to speak of Rousseau's "general will" as a Platonic "idea" merely because Rousseau himself uses the words "Form" and "Idea." But even without reference to this precise use of words, many commentators have noted the strong influence of Plato on Rousseau's thought: for example, Vaughan, I, 2–3; Charles W. Hendel, *Jean-Jacques Rousseau: Moralist* (Indianapolis, Ind.: Library of Liberal Arts, 1962), I, 15–19, 27–29, et passim; ed. de Jouvenel, pp. 21, 35–38, 141–143. That Rousseau viewed his philosophy as a modern response to Plato is particularly evident in the *Émile*: see Masters, *Political Philosophy of Rousseau*, pp. 98–105.

[35]See the passage of the *Confessions* cited in editorial note 4 to the *Social Contract*. In the *Social Contract* itself, there are two favorable references to Plato's *Statesman* (II, vii and III, vi) and another to Plato himself (II, viii), but no mention is made of the *Republic*. Rousseau's "Principles of Political Right" are in part inspired by Plato, but intended to provide a modern replacement for the *Republic*.

[36]See *État de Guerre* (Pléiade, III, 606), cited in Masters, *The Political Philosophy of Rousseau*, p. 286. On the analogy of the State and a machine, see ibid., pp. 260–261, 287–288, and compare note 25 to this Introduction.

[37]For an analysis, see Masters, *The Political Philosophy of Rousseau*, chap. viii.

[38]"All political societies are composed of other, smaller societies of different types, each of which has its interests and maxims. . . . The will of these particular societies always has two relations: for the members of the association, it is a general will; for the large society, it is a private will" (*Political Economy*, p. 212; Pléiade, III, 245–246).

[39]Compare *Political Economy:* "Since particular societies are always subordinate to those that contain them, one ought to obey the latter in preference to the former; the citizen's duties take precedence over the senator's, and the man's over the citizen's. But unfortunately personal interest is always found in inverse ratio to duty, and it increases in proportion as the association becomes narrower and the engagement less sacred—invincible proof that the most general will is also always the most just, and that the voice of the people is in fact the voice of God" (p. 213; Pléiade, III, 246).

[40]In this passage, Rousseau uses the word "prince" to refer to the entire body of magistrates (compare III, i). Although supposedly justified by the usage of the Republic of Venice, Rousseau's unconventional definition has the same antimonarchical bias as his use of the word "sovereign."

[41]Bertrand de Jouvenel, "Rousseau's Theory of the Forms of Government," in *Hobbes and Rousseau*, ed. Cranston and Peters, p. 496. Among recent commentators, de Jouvenel has the immense merit of having focused on the importance of what Rousseau called his "maxims" of politics, and of relating them to his generally "pessimistic" view of human history.

[42]*Confessions*, I (Pléiade, I, 5). This extraordinary opening passage, in which the first person singular appears fifteen times in seven sentences, was considered scandalously egocentric when it first became known (Pléiade, I, 1231).

[43]*Rêveries*, First Promenade (Pléiade, I, 995). Is it necessary to underline the extent to which Jean-Jacques attributes his isolation to something like a social contract?

[44]See Michel Launay's invaluable *Jean-Jacques Rousseau Écrivain Politique* (Grenoble, France: A.C.E.R., 1971), especially chap. 1. For those seeking to balance Rousseau's autobiographic writings, the best biography is probably Jean Guehenno, *Jean-Jacques Rousseau*, 2 vols. (London: Routledge and Kegan Paul, 1966).

[45]*Confessions*, IX (Pléiade, I, 416–417).

[46]Ibid. For a view of the "intellectual world" in which Rousseau moved, see Arthur M. Wilson, *Diderot* (New York: Oxford University Press, 1972) and Peter Gay, *The Enlightenment: An Interpretation* (New York: Knopf, 1966). Wilson's biography is particularly valuable since it provides a very well-balanced description of the friendship—and subsequent break—between Diderot and Rousseau.

[47]Vaughan, I, 21. Compare ed. Halbwachs, pp. 125–127. In contrast to Vaughan's argument for a basic continuity is J. C. Hall, "The Development of Rousseau's Political Philosophy," in ed. Brumfitt and Hall, pp. xlv–xlix. According to Hall, in *Political Economy* Rousseau's "interest is at first in discovering what kind of activity on the part of government will make men virtuous rather than corrupt them. . . . By the time he wrote the material copied in the *Geneva Manuscript* his interest shifted to the formal conditions that must be fulfilled if any government is to be legitimate. . . . Finally, in the latest additions to the *Social Contract*, he is concerned with finding a specific constitution that will guarantee that the general will can always be expressed. At this

stage his interest has narrowed. Whereas in the parts found in the *Geneva Manuscript* he shows a concern for the legitimate government of all peoples, in the latest parts he shows interest only in city-states, particularly Geneva" (ed. Brumfitt and Hall, p. xlix). Such a hypothesis confronts several massive difficulties. First of all, the Dedicatory Epistle of the *Second Discourse*, written in 1754, treats Geneva as "that people which, of all others, seems to me to possess society's greatest advantages and to have best prevented its abuse" (ed. Masters, p. 78). Second, the "latest part" of the *Social Contract* in unquestionably the chapter on "Civil Religion" (IV, viii), which does not fit Hall's hypothesis at all; indeed, one could say that Rousseau's civil religion is concerned with making citizens "virtuous"—for Hall the focus of the *Political Economy*. And finally, Hall's entire interpretation rests on the unproven and unprovable assumption that "the parts of the *Social Contract* that are found only in the final version" were written after the *Geneva Manuscript* which has survived. As a matter of fact, however, that manuscript is a notebook which is torn in half, with the second half missing (so that the text breaks off at Book III, chap. i). Since the *Geneva Manuscript* was written out in a fair hand as if for the printer (Pléiade, III, 1866), one could as well argue that the missing second half of the notebook was used, virtually unchanged, in the final version. In any event, it is hard to see why it is necessary to engage in complex explanations that require hunches or guesses about unknown historical details.

[48]For example, Jean Starobinski, *Jean-Jacques Rousseau: le transparence et l'obstacle* (Paris: Plon, 1957). As the Frenchman of *Rousseau Juge de Jean-Jacques* remarks: "Where could the painter and apologist of nature, today so disfigured and calomnied, have found his model if not in his own heart? . . . it was necessary for a man to paint himself to show us primitive man in this way" (Dialogue III [Pléiade, I, 936]).

[49]See *Rousseau Juge de Jean-Jacques,* Dialogue II (Pléiade, I, 932); and letter to Rey (Rousseau's publisher), April 4, 1762, cited in Masters, *Political Philosophy of Rousseau,* p. 306. As Rousseau puts it in the *Social Contract* (III, i): "I do not know the art of being clear for those who are not willing to be attentive."

On The Social Contract

Contents

BOOK I

Inquiring how man passed from the state of
nature to the civil state, and what the
essential conditions of the compact are.

BOOK II

Discussing legislation.

BOOK III

Discussing political laws; that is,
the form of the government.

BOOK IV

Continuing the discussion of political laws,
the ways to strengthen the constitution of the
State are presented.

ON THE SOCIAL CONTRACT

OR

PRINCIPLES OF POLITICAL RIGHT[1]

By J. J. Rousseau
Citizen of Geneva[2]

—foederis aequas
Dicamus leges.
Aeneid XI[3]

FOREWORD

This short treatise is taken from a more extensive work, which I undertook in the past without considering my strength, and have long since abandoned. Of the various segments that could be taken from what had been done, this is the most considerable, and seemed to me the least unworthy of being offered to the public. The rest no longer exists.[4]

BOOK I

I want to inquire whether there can be a legitimate and reliable rule of administration in the civil order, taking men as they are and laws as they can be. I shall try always to reconcile in this research what right permits with what interest prescribes, so that justice and utility are not at variance.[5]

I start in without proving the importance of my subject. It will be asked if I am a prince or a legislator to write about politics. I reply that I am neither, and that is why I write about politics. If I were a prince or a legislator, I would not waste my time saying what has to be done. I would do it, or keep silent.[6]

Born a citizen of a free State, and a member of the sovereign, the right to vote there is enough to impose on me the duty of learning about public affairs, no matter how feeble the influence of my voice may be. And I am happy, every time I meditate about governments, always to find in my research new reasons to love that of my country![7]

Chapter I: Subject of This First Book

Man was/is born free, and everywhere he is in chains.[8] One who believes himself the master of others is nonetheless a greater slave than they. How did this change occur? I do not know. What can make it legitimate? I believe I can answer this question.

If I were to consider only force and the effect it produces, I would say that as long as a people is constrained to obey and does so, it does well; as soon as it can shake off the yoke and does so, it does even better. For in recovering its freedom by means of the same right used to steal it, either the people is justified in taking it back, or those who took it away were not jus-

social order is conventional

tified in doing so. But the social order is a sacred right that serves as a basis for all the others. However, this right does not come from nature; it is therefore based on conventions. The problem is to know what these conventions are. Before coming to that, I should establish what I have just asserted.

Chapter II: On the First Societies

The most ancient of all societies, and the only natural one, is that of the family.[9] Yet children remain bound to the father only as long as they need him for self-preservation. As soon as this need ceases, the natural bond dissolves. The children, exempt from the obedience they owed the father, and the father, exempt from the care he owed the children, all return equally to independence. If they continue to remain united, it is no longer naturally but voluntarily, and the family itself is maintained only by convention.[10]

This common freedom is a consequence of man's nature. His first law is to attend to his own preservation, his first cares are those he owes himself; and as soon as he has reached the age of reason, as he alone is the judge of the proper means of preserving himself, he thus becomes his own master.

The family is therefore, so to speak, the prototype of political societies. The leader is like the father, the people are like the children; and since all are born equal and free, they only alienate their freedom for their utility. The entire difference is that in the family, the father's love for his children rewards him for the care he provides; whereas in the State, the pleasure of commanding substitutes for this love, which the leader does not have for his people.

Grotius denies that all human power is established for the benefit of those who are governed. He cites slavery as an example.[11] His most persistent mode of reasoning is always to establish right by fact.[*] One could use a more rational method, but not one more favorable to tyrants.

It is therefore doubtful, according to Grotius, whether the human race belongs to a hundred men, or whether these hundred men belong to the human race; and throughout his book he appears to lean toward the former view. This is Hobbes's sentiment as well. Thus the human species is divided into herds of livestock, each with its leader, who tends it in order to devour it.[13]

As a herdsman's nature is superior to that of his herd, so the shepherds of men, who are their leaders, are also superior in nature to their peoples. The emperor Caligula reasoned thus, according to Philo, concluding rather logically from this analogy that the kings were Gods or that people were beasts.

[*]"Learned research on public right is often merely the history of ancient abuses, and people have gone to a lot of trouble for nothing when they have bothered to study it too much." *Treatise on the Interests of France in Relation to her Neighbors, by M. le Marquis d'Argenson* (printed by Rey in Amsterdam).[12] This is exactly what Grotius has done.

critique of Hobbes

Caligula's reasoning amounts to the same thing as that of Hobbes and Grotius. Before any of them, Aristotle too had said that men are not naturally equal, but that some are born for slavery and others for domination.[14]

Aristotle was right, but he mistook the effect for the cause. Every man born in slavery is born for slavery; nothing could be more certain. Slaves lose everything in their chains, even the desire to be rid of them. They love their servitude as the companions of Ulysses loved their brutishness.* If there are slaves by nature, therefore, it is because there have been slaves contrary to nature. Force made the first slaves; their cowardice perpetuated them.

I have said nothing about king Adam or emperor Noah, father of three great monarchs who divided up the universe among themselves, as did the children of Saturn who have been identified with them. I hope this moderation will be appreciated, for as I am a direct descendant of one of these princes, and perhaps of the eldest branch, how am I to know whether, through the verification of titles, I would not discover that I am the legitimate king of the human race? However that may be, it cannot be denied that Adam was sovereign of the world, like Crusoe of his island, as long as he was its only inhabitant. And what was convenient in that empire was that the monarch, secure on his throne, had neither rebellions, nor wars, nor conspirators to fear.[16]

Chapter III: On the Right of the Strongest

The strongest is never strong enough to be the master forever unless he transforms his force into right and obedience into duty.[17] This leads to the right of the strongest, a right that is in appearance taken ironically and in principle really established. But won't anyone ever explain this word to us? Force is a physical power. I do not see what morality can result from its effects. Yielding to force is an act of necessity, not of will. At most, it is an act of prudence. In what sense could it be a duty?

Let us suppose this alleged right for a moment. I say that what comes of it is nothing but inexplicable confusion. For as soon as force makes right, the effect changes along with the cause. Any force that overcomes the first one succeeds to its right. As soon as one can disobey without punishment, one can do so legitimately, and since the strongest is always right, the only thing to do is to make oneself the strongest. But what is a right that perishes when force ceases? If it is necessary to obey by force, one need not obey by duty, and if one is no longer forced to obey, one is no longer obligated to do so. It is apparent, then, that this word right adds nothing to force. It is meaningless here.

Obey those in power.[18] If that means yield to force, the precept is good, but superfluous; I reply that it will never be violated. All power comes from

*See a short treatise by Plutarch entitled *That Animals Reason*.[15]

God, I admit, but so does all illness. Does this mean it is forbidden to call the doctor? If a brigand takes me by surprise at the edge of a woods, must I not only give up my purse by force; am I obligated by conscience to give it even if I could keep it away? After all, the pistol he holds is also a power.

Let us agree, therefore, that might does not make right, and that one is only obligated to obey legitimate powers. Thus my original question still remains.

Chapter IV: On Slavery

Since no man has any natural authority over his fellow man, and since force produces no right, there remain only conventions as the basis of all legitimate authority among men.[19]

If a private individual, says Grotius, can alienate his freedom and enslave himself to a master, why can't a whole people alienate its freedom and subject itself to a king?[20] There are many equivocal words in this that need explaining, but let us limit ourselves to the word *alienate*. To alienate is to give or to sell. Now a man who makes himself another's slave does not give himself, he sells himself, at the least for his subsistence. But why does a people sell itself? Far from furnishing the subsistence of his subjects, a king derives his own only from them, and according to Rabelais a king does not live cheaply. Do the subjects give their persons, then, on condition that their goods will be taken too? I do not see what remains for them to preserve.

It will be said that the despot guarantees civil tranquillity to his subjects. Perhaps so, but what have they gained if the wars that his ambition brings on them, if his insatiable greed, if the harassment of his ministers are a greater torment than their dissensions would be? What have they gained, if this tranquillity is one of their miseries? Life is tranquil in jail cells, too. Is that reason enough to like them? The Greeks lived tranquilly shut up in the Cyclop's cave as they awaited their turn to be devoured.[21]

To say that a man gives himself gratuitously is to say something absurd and inconceivable. Such an act is illegitimate and null, if only because he who does so is not in his right mind. To say the same thing about an entire people is to suppose a people of madmen. Madness does not make right.

Even if everyone could alienate himself, he could not alienate his children. They are born men and free. Their freedom belongs to them; no one but themselves has a right to dispose of it. Before they have reached the age of reason, their father can, in their name, stipulate conditions for their preservation, for their well-being; but he cannot give them irrevocably and unconditionally, because such a gift is contrary to the ends of nature and exceeds the rights of paternity. For an arbitrary government to be legitimate, it would therefore be necessary for the people in each generation to be master of its acceptance or rejection. But then this government would no longer be arbitrary.

To renounce one's freedom is to renounce one's status as a man, the rights of humanity and even its duties.[22] There is no possible compensation for anyone who renounces everything. Such a renunciation is incompatible with the nature of man, and taking away all his freedom of will is taking away all morality from his actions. Finally, it is a vain and contradictory convention to stipulate absolute authority on one side and on the other unlimited obedience. Isn't it clear that one is in no way engaged toward a person from whom one has the right to demand everything, and doesn't this condition alone—without equivalent and without exchange—entail the nullification of the act? For what right would my slave have against me, since all he has belongs to me, and his right being mine, my right against myself is a meaningless word?

Grotius and others derive from war another origin of the alleged right of slavery.[23] As the victor has the right to kill the vanquished, according to them, the latter can buy back his life at the cost of his freedom—a convention all the more legitimate in that it is profitable for both of them.

But it is clear that this alleged right to kill the vanquished in no way results from the state of war. Men are not naturally enemies, if only because when living in their original independence, they do not have sufficiently stable relationships among themselves to constitute either the state of peace or the state of war. It is the relationship between things, not between men, that constitutes war; and as the state of war cannot arise from simple, personal relations, but only from proprietary relations, private war between one man and another can exist neither in the state of nature, where there is no stable property, nor in the social state, where everything is under the authority of the laws.

Individual combats, duels, encounters are not acts that constitute a state.[24] And with regard to private wars, authorized by the establishments of King Louis IX of France and suspended by the peace of God, they are abuses of feudal government, an absurd system if there ever was one, contrary to the principles of natural right and to every good polity.

War is not, therefore, a relation between man and man, but between State and State, in which private individuals are enemies only by accident, not as men, nor even as citizens,* but as soldiers; not as members of the homeland but as its defenders. Finally, each State can have only other States, and not men, as enemies, since no true relationship can be established between things of differing natures.

This principle even conforms with the established maxims of all ages

---

*The Romans, who understood and respected the right of war better than any nation in the world, were so scrupulous in this respect that a citizen was not allowed to serve as a volunteer unless he had expressly engaged himself against the enemy, and against the particular enemy by name. When a legion in which Cato the Younger was serving for the first time under Popilius had been reorganized, Cato the Elder wrote to Popilius that if he wanted his son to continue to serve under him, Popilius would have to have

and with the constant practice of all civilized peoples. Declarations of war are not so much warnings to those in power as to their subjects. The foreigner—whether he be king, private individual, or people—who robs, kills, or imprisons subjects without declaring war on the prince, is not an enemy, but a brigand.[26] Even in the midst of war, a just prince may well seize everything in an enemy country that belongs to the public, but he respects the person and goods of private individuals. He respects rights on which his own are based. The end of war being the destruction of the enemy State, one has the right to kill its defenders as long as they are armed. But as soon as they lay down their arms and surrender, since they cease to be enemies or instruments of the enemy, they become simply men once again, and one no longer has a right to their lives. Sometimes it is possible to kill the State without killing a single one of its members. War confers no right that is not necessary to its end. These principles are not those of Grotius; they are not based on the authority of poets, but are derived from the nature of things, and are based on reason.

With regard to the right of conquest, it has no basis other than the law of the strongest. If war does not give the victor the right to massacre the vanquished peoples, this right he does not have cannot establish the right to enslave them. One only has the right to kill the enemy when he cannot be made a slave. The right to make him a slave does not come, then, from the right to kill him. It is therefore an iniquitous exchange to make him buy his life, over which one has no right, at the cost of his freedom. By establishing the right of life and death on the right of slavery, and the right of slavery on the right of life and death, isn't it clear that one falls into a vicious circle?

Even assuming this terrible right to kill everyone, I say that a man enslaved in war or a conquered people is in no way obligated toward his master, except to obey for as long as he is forced to do so. In taking the equivalent of his life, the victor has not spared it; rather than to kill him purposelessly, he has killed him usefully. Therefore, far from the victor having acquired any authority over him in addition to force, the state of war subsists between them as before; their relation itself is its effect, and the customs of the right of war suppose that there has not been a peace treaty. They made a convention, true; but that convention, far from destroying the state of war, assumes its continuation.

Thus, from every vantage point, the right of slavery is null, not merely because it is illegitimate, but because it is absurd and meaningless. These words *slavery* and *right* are contradictory; they are mutually exclusive.

him take the military oath again, because the first oath being annulled, he could no longer bear arms against the enemy. And the same Cato wrote his son to be careful not to appear in combat without swearing this new oath. I know that the siege of Clusium and other specific events can be raised in contradiction to this, but I cite laws and practices. The Romans were the people who least often transgressed their laws, and they are the only people who had such fine ones.[25]

Whether it is said by one man to another or by a man to a people, the following speech will always be equally senseless: *I make a convention with you that is entirely at your expense and entirely for my benefit; that I shall observe for as long as I want, and that you shall observe for as long as I want.*

Chapter V: That It Is Always Necessary to Go Back to a First Convention

Even if I were to grant everything I have thus far refuted, the proponents of despotism would be no better off.[27] There will always be a great difference between subjugating a multitude and governing a society. If scattered men, however many there may be, are successively enslaved by one individual, I see only a master and slaves; I do not see a people and its leader. It is an aggregation, if you wish, but not an association. It has neither public good nor body politic. That man, even if he had enslaved half the world, is nothing but a private individual. His interest, separate from that of the others, is still nothing but a private interest. If this same man dies, thereafter his empire is left scattered and without bonds, just as an oak tree disintegrates and falls into a heap of ashes after fire has consumed it.

A people, says Grotius, can give itself to a king. According to Grotius, a people is therefore a people before it gives itself to a king. This gift itself is a civil act; it presupposes a public deliberation. Therefore, before examining the act by which a people elects a king, it would be well to examine the act by which a people becomes a people. For this act, being necessarily prior to the other, is the true basis of society.

Indeed, if there were no prior convention, what would become of the obligation for the minority to submit to the choice of the majority, unless the election were unanimous; and where do one hundred who want a master get the right to vote for ten who do not? The law of majority rule is itself an established convention, and presupposes unanimity at least once.[28]

Chapter VI: On the Social Compact

I assume that men have reached the point where obstacles to their self-preservation in the state of nature prevail by their resistance over the forces each individual can use to maintain himself in that state.[29] Then that primitive state can no longer subsist and the human race would perish if it did not change its way of life.

Now since men cannot engender new forces, but merely unite and direct existing ones, they have no other means of self-preservation except to form, by aggregation, a sum of forces that can prevail over the resistance; set them to work by a single motivation; and make them act in concert.

This sum of forces can arise only from the cooperation of many. But since each man's force and freedom are the primary instruments of his self-preservation, how is he to engage them without harming himself and without neglecting the cares he owes to himself? In the context of my subject, this difficulty can be stated in these terms:

"Find a form of association that defends and protects the person and goods of each associate with all the common force, and by means of which each one, uniting with all, nevertheless obeys only himself and remains as free as before." This is the fundamental problem which is solved by the social contract.

The clauses of this contract are so completely determined by the nature of the act that the slightest modification would render them null and void. So that although they may never have been formally pronounced, they are everywhere the same, everywhere tacitly accepted and recognized, until the social compact is violated, at which point each man recovers his original rights and resumes his natural freedom, thereby losing the conventional freedom for which he renounced it.[30]

Properly understood, all of these clauses come down to a single one, namely the total alienation of each associate, with all his rights, to the whole community. For first of all, since each one gives his entire self, the condition is equal for everyone, and since the condition is equal for everyone, no one has an interest in making it burdensome for the others.

Furthermore, as the alienation is made without reservation, the union is as perfect as it can be, and no associate has anything further to claim. For if some rights were left to private individuals, there would be no common superior who could judge between them and the public. Each man being his own judge on some point would soon claim to be so on all; the state of nature would subsist and the association would necessarily become tyrannical or ineffectual.

Finally, as each gives himself to all, he gives himself to no one; and since there is no associate over whom one does not acquire the same right one grants him over oneself, one gains the equivalent of everything one loses, and more force to preserve what one has.[31]

If, then, everything that is not of the essence of the social compact is set aside, one will find that it can be reduced to the following terms. *Each of us puts his person and all his power in common under the supreme direction of the general will, and in a body we receive each member as an indivisible part of the whole.*

Instantly, in place of the private person of each contracting party, this act of association produces a moral and collective body, composed of as many members as there are voices in the assembly, which receives from this same act its unity, its common *self*, its life, and its will. This public person, formed thus by the union of all the others, formerly took the name *City,** and now takes that of *Republic* or *body politic,* which its members call *State* when it is passive, *Sovereign* when active, *Power* when comparing it to similar bodies. As for the associates, they collectively take the name *people;* and individually are called *Citizens* as participants in the sovereign authority, and *Subjects* as subject to the laws of the State. But these terms are often mixed up and mistaken for one another. It is enough to know how to distinguish them when they are used with complete precision.

Chapter VII: On the Sovereign

This formula shows that the act of association includes a reciprocal engagement between the public and private individuals, and that each individual, contracting with himself so to speak, finds that he is doubly engaged, namely toward private individuals as a member of the sovereign and toward the sovereign as a member of the State.[33] But the maxim of civil right that no one can be held responsible for engagements toward himself cannot be applied here, because there is a great difference between being obligated to oneself, or to a whole of which one is a part.

It must further be noted that the public deliberation that can obligate all of the subjects to the sovereign—due to the two different relationships in which each of them is considered—cannot for the opposite reason obligate the sovereign toward itself; and that consequently it is contrary to the nature of the body politic for the sovereign to impose on itself a law it cannot break. Since the sovereign can only be considered in a single relationship, it is then in the situation of a private individual contracting with himself. It is apparent from this that there is not, nor can there be, any kind of fundamental law that is obligatory for the body of the people, not even the social contract. This does not mean that this body cannot perfectly well enter an engagement toward another with respect to things that do not violate this contract. For with reference to the foreigner, it becomes a simple being or individual.

*The true meaning of this word has been almost entirely lost among modern men. Most of them mistake a town for a City, and a bourgeois for a citizen. They do not know that houses make the town, but that citizens make the City. This same error was very costly to the Carthaginians long ago. I have not read that the title *cives* has ever been given to the subjects of any prince—even in ancient times to the Macedonians or currently to the English, although they are closer to freedom than all others. Only the French use the name *citizens* with complete familiarity, because they have no true idea of its meaning, as can be seen from their dictionaries. If this were not the case, in usurping it they would be guilty of the crime of high treason. For the French, this name expresses a virtue and not a right. When Bodin wanted to talk about our citizens and bourgeois, he made a gross blunder in taking one for the other. M. d'Alembert did not confuse them, and in his article *Geneva* carefully distinguished the four orders of men (even five counting simple foreigners) who are in our town, and of whom only two compose the Republic. No other French author, to my knowledge, has understood the true meaning of the word *citizen.*[32]

forced to be free

But the body politic or the sovereign, deriving its being solely from the sanctity of the contract, can never obligate itself, even toward another, to do anything that violates that original act, such as to alienate some part of itself or to subject itself to another sovereign. To violate the act by which it exists would be to destroy itself, and whatever is nothing, produces nothing.[34]

As soon as this multitude is thus united in a body, one cannot harm one of the members without attacking the body, and it is even less possible to harm the body without the members feeling the effects. Thus duty and interest equally obligate the two contracting parties to mutual assistance, and the same men should seek to combine in this double relationship all the advantages that are dependent on it.

all for one, one for all

Now the sovereign, formed solely by the private individuals composing it, does not and cannot have any interest contrary to theirs. Consequently, the sovereign power has no need of a guarantee toward the subjects, because it is impossible for the body ever to want to harm all its members, and we shall see later that it cannot harm any one of them as an individual. The sovereign, by the sole fact of being, is always what it ought to be.[35]

But the same is not true of the subjects in relation to the sovereign, which, despite the common interest, would have no guarantee of the subjects' engagements if it did not find ways to be assured of their fidelity.

Indeed, each individual can, as a man, have a private will contrary to or differing from the general will he has as a citizen. His private interest can speak to him quite differently from the common interest. His absolute and naturally independent existence can bring him to view what he owes the common cause as a free contribution, the loss of which will harm others less than its payment burdens him. And considering the moral person of the State as an imaginary being because it is not a man, he might wish to enjoy the rights of the citizen without wanting to fulfill the duties of a subject, an injustice whose spread would cause the ruin of the body politic.[36]

free rider issue

Therefore, in order for the social compact not to be an ineffectual formula, it tacitly includes the following engagement, which alone can give force to the others: that whoever refuses to obey the general will shall be constrained to do so by the entire body; which means only that he will be forced to be free.[37] For this is the condition that, by giving each citizen to the homeland, guarantees him against all personal dependence; a condition that creates the ingenuity and functioning of the political machine, and alone gives legitimacy to civil engagements which without it would be absurd, tyrannical, and subject to the most enormous abuses.

e.g. to pay taxes

Chapter VIII: On the Civil State

This passage from the state of nature to the civil state produces a remarkable change in man, by substituting justice for instinct in his behavior and giving his actions the morality they previously lacked.[38] Only then, when the voice of duty replaces physical impulse and right replaces appetite, does man, who until that time only considered himself, find himself forced to act upon other principles and to consult his reason before heeding his inclinations. Although in this state he deprives himself of several advantages given him by nature, he gains such great ones, his faculties are exercised and developed, his ideas broadened, his feelings ennobled, and his whole soul elevated to such a point that if the abuses of this new condition did not often degrade him beneath the condition he left, he ought ceaselessly to bless the happy moment that tore him away from it forever, and that changed him from a stupid, limited animal into an intelligent being and a man.

Let us reduce the pros and cons to easily compared terms. What man loses by the social contract is his natural freedom and an unlimited right to everything that tempts him and that he can get; what he gains is civil freedom and the proprietorship of everything he possesses. In order not to be mistaken about these compensations, one must distinguish carefully between natural freedom, which is limited only by the force of the individual, and civil freedom, which is limited by the general will; and between possession, which is only the effect of force or the right of the first occupant, and property, which can only be based on a positive title.

To the foregoing acquisitions of the civil state could be added moral freedom, which alone makes man truly the master of himself. For the impulse of appetite alone is slavery, and obedience to the law one has prescribed for oneself is freedom. But I have already said too much about this topic, and the philosophic meaning of the word *freedom* is not my subject here.

Chapter IX: On Real Estate

Each member of the community gives himself to it at the moment of its formation, just as he currently is—both himself and all his force, which includes the goods he possesses.[39] It is not that by this act possession, in changing hands, changes its nature and becomes property in the hands of the sovereign. But as the force of the City is incomparably greater than that of a private individual, public possession is by that very fact stronger and more irrevocable, without being more legitimate, at least as far as foreigners are concerned. For with regard to its members, the State is master of all their goods through the social contract, which serves within the State as the basis of all rights. But with regard to other powers, it is master only through the right of the first occupant, which it derives from the private individuals.

The right of the first occupant, although more real than the right of the strongest, becomes a true right only after the establishment of the right of property. Every man naturally has a right to everything he needs; but the positive act that makes him the proprietor of some good excludes him from all the rest. Once his portion is designated, he should limit himself to it, and

not so in US + OZ

no longer has any right to the community's goods. That is why the right of the first occupant, so weak in the state of nature, is respectable to every civilized man. In this right, one respects not so much what belongs to others as what does not belong to oneself.

In general, the following conditions are necessary to authorize the right of the first occupant to any land whatsoever. First, that this land not yet be inhabited by anyone. Second, that one occupy only the amount needed to subsist. Third, that one take possession not by a vain ceremony, but by labor and cultivation, the only sign of property that others ought to respect in the absence of legal titles. — *Indians + Aborigines did not do*

Indeed, by granting the right of the first occupant to need and labor, hasn't it been extended as far as possible? Is it impossible to establish limits *This* to this right? Will setting foot on a piece of common ground be sufficient to *always* claim on the spot to be its master? Will having the force to disperse other men for a moment be sufficient to take away forever their right to return? *good* How can a man or a people seize an immense territory and deprive the whole human race of it except through punishable usurpation, since this act takes away from the remaining men the dwelling place and foods that nature gives them in common? When Nuñez Balboa, standing on the shore, took possession of the South Sea and all of South America in the name of the crown of Castile, was this enough to dispossess all the inhabitants and exclude all the princes of the world? On that basis such ceremonies multiplied rather ineffectually, and all the Catholic King had to do was to take possession of the entire universe all at once from his study, subsequently eliminating from his empire what had previously been possessed by other princes.

It is understandable how the combined and contiguous lands of private individuals become public territory, and how the right of sovereignty, extending from the subjects to the ground they occupy, comes to include both property and persons, which places those who possess land in a greater dependency and turns even their force into a guarantee of their loyalty. This advantage does not appear to have been well understood by ancient kings who, only calling themselves Kings of the Persians, the Scythians, the Macedonians, seem to have considered themselves leaders of men rather than masters of the country. Today's kings more cleverly call themselves Kings of France, Spain, England, etc. By thus holding the land, they are quite sure to hold its inhabitants.

What is extraordinary about this alienation is that far from plundering private individuals of their goods, by accepting them the community thereby only assures them of legitimate possession, changes usurpation into a true right, and use into property. Then, since the possessors are considered as trustees of the public goods, and since their rights are respected by all the members of the State and maintained with all its force against foreigners, through a transfer that is advantageous to the public and even more so to themselves, they have, so to speak, acquired all they have given. This paradox is easily explained by the distinction between the rights of the sovereign and of the proprietor to the same resource, as will be seen hereafter.

It can also happen that men start to unite before possessing anything and that subsequently taking over a piece of land sufficient for all, they use it in common or divide it among themselves, either equally or according to proportions established by the sovereign. However this acquisition is made, the right of each private individual to his own resources is always subordinate to the community's right to all, without which there would be neither solidity in the social bond nor real force in the exercise of sovereignty.

I shall end this chapter and this book with a comment that ought to serve as the basis of the whole social system. It is that rather than destroying natural equality, the fundamental compact on the contrary substitutes a moral and legitimate equality for whatever physical inequality nature may have placed between men, and that although they may be unequal in force or in genius, they all become equal through convention and by right.*

END OF THE FIRST BOOK

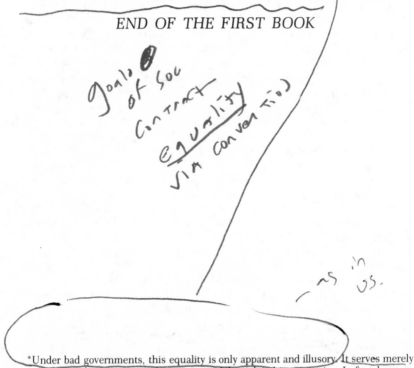

*Under bad governments, this equality is only apparent and illusory. It serves merely to maintain the poor man in his misery and the rich in his usurpation. In fact, laws are always useful to those who have possessions and harmful to those who have nothing. It follows from this that the social state is only advantageous to men insofar as they all have something and none of them has anything superfluous.[40]

BOOK II

No representative gov't. (handwritten)

Chapter I: That Sovereignty Is Inalienable

The first and most important consequence of the principles established above is that the general will alone can guide the forces of the State according to the end for which it was instituted, which is the common good.[41] For if the opposition of private interests made the establishment of societies necessary, it is the agreement of these same interests that made it possible. It is what these different interests have in common that forms the social bond, and if there were not some point at which all the interests are in agreement, no society could exist. Now it is uniquely on the basis of this common interest that society ought to be governed.

I say, therefore, that sovereignty, being only the exercise of the general will, can never be alienated, and that the sovereign, which is only a collective being, can only be represented by itself. Power can perfectly well be transferred, but not will.

Indeed, though it is not impossible for a private will to agree with the general will on a given point, it is impossible, at least, for this agreement to be lasting and unchanging. For the private will tends by its nature toward preferences, and the general will toward equality. It is even more impossible for there to be a guarantee of this agreement even should it always exist. It would not be the result of art, but of chance. The sovereign may well say, "I currently want what a particular man wants, or at least what he says he wants." But it cannot say, "What that man will want tomorrow, I shall still want," since it is absurd for the will to tie itself down for the future and since no will can consent to anything that is contrary to the good of the being that wills. Therefore, if the people promises simply to obey, it dissolves itself by that act; it loses the status of a people. The moment there is a master, there is no longer a sovereign, and from then on the body politic is destroyed.

This is not to say that the commands of leaders cannot pass for expressions of the general will, as long as the sovereign, being free to oppose them, does not do so. In such a case, one ought to presume the consent of the people from universal silence. This will be explained at greater length.

Chapter II: That Sovereignty Is Indivisible

For the same reason that sovereignty is inalienable, it is indivisible.[42] Because either the will is general* or it is not. It is the will of the people as a

---

*In order for a will to be general, it is not always necessary for it to be unanimous, but it is necessary that all votes be counted. Any formal exclusion destroys the generality.

body, or of only a part. In the first case, this declared will is an act of sovereignty and constitutes law. In the second case, it is merely a private will or an act of magistracy; it is at most a decree.

But our political theorists, unable to divide the principle of sovereignty, divide it in its object. They divide it into force and will; into legislative power and executive power; into rights of taxation, justice, and war; into internal administration and power to negotiate with foreigners. Sometimes they mix all these parts together, sometimes they separate them. They turn the sovereign into a fantastic body formed of bits and pieces. It is as though they constructed a man out of several bodies, one of which would have eyes, another arms, another feet, and nothing more. Japanese charlatans are said to cut up a child right in front of the audience; then, tossing all the parts into the air one after another, they make the child come back down alive and in one piece. The juggling acts of our political theorists are about like that. After they have taken the social body apart by a trick worthy of a carnival, they put the pieces back together in some unknown way.

This error comes from not having developed precise concepts of sovereign authority, and from having mistaken for parts of that authority what were merely emanations from it. Thus, for example, the acts of declaring war and making peace have been regarded as acts of sovereignty, which they are not, since each of these acts is not a law but merely an application of the law, a particular act which determines the legal situation, as will be clearly seen when the idea attached to the word *law* is established.[43]

By examining the other divisions in the same way, it would be found that every time it is thought that sovereignty is divided, a mistake has been made, and that the rights that are mistaken for parts of that sovereignty are always subordinate to it and always presuppose supreme wills which these rights merely execute.

It is hard to overestimate how much this lack of precision has obscured the decisions of those who have written on the subject of political right when they wanted to judge the respective rights of kings and peoples on the basis of the principles they had established. In chapters III and IV of the first book of Grotius, anyone can see how this learned man and his translator Barbeyrac get entangled and trapped in their sophisms, for fear of saying too much or not enough according to their viewpoints, and of offending the interests they needed to reconcile. Grotius—taking refuge in France, discontent with his homeland, and wanting to pay court to Louis XIII to whom his book is dedicated—spares nothing to divest the people of all their rights and to endow kings with them as artfully as possible. This would certainly have been the preference of Barbeyrac, too, who dedicated his translation to King George I of England. But unfortunately the expulsion of James II, which he calls abdication, forced him to be cautious, evasive, and equivocal so as not to make William appear to be a usurper. If these two writers had adopted the true principles, all their difficulties would have been avoided and

Will of all

they would always have been consistent. But they would have told the truth with regret and paid court only to the people. For truth does not lead to fortune, and the people does not confer embassies, professorships, or pensions.

Chapter III: Whether the General Will Can Err

From the foregoing it follows that the general will is always right and always tends toward the public utility. But it does not follow that the people's deliberations always have the same rectitude. One always wants what is good for oneself, but one does not always see it. The people is never corrupted, but it is often fooled, and only then does it appear to want what is bad.

There is often a great difference between the will of all and the general will. The latter considers only the common interest; the former considers private interest, and is only a sum of private wills. But take away from these same wills the pluses and minuses that cancel each other out,* and the remaining sum of the differences is the general will.

If, when an adequately informed people deliberates, the citizens were to have no communication among themselves, the general will would always result from the large number of small differences, and the deliberation would always be good. But when factions, partial associations at the expense of the whole, are formed, the will of each of these associations becomes general with reference to its members and particular with reference to the State. One can say, then, that there are no longer as many voters as there are men, but merely as many as there are associations. The differences become less numerous and produce a result that is less general. Finally, when one of these associations is so big that it prevails over all the others, the result is no longer a sum of small differences, but a single difference. Then there is no longer a general will, and the opinion that prevails is merely a private opinion.

In order for the general will to be well expressed, it is therefore important that there be no partial society in the State, and that each citizen give only his own opinion.** Such was the unique and sublime system instituted by the great Lycurgus. If there are partial societies, their number must be multiplied and their inequality prevented, as was done by Solon, Numa, and

---

Each interest, says the Marquis d'Argenson, *has different principles. The agreement of two private interests is formed in opposition to the interest of a third.*[44] He could have added that the agreement of all interests is formed in opposition to the interest of each. If there were no different interests, the common interest, which would never encounter any obstacle, would scarcely be felt. Everything would run smoothly by itself and politics would cease to be an art.

**Vera cosa è,* says Machiavelli, *che alcune divisioni nuocono alle Republiche, a alcune giovano: quelle nuocono che sono dalle sette e da partigiani accompagnate: quelle giovano che senza sette, senza partigiani si mantengono. Non potendo adunque provedere un fondatore d'una Republica che non siano nimicizie in quella, hà da proveder almeno che non vi siano sette.* History of Florence, Book VII.[45]

Servius. These precautions are the only valid means of ensuring that the general will is always enlightened and that the people is not deceived.[46]

Chapter IV: On the Limits of the Sovereign Power

If the State or the City is only a moral person whose life consists in the union of its members, and if the most important of its concerns is that of its own preservation, it must have a universal, compulsory force to move and arrange each part in the manner best suited to the whole.[47] Just as nature gives each man absolute power over all his members, the social compact gives the body politic absolute power over all its members, and it is this same power, directed by the general will, which as I have said bears the name sovereignty.

But in addition to the public person, we have to consider the private persons who compose it and whose life and freedom are naturally independent of it. It is a matter, then, of making a clear distinction between the respective rights of the citizens and the sovereign,* and between the duties that the former have to fulfill as subjects and the natural rights to which they are entitled as men.

It is agreed that each person alienates through the social compact only that part of his power, goods, and freedom whose use matters to the community; but it must also be agreed that the sovereign alone is the judge of what matters.[49]

A citizen owes the State all the services he can render it as soon as the sovereign requests them. But the sovereign, for its part, cannot impose on the subjects any burden that is useless to the community. It cannot even will to do so, for under the law of reason nothing is done without a cause, any more than under the law of nature.

The engagements that bind us to the social body are obligatory only because they are mutual, and their nature is such that in fulfilling them one cannot work for someone else without also working for oneself. Why is the general will always right and why do all constantly want the happiness of each, if not because there is no one who does not apply this word *each* to himself, and does not think of himself as he votes for all? Which proves that the equality of right, and the concept of justice it produces, are derived from each man's preference for himself and consequently from the nature of man; that the general will, to be truly such, should be general in its object as well as in its essence; that it should come from all to apply to all; and that it loses its natural rectitude when it is directed toward any individual, determinate object. Because then, judging what is foreign to us, we have no true principle of equity to guide us.

Indeed, as soon as it is a matter of fact or a particular right concerning a

---

*Attentive readers, please do not be in a hurry to accuse me of inconsistency here. I have been unable to avoid it in my terminology, given the poverty of the language. But wait.[48]

[handwritten annotations in top margin: "acting as sovereign — general rulier", "u u Magistrate — spec. acts"]

point that has not been regulated by a prior, general convention, the affair is in dispute. It is a lawsuit where the interested private individuals constitute one party and the public the other, but in which I see neither what law must be followed nor what judge should decide. In this case it would be ridiculous to want to turn to an express decision of the general will, which can only be the conclusion of one of the parties and which, for the other party, is consequently only a foreign, private will, showing injustice on this occasion and subject to error. Thus just as a private will cannot represent the general will, the general will in turn changes its nature when it has a particular object; and as a general will it cannot pass judgment on either a man or a fact. When the people of Athens, for example, appointed or dismissed its leaders, awarded honors to one or imposed penalties on another, and by means of a multitude of particular decrees performed indistinguishably all the acts of government, the people then no longer had a general will properly speaking. It no longer acted as sovereign, but as magistrate. This will appear contrary to commonly held ideas, but you must give me time to present my own.

It should be understood from this that what generalizes the will is not so much the number of votes as the common interest that unites them, because in this institution everyone necessarily subjects himself to the conditions he imposes on others, an admirable agreement between interest and justice which confers on common deliberations a quality of equity that vanishes in the discussion of private matters, for want of a common interest that unites and identifies the rule of the judge with that of the party.

[handwritten margin annotations right side: "Kant &", "Rawls", "which is what he wants —", "Morality", "+", "Utility"]

However one traces the principle, one always reaches the same conclusion, namely that the social compact established an equality between the citizens such that they all engage themselves under the same conditions and should all benefit from the same rights. Thus by the very nature of the compact, every act of sovereignty, which is to say every authentic act of the general will, obligates or favors all citizens equally, so that the sovereign knows only the nation as a body and makes no distinctions between any of those who compose it. What really is an act of sovereignty then? It is not a convention between a superior and an inferior, but a convention between the body and each of its members. A convention that is legitimate because it has the social contract as a basis; equitable, because it is common to all; useful, because it can have no other object than the general good; and solid, because it has the public force and the supreme power as guarantee. As long as subjects are subordinated only to such conventions, they do not obey anyone, but solely their own will; and to ask how far the respective rights of the sovereign and of citizens extend is to ask how far the latter can engage themselves to one another, each to all and all to each.

It is apparent from this that the sovereign power, albeit entirely absolute, entirely sacred, and entirely inviolable, does not and cannot exceed the limits of the general conventions, and that every man can fully dispose of the part of his goods and freedom that has been left to him by these conventions. So that the sovereign never has the right to burden one subject more than another, because then the matter becomes individual, and its power is no longer competent.

Once these distinctions are acknowledged, it is so false that the social contract involves any true renunciation on the part of private individuals that their situation, by the effect of this contract, is actually preferable to what it was beforehand; and instead of an alienation, they have only exchanged to their advantage an uncertain, precarious mode of existence for another that is better and safer; natural independence for freedom; the power to harm others for their personal safety; and their force, which others could overcome, for a right which the social union makes invincible. Their life itself, which they have dedicated to the State, is constantly protected by it; and when they risk it for the State's defense, what are they then doing except to give back to the State what they have received from it? What are they doing that they did not do more often and with greater danger in the state of nature, when waging inevitable fights they defend at the risk of their life that which preserves it for them? It is true that everyone has to fight, if need be, for the homeland, but also no one ever has to fight for himself. Don't we still gain by risking, for something that gives us security, a part of what we would have to risk for ourselves as soon as our security is taken away?

Chapter V: On the Right of Life and Death

It is asked how private individuals who have no right to dispose of their own lives can transfer to the sovereign a right they do not have.[50] This question appears hard to resolve only because it is badly put. Every man has a right to risk his own life in order to preserve it. Has it ever been said that someone who jumps out of a window to escape a fire is guilty of suicide? Has this crime ever even been imputed to someone who dies in a storm, although he was aware of the danger when he set off?

The social treaty has the preservation of the contracting parties as its end. Whoever wants the end also wants the means, and these means are inseparable from some risks, even from some losses. Whoever wants to preserve his life at the expense of others should also give it up for them when necessary. Now the citizen is no longer judge of the risk to which the law wills that he be exposed, and when the prince has said to him, "It is expedient for the State that you should die," he ought to die. Because it is only under this condition that he has lived in safety up to that point, and because his life is no longer only a favor of nature, but a conditional gift of the State.

The death penalty inflicted on criminals can be considered from approximately the same point of view: it is in order not to be the victim of a murderer that a person consents to die if he becomes one. Under this treaty, far from disposing of one's own life, one only thinks of guaranteeing it; and it cannot be presumed that any of the contracting parties is at that time planning to have himself hanged.

of Locke

Besides, every offender who attacks the social right becomes through his crimes a rebel and traitor to his homeland; he ceases to be one of its members by violating its laws, and he even wages war against it. Then the State's preservation is incompatible with his own, so one of the two must perish; and when the guilty man is put to death, it is less as a citizen than as an enemy. The proceedings and judgment are the proofs and declaration that he has broken the social treaty, and consequently is no longer a member of the State. Now as he had acknowledged himself to be such, at the very least by his residence, he ought to be removed from it by exile as a violator of the compact or by death as a public enemy. For such an enemy is not a moral person but a man, and in this case the right of war is to kill the vanquished.

But it will be said that the condemnation of a criminal is a particular act. Agreed—hence this condemnation is not to be made by the sovereign. It is a right the sovereign can confer without itself being able to exercise it. All of my ideas fit together, but I can hardly present them simultaneously.

Moreover, frequent corporal punishment is always a sign of weakness or laziness in the government. There is no wicked man who could not be made good for something. One only has the right to put to death, even as an example, someone who cannot be preserved without danger.

With regard to the right to pardon, or to exempt a guilty man from the penalty prescribed by the law and pronounced by the judge, this belongs only to one who is above the judge and the law—which is to say, to the sovereign. Yet its right in this matter is not very clear and the cases in which it is applied are very rare. In a well-governed State, there are few punishments, not because many pardons are given, but because there are few criminals. When the State declines, a high number of crimes guarantees their impunity. Under the Roman Republic, the senate and consuls never tried to pardon. The people itself did not do so, although it sometimes revoked its own judgment. Frequent pardons indicate that crimes will soon have no further need of them, and everyone sees where that leads. But I feel that my heart murmurs and holds back my pen. Let these questions be discussed by the just man who has never transgressed and who never needed pardon himself.

Chapter VI: On Law

Through the social compact we have given the body politic existence and life; the issue now is to give it movement and will through legislation.[51] For the original act which forms and unites this body does not thereby determine anything about what it should do to preserve itself.

Whatever is good and in accordance with order is so by the nature of things, independently of human conventions. All justice comes from God; He alone is its source. But if we knew how to receive it from on high, we would need neither government nor laws. There is without doubt a universal justice emanating from reason alone;[52] but to be acknowledged among us, this justice must be reciprocal. Considering things from a human point of view, the laws of justice are ineffectual among men for want of a natural sanction. They merely benefit the wicked man and harm the just, when the latter observes them toward everyone while no one observes them toward him. Therefore, there must be conventions and laws to combine rights with duties and to bring justice back to its object. In the state of nature where everything is in common, I owe nothing to those to whom I have promised nothing; I recognize as belonging to someone else only what is useless to me. It is not the same in the civil state where all rights are fixed by the law.

But what is a law after all? As long as people are satisfied to attach only metaphysical ideas to this word, they will continue to reason without understanding each other, and when they have stated what a law of nature is, they will not thereby have a better idea of what a law of the State is.

I have already said that there is no general will concerning a particular object. Indeed, that particular object is either within the State or outside of the State. If it is outside of the State, a will that is foreign to it is not general in relation to it. And if within the State, that object is part of it. Then a relation between the whole and its parts is formed which makes of them two separate entities, one of which is the part and the other of which is the whole minus that part. But the whole minus a part is not the whole, and for as long as this relationship lasts, there is no whole, but rather two unequal parts. It follows from this that the will of one of them is no longer general in relation to the other.

But when the entire people enacts something concerning the entire people, it considers only itself, and if a relationship is formed then, it is between the whole object viewed in one way and the whole object viewed in another, without any division of the whole. Then the subject matter of the enactment is general like the will that enacts. It is this act that I call a law.

When I say that the object of the laws is always general, I mean that the law considers the subjects as a body and actions in the abstract, never a man as an individual or a particular action. Thus the law can very well enact that there will be privileges, but it cannot confer them on anyone by name. The law can create several classes of citizens, and even designate the qualities determining who has a right to these classes, but it cannot name the specific people to be admitted to them. It can establish a royal government and hereditary succession, but it cannot elect a king or name a royal family. In short, any function that relates to an individual object does not belong to the legislative power.

Given this idea, one sees immediately that it is no longer necessary to ask who should make laws, since they are acts of the general will; nor whether the prince is above the laws, since he is a member of the State; nor whether the law can be unjust, since no one is unjust toward himself; nor how one is free yet subject to the laws, since they merely record our wills.

Furthermore, one sees that since the law combines the universality of the will and that of the object, what any man, whoever he may be, orders on his own authority is not a law. Whatever is ordered even by the sovereign concerning a particular object is not a law either, but rather a decree; nor is it an act of sovereignty, but of magistracy.

I therefore call every State ruled by laws a republic, whatever the form of administration may be, for then alone the public interest governs and the commonwealth really exists. Every legitimate government is republican.* I shall explain later what government is.

Laws are properly speaking only the conditions of the civil association. The people that is subject to the laws ought to be their author. Only those who are forming an association have the right to regulate the conditions of the society. But how will they regulate these conditions? Will it be in common accord, by sudden inspiration? Does the body politic have an organ to enunciate its will? Who will give it the necessary foresight to formulate acts and publish them in advance, or how will it pronounce them in time of need? How will a blind multitude, which often does not know what it wants because it rarely knows what is good for it, carry out by itself an undertaking as vast and as difficult as a system of legislation? By itself, the people always wants the good, but by itself it does not always see it. The general will is always right, but the judgment that guides it is not always enlightened. It must be made to see objects as they are, or sometimes as they should appear to be; shown the good path it seeks; safeguarded against the seduction of private wills; shown how to assimilate considerations of time and place; taught to weigh the attraction of present, tangible advantages against the danger of remote, hidden ills. Private individuals see the good they reject; the public wants the good it does not see. All are equally in need of guides. The former must be obligated to make their wills conform to their reason. The latter must be taught to know what it wants. Then public enlightenment results in the union of understanding and will in the social body; hence the complete cooperation of the parts, and finally the greatest force of the whole. From this arises the necessity for a legislator.

Chapter VII: On the Legislator

The discovery of the best rules of society suited to nations would require a superior intelligence, who saw all of men's passions yet experienced none of them; who had no relationship at all to our nature yet knew it thoroughly; whose happiness was independent of us, yet who was nevertheless willing to attend to ours; finally one who, preparing for himself a future

*By this word I do not mean only an aristocracy or a democracy, but in general any government guided by the general will, which is the law. In order to be legitimate, the government must not be confounded with the sovereign, but must be its minister. Then monarchy itself is a republic. This will become clearer in the next book.

glory with the passage of time, could work in one century and enjoy the reward in another.*[53] Gods would be needed to give laws to men.

The same reasoning Caligula used with respect to fact was used by Plato with respect to right in defining the civil or royal man he seeks in the *Statesman*. But if it is true that a great prince is a rare man, what about a great legislator? The former only has to follow the model that the latter should propose. The latter is the mechanic who invents the machine; the former is only the workman who puts it together and starts it running. At the birth of societies, says Montesquieu, the leaders of republics create the institutions; thereafter, it is the institutions that form the leaders of republics.[54]

One who dares to undertake the founding of a people should feel that he is capable of changing human nature, so to speak; of transforming each individual, who by himself is a perfect and solitary whole, into a part of a larger whole from which this individual receives, in a sense, his life and his being; of altering man's constitution in order to strengthen it; of substituting a partial and moral existence for the physical and independent existence we have all received from nature. He must, in short, take away man's own forces in order to give him forces that are foreign to him and that he cannot make use of without the help of others. The more these natural forces are dead and destroyed, and the acquired ones great and lasting, the more the institution as well is solid and perfect. So that if each citizen is nothing, and can do nothing, except with all the others, and if the force acquired by the whole is equal or superior to the sum of the natural forces of all the individuals, it may be said that legislation has reached its highest possible point of perfection.

The legislator is an extraordinary man in the State in all respects. If he should be so by his genius, he is no less so by his function. It is not magistracy, it is not sovereignty. This function, which constitutes the republic, does not enter into its constitution. It is a particular and superior activity that has nothing in common with human dominion. For if one who has authority over men should not have authority over laws, one who has authority over laws should also not have authority over men. Otherwise his laws, ministers of his passions, would often only perpetuate his injustices, and he could never avoid having private views alter the sanctity of his work.

When Lycurgus gave his homeland laws, he began by abdicating the throne. It was the custom of most Greek cities to entrust the establishment of their laws to foreigners. The modern republics of Italy often imitated this practice. The republic of Geneva did so too, with good results.** During its finest period Rome saw all the crimes of tyranny revived in its midst, and

---

*A people only becomes famous when its legislation starts to decline. It is not known for how many centuries the institutions founded by Lycurgus created the happiness of the Spartans before the rest of Greece became aware of them.

**Those who only consider Calvin as a theologian do not understand the extent of his genius. The drawing up of our wise edicts, in which he played a large part, does him as

nearly perished as a result of combining legislative authority and sovereign power in the same hands.

However even the Decemvirs never took upon themselves the right to have any law passed solely on their authority. *Nothing that we propose,* they said to the people, *can become law without your consent. Romans, be yourselves the authors of the laws that should create your happiness.*[56]

He who drafts the laws, therefore, does not or should not have any legislative right. And the people itself cannot, even if it wanted to, divest itself of this incommunicable right, because according to the fundamental compact, only the general will obligates private individuals, and one can never be assured that a private will is in conformity with the general will until it has been submitted to the free vote of the people. I have already said this, but it is not useless to repeat it.

Thus one finds combined in the work of legislation two things that seem incompatible: an undertaking beyond human force and, to execute it, an authority that amounts to nothing.

Another difficulty deserves attention. Wise men who want to use their own language, rather than that of the common people, cannot be understood by the people. Now there are a thousand kinds of ideas that are impossible to translate into the language of the people. Overly general views and overly remote objects are equally beyond its grasp. Each individual, appreciating no other aspect of government than the one that relates to his private interest, has difficulty perceiving the advantages he should obtain from the continual deprivations imposed by good laws. In order for an emerging people to appreciate the healthy maxims of politics, and follow the fundamental rules of statecraft, the effect would have to become the cause; the social spirit, which should be the result of the institution, would have to preside over the founding of the institution itself; and men would have to be prior to laws what they ought to become by means of laws. Since the legislator is therefore unable to use either force or reasoning, he must necessarily have recourse to another order of authority, which can win over without violence and persuade without convincing.

This is what has always forced the fathers of nations to have recourse to the intervention of heaven and to attribute their own wisdom to the Gods, so that the peoples, subjected to the laws of the State as to those of nature, and recognizing the same power in the formation of man and of the City, might obey with freedom and bear with docility the yoke of public felicity.

It is this sublime reason, which rises above the grasp of common men, whose decisions the legislator places in the mouth of the immortals in order to convince by divine authority those who cannot be moved by human

---

much honor as his *Institutes*. Whatever revolution time may bring about in our cult, as long as love of the homeland and liberty is not extinguished among us, the memory of that great man will never cease to be blessed.[55]

prudence.* But it is not every man who can make the Gods speak or be believed when he declares himself their interpreter. The legislator's great soul is the true miracle that should prove his mission. Any man can engrave stone tablets, buy an oracle, pretend to have a secret relationship with some divinity, train a bird to talk in his ear, or find other crude ways to impress the people. One who knows only that much might even assemble, by chance, a crowd of madmen, but he will never found an empire, and his extravagant work will soon die along with him. False tricks can form a fleeting bond; wisdom alone can make it durable. The Jewish law, which is still in existence, and the law of the son of Ishmael, which has ruled half the world for ten centuries, still bear witness today to the great men who formulated them. And whereas proud philosophy or blind partisan spirit regards them merely as lucky imposters, the true political theorist admires in their institutions that great and powerful genius which presides over lasting establishments.[58]

One must not conclude from all this, as Warburton does, that politics and religion have a common object for us, but rather that at the origin of nations, one serves as an instrument of the other.[59]

Chapter VIII: On the People

Just as an architect, before putting up a big building, observes and tests the ground to see whether it can bear the weight, so the wise founder does not start by drafting laws that are good in themselves, but first examines whether the people for whom he intends them is suited to bear them.[60] For this reason, Plato refused to give laws to the Arcadians and Cyrenians, knowing that these two peoples were rich and could not tolerate equality. For this reason, there were good laws and wicked men in Crete, because Minos had disciplined only a people full of vices.

A thousand nations that have flourished on earth could never have tolerated good laws, and even those that could were only so disposed for a very short time during their entire existence. Most peoples, like men, are docile only in their youth. They become incorrigible as they grow older. Once customs are established and prejudices have taken root, it is a dangerous and foolhardy undertaking to want to reform them. The people cannot even tolerate having their ills touched for the purpose of destroying them, like those stupid and cowardly patients who tremble at the sight of a doctor.

To be sure, just as men's minds are unhinged and their memory of the past erased by some illnesses, so there sometimes occur during the lifetime of States violent periods when revolutions have the same effect on peoples as

---

*E veramente, says Machiavelli, mai non fu alcuno ordinatore di leggi straordinarie in un popolo, che non ricorresse a Dio, perche altrimenti non sarebbero accettate; perche sono molti beni conosciuti da uno prudente, i quali non hanno in se raggioni evidenti da potergli persuadere ad altrui. Discourses on Titus Livy, Book I, chapter 11.[57]

do certain crises on individuals; when horror of the past is equivalent to amnesia, and when the State, set afire by civil wars, is reborn so to speak from its ashes and resumes the vigor of youth by escaping from death's clutches. Sparta in the time of Lycurgus and Rome after the Tarquins were like this, and among us so were Holland and Switzerland after the expulsion of the tyrants.

But these events are rare: they are exceptions that can always be explained by the particular constitution of the exceptional State. They cannot even occur twice for the same people; for it can liberate itself as long as it is merely barbarous, but can no longer do so when the civil machinery is worn out. Then, disturbances can destroy it, but revolutions cannot reestablish it, and as soon as its chains are broken, it falls apart and no longer exists. Henceforth it must have a master and not a liberator. Free peoples, remember this maxim: Freedom can be acquired, but it can never be recovered.

Youth is not childhood. For nations as for men there is a time of youth, or maturity if you prefer, that must be awaited before subjecting them to laws. But the maturity of a people is not always easy to recognize, and if it is anticipated, the work is ruined. One people is capable of discipline at birth, another is not after ten centuries. The Russians will never be truly civilized because they were civilized too early. Peter had the genius of imitation. He did not have true genius, the kind that creates and makes everything from nothing. A few of the things he did were good; most were out of place. He saw that his people was barbarous; he did not see that it was not ripe for a political order. He wanted to make it cultured when it only needed to be made warlike. He wanted first to make Germans and Englishmen, whereas it was necessary to begin by making Russians. He prevented his subjects from ever becoming what they could be by convincing them that they were what they are not. It is like the way a French tutor molds his pupil to shine briefly during his childhood and thereafter never to amount to anything. The Russian empire would like to subjugate Europe and will itself be subjugated. The Tartars, its subjects or its neighbors, will become its masters and ours. This revolution appears inevitable to me. All the kings of Europe are working together to hasten it.

Chapter IX: Continued — on small states

Just as nature has set limits to the stature of a well-formed man, beyond which there are only giants or dwarfs, so with regard to the best constitution of a State there are limits to the dimensions it can have in order that it be neither too large to be well governed nor too small to be self-sustaining.[61] There is a maximum force in every body politic which it cannot exceed and of which it often falls short by growing larger. The more the social bond stretches, the looser it becomes, and in general a small State is proportionately stronger than a large one.

A thousand reasons prove this maxim. First, administration becomes more difficult over long distances, as a weight becomes heavier at the end of a bigger lever. It also becomes more burdensome as the number of levels multiplies, because each city first has its own administration paid for by the people; each district has one, again paid for by the people; next each province, then the large-scale governments—the satrapies and vice-royalties—that cost more the higher up one goes, and always at the expense of the unfortunate people. Finally there is the supreme administration which crushes everything. Such overtaxing continually exhausts the subjects. Far from being better governed by these different levels, they are less well governed than if there were only one over them. As it is, there barely remain resources for emergencies, and when it is necessary to have recourse to them, the State is always on the brink of ruin.

That is not all. Not only does the government have less vigor and speed to enforce the laws, prevent harassment, correct abuses, and forestall seditious undertakings that may occur in distant places, but also the people has less affection for leaders it never sees, for the homeland which is like the whole world in its eyes, and for its fellow citizens, most of whom are foreigners to it. The same laws cannot be suited to such a variety of provinces, which have different mores, live in contrasting climates, and cannot tolerate the same form of government. Different laws only produce discord and confusion among peoples who, living under the same leaders and in constant communication, move or get married in each other's areas and, being subjected to other customs, never know whether their patrimony is really theirs. Talents are buried, virtues unknown, vices unpunished in this multitude of men who do not know one another and who are gathered together in one place by the location of the supreme administration. Leaders overburdened with work see nothing by themselves; functionaries govern the State. Finally, all the public attention is absorbed by the steps that must be taken to maintain the general authority, which so many distant officials want to avoid or abuse. Nothing is left for the people's happiness, and there is barely anything left for its defense if necessary. And thus a State that is too big for its constitution collapses and perishes, crushed by its own weight.

On the other hand, the State ought to procure a sufficient basis to be solid, to withstand the upheavals it is sure to go through and the efforts it will have to make to sustain itself. For all peoples have a kind of centrifugal force by which they constantly act upon each other and tend to grow at the expense of their neighbors, like Descartes's vortices. Thus the weak risk being rapidly swallowed up, and none can hope to preserve itself except by establishing a kind of equilibrium with all the others, which approximately equalizes the pressure on all.

It is apparent from this that there are reasons to expand and reasons to shrink, and it is not the least of political theorist's talents to find among these reasons the proportion most advantageous to the preservation of the State. In general, it can be said that the former, being merely external and relative, should be subordinated to the latter, which are internal and absolute. A healthy, strong constitution is the first thing that must be sought, and one should rely more on the vigor born of a good government than on the resources furnished by a large territory.

Besides, there have been States so constituted that the necessity for conquests entered into their constitution itself, and that were forced to grow endlessly to maintain themselves. Perhaps they took great pride in this happy necessity, though it showed them, along with the limit of their size, the inevitable moment of their downfall.

Chapter X: Continued

[handwritten annotation: assumes agriculture as economic basis of the state]

A body politic can be measured in two ways, namely by the extent of its territory and by the number of its people; and there is an appropriate ratio between these two measures if the State is to be given its true size.[62] It is men who make up the State and the land feeds the men. This ratio therefore consists in there being enough land for the maintenance of its inhabitants and as many inhabitants as can be fed by the land. The maximum force of a given number of people is to be found in this proportion; for if there is too much land, its defense is burdensome, its cultivation inadequate, its output superfluous. This is the immediate cause of defensive wars. If there is not enough land, the State finds itself at the discretion of its neighbors for the supplement. This is the immediate cause of offensive wars. Every people whose position only gives it the alternative between commerce and war is intrinsically weak. It is dependent on its neighbors; it is dependent on events. It never has anything except an uncertain and brief existence. Either it conquers and alters its situation or it is conquered and reduced to nothing. It cannot preserve its freedom except through smallness or greatness.

One cannot calculate arithmetically a fixed ratio between the extent of land and the number of men that are mutually sufficient, as much because of differences in qualities of the terrain, its degrees of fertility, the nature of its products, and the influence of climate, as because of differences to be noted in the temperaments of the men who inhabit them, some of whom consume little in a fertile country, others a great deal on more sterile soil. Attention must also be paid to the greater or lesser fecundity of women, to what the country offers that is more or less favorable to population, to the number of people that the legislator can hope to attract there by means of what he establishes. Hence, the legislator's judgment should not be based on what he sees, but on what he foresees; nor should he give as much consideration to the present state of the population as to the state it should naturally attain. Finally, there are a thousand occasions when the peculiarities of a place require or permit the inclusion of more land than appears necessary. Thus one expands considerably in mountainous country where natural products, namely woods and pastures, require less work; where experience shows that women are more fecund than on the plains; and where a large amount of sloping land provides only a small horizontal area, which is all that can be counted on for vegetation. On the contrary, it is possible to shrink by the sea, even on nearly barren rocks and sand, because fishing can substitute substantially for products of the land, because men should be gathered more closely together to repulse pirates, and because it is, in addition, easier to relieve the country of surplus inhabitants by means of colonies.

To these conditions for founding a people must be added one that cannot substitute for any other, but without which all the rest are useless: the enjoyment of prosperity and peace. For the time when a State is organized, like that when a battalion is formed, is the instant when the body is least capable of resisting and easiest to destroy. There would be better resistance during absolute disorder than during a moment of ferment, when everyone is concerned about his status rather than the danger. Should a war, famine, or sedition occur in this time of crisis, the State is inevitably overthrown.

To be sure, many governments are established during such storms, but then it is these very governments that destroy the State. Usurpers always bring about or choose these times of troubles, taking advantage of public panic to pass destructive laws that the people would never adopt when calm. The choice of the moment of the founding is one of the surest ways to distinguish the work of a legislator from that of a tyrant.

What people, then, is suited for legislation? One that, though already bound by some union of origin, interest, or convention, has not yet borne the true yoke of laws. One that has neither customs nor superstitions that are deeply entrenched. One that does not fear being crushed by a sudden invasion and can, without becoming involved in its neighbors' quarrels, resist each of them by itself or use the help of one to drive away another. One where each member can be known to all, and where it is not necessary to impose on any man a greater burden than a man can bear. One that does not depend on other peoples, and on whom no other people depends.* One that is neither rich nor poor, and can be self-sufficient. Finally, one that combines the stability of an ancient people with the docility of a new people. What makes the work of legislation difficult is not so much what must be established as what must be destroyed. And what makes success so rare is the impossibility of finding the simplicity of nature together with the needs of so-

---

*If one of two neighboring peoples could not do without the other, the situation would be very hard for the former and very dangerous for the latter. In such a case, any wise nation will very quickly try to relieve the other of its dependency. The republic of Thlascala, an enclave within the Mexican empire, preferred doing without salt to buying it from the Mexicans, and even to accepting it free of charge. The wise Thlascalans saw the trap hidden beneath this generosity. They preserved their freedom; and this small State, enclosed within this great empire, was finally the instrument of its ruin.

ciety. All these conditions, it is true, are hard to find together. Hence one sees few well-constituted States.

In Europe there is still one country capable of legislation: it is the island of Corsica. The valor and perseverance with which this courageous people was able to recover and defend its freedom would well deserve that some wise man should teach them how to preserve it. I have a feeling that some day this little island will astound Europe.

Chapter XI: On the Various Systems of Legislation

If one seeks to define precisely what constitutes the greatest good of all, which ought to be the end of every system of legislation, one will find that it comes down to these two principal objects: *freedom* and *equality*.[63] Freedom because all private dependence is that much force subtracted from the body of the State; equality because freedom cannot last without it.

I have already said what civil freedom is. With regard to equality, this word must not be understood to mean that degrees of power and wealth should be exactly the same, but rather that with regard to power, it should be incapable of all violence and never exerted except by virtue of status and the laws; and with regard to wealth, no citizen should be so opulent that he can buy another, and none so poor that he is constrained to sell himself. This presumes moderation in goods and influence on the part of the upper classes and moderation in avarice and covetousness on the part of the lower classes.*

This equality is said to be a speculative fantasy that cannot exist in practice. But if abuse is inevitable, does it follow that it must not at least be regulated? It is precisely because the force of things always tends to destroy equality that the force of legislation should always tend to maintain it.

But these general objects of all good institutions should be modified in each country according to the relationships that arise as much from the local situation as from the character of the inhabitants, and it is on the basis of these relationships that each people must be assigned a particular system of institutions that is the best, not perhaps in itself, but for the State for which it is intended. For example, is the soil unprofitable and barren, or the country too small for its inhabitants? Turn to industry and the arts, the products of which can be exchanged for the foodstuffs you lack. On the contrary, do you inhabit rich plains and fertile hillsides? Do you lack inhabitants on good terrain? Apply all your efforts to agriculture, which multiplies men, and chase out the arts, which would merely complete the country's depopulation by

---

*Do you then want to give stability to the State? Bring the extremes as close together as possible: tolerate neither opulent people nor beggars. These two conditions, naturally inseparable, are equally fatal to the common good. From the one come those who foment tyranny and from the other the tyrants. It is always between them that trafficking in the public freedom takes place. The one buys it and the other sells it.

concentrating its small number of inhabitants in a few locations.* Do you inhabit extensive, convenient shores? Cover the sea with ships; cultivate commerce and navigation. You will have a brilliant and brief existence. Is your coast merely a place where the sea meets almost inaccessible rocks? Remain barbarians and fish eaters; you will live more peacefully, better perhaps, and surely more happily. In short, apart from the maxims common to all, each people contains within itself some cause that organizes it in a particular manner and renders its legislation appropriate for it alone. Thus the Hebrews long ago and the Arabs recently have had religion as their principal object; the Athenians, letters; Carthage and Tyre, commerce; Rhodes, navigation; Sparta, war; and Rome, virtue. The author of *The Spirit of Laws* has given large numbers of examples of the art by which the legislator directs the institutions toward each of these objects.[65]

The constitution of a State is made truly solid and enduring when matters of expediency are so well satisfied that natural relationships and the laws always agree on the same points, and the latter only secure, accompany, and rectify, so to speak, the former. But if the legislator makes a mistake about his objective and adopts a different principle from the one arising from the nature of things—whether one tends toward servitude and the other toward freedom, one toward wealth and the other toward population growth, or one toward peace and the other toward conquest—the laws will imperceptibly weaken, the constitution will be altered, and the State will not cease being agitated until it is either destroyed or changed, and invincible nature has regained its dominion.[66]

Chapter XII: Classification of Laws

Various relations have to be considered in order to organize the whole or give the commonwealth the best possible form.[67] First the action of the entire body acting upon itself—that is, the relationship of the whole to the whole, or of the sovereign to the State; and this relationship is composed of the relationship of intermediary terms, as we shall see later.

The laws that regulate this relationship are named political laws, and are also called fundamental laws, not without a degree of reason if these laws are wise. For if there is only one correct way to organize each State, the people that has found it should abide by it; but if the established order is bad, why should one accept, as fundamental, laws that prevent it from being good? Besides, in any event a people is always the master to change its laws—even the best laws; for if it wishes to do itself harm, who has the right to prevent it from doing so?

Any type of foreign commerce, says the Marquis d'Argenson, creates almost nothing but a deceptive utility for a kingdom in general. It can enrich some private individuals, even some towns; but the whole nation gains nothing from it and the people is not better off because of it.[64]

The second relation is that of the members to each other or to the entire body. And this relationship should be as small as possible with respect to the former and as large as possible with respect to the latter, so that each citizen is in a position of perfect independence from all the others and of excessive dependence upon the City. This is always achieved by the same means, because only the force of the State creates the freedom of its members. It is from this second relationship that civil laws arise.

It is possible to consider a third type of relation between man and the law, namely that of disobedience and penalty. And this gives rise to the establishment of criminal laws, which are basically not so much a particular type of law as a sanction for all the others.

To these three types of laws is added a fourth, the most important of all; which is not engraved on marble or bronze, but in the hearts of the citizens; which is the true constitution of the State; which gains fresh force each day; which, when other laws age or die out, revives or replaces them, preserves a people in the spirit of its institution, and imperceptibly substitutes the force of habit for that of authority. I am speaking of mores, customs, and especially of opinion—a part of the laws unknown to our political theorists, but on which the success of all the others depends; a part to which the great legislator attends in secret while appearing to limit himself to the particular regulations that are merely the sides of the arch of which mores, slower to arise, form at last the unshakable keystone.

Among these various classes, political laws, which constitute the form of government, are the only ones relevant to my subject.

END OF THE SECOND BOOK

BOOK III

Before discussing the various forms of government, let us try to define the precise meaning of this word, which has not yet been very well explained.

Chapter I: On Government in General

I warn the reader that this chapter should be read carefully, and that I do not know the art of being clear for those who are not willing to be attentive.[68]

Every free action has two causes that combine to produce it. One is moral, namely the will that determines the act; the other is physical, namely the power that executes it. When I walk toward an object, I must first want to go there, and in the second place my feet must take me there. A paralyzed man who wants to run, or an agile man who does not want to do so, will both remain where they are.[69] The body politic has the same motivating causes; force and will are distinguishable within it in the same sense, the latter under the name *legislative power* and the former under the name *executive power*. Nothing is or should be done there without their cooperation.

We have seen that the legislative power belongs to the people and can belong only to it. It is easy to see, on the contrary, by the principles already established, that the executive power cannot belong to the general public in its legislator's or sovereign capacity, because this power consists solely of particular acts which are not within the jurisdiction of the law, nor consequently of the sovereign, all of whose acts can only be laws.

The public force must therefore have its own agent, which unites it and puts it into operation according to the directions of the general will; which serves as a means of communication between the State and the sovereign; and which does in a sense for the public person what the union of the soul and the body does in man. This is the reason why, in the State, there is government, which has been incorrectly confounded with the sovereign, of which it is only the minister.

What is the government then? An intermediate body established between the subjects and the sovereign for their mutual communication, and charged with the execution of the laws and the maintenance of civil as well as political freedom.

The members of this body are called magistrates or *kings*, that is to say *governors;* and the body as a whole bears the name *prince.** Thus those who claim that the act by which a people subjects itself to leaders is not a contract are entirely right. It is absolutely nothing but a commission, a function in which, as simple officers of the sovereign, they exercise in its name the power that has been entrusted to them by the sovereign, and that the sovereign can limit, modify, and take back whenever it pleases, since the alienation of such a right is incompatible with the nature of the social body and contrary to the goal of the association.

I therefore give the name *government* or supreme administration to the legitimate exercise of the executive power, and Prince or magistrate to the man or the body charged with that administration.

It is in the government that are found the intermediate forces whose relationships compose the relationship of the whole to the whole or of the sovereign to the State. The latter relationship can be represented by the extremes of a continuous proportion, of which the proportional mean is the government. The government receives from the sovereign the orders that it gives to the people; and in order for the State to be in good equilibrium, all things considered, the product or power of the government, taken by itself, must be equal to the product or power of the citizens, who are sovereigns on the one hand and subjects on the other.[71]

Moreover, none of the three terms could be altered without simultaneously destroying the proportion. If the sovereign wants to govern, or if the magistrate wants to make laws, or if the subjects refuse to obey, disorder replaces rule, force and will no longer act in concert, and the dissolved State thereby falls into despotism or anarchy. Finally, since there is only one proportional mean for each relationship, there is no more than one good government possible in a State. But as a thousand events can change the relationships of a people, not only can different governments be suited to various peoples, but also to the same people at different times.

To try to give some idea of the various relationships that can exist between these two extremes, I shall take as an example the number of people, which is a comparatively easy relationship to express.

Let us suppose that the State is composed of ten thousand citizens. The sovereign can only be considered collectively and as a body. But each private individual in his status as a subject is considered as an individual. Thus the sovereign is to the subject as ten thousand is to one. Which is to say that the share of each member of the State is only one ten-thousandth of the sovereign authority, even though he is totally subjected to it. If the people is composed of one hundred thousand men, the condition of the subjects does

---

*Thus in Venice the college is given the name *most serene prince* even when the Doge is not in attendance.[70]

not change, and each is equally under the whole dominion of the laws, while his vote, reduced to one hundred-thousandth, has ten times less influence on their drafting. Thus since the subject always remains one, the ratio of the sovereign to the subject increases in proportion to the number of citizens.[72] From which it follows that the larger the State grows, the less freedom there is.

When I say that the ratio increases, I mean that it grows further away from equality. Thus the greater the ratio in the geometrician's sense, the less relationship there is in the ordinary sense.[73] In the former, the ratio—considered in terms of quantity—is measured by the quotient, and in the latter, the relationship—considered in terms of likeness—is estimated by the similarity.

Now the less relationship there is between private wills and the general will, that is between the mores and the laws, the more repressive force should increase. Thus, in order for the government to be good, it ought to be relatively stronger in proportion as the people is more numerous.

On the other hand, as the enlargement of the State gives those entrusted with the public authority more temptations and means to abuse their power, the more force the government should have to restrain the people, the more the sovereign should have in turn to restrain the government. I am not speaking here of absolute force, but of the relative force of the various parts of the State.

It follows from this double relationship that the continuous proportion between the sovereign, the prince, and the people is no arbitrary idea, but rather a necessary consequence of the nature of the body politic. It also follows that since one of the extremes, namely the people as subject, is fixed and represented by unity, whenever the doubled ratio increases or decreases, the simple ratio increases or decreases similarly; and that consequently the middle term is changed.[74] This shows that there is no unique and absolute constitution of government, but that there can be as many governments of different natures as there are States of different sizes.

If in ridiculing this system, it was said that in order to find this proportional mean and form the body of the government, it is only necessary, according to me, to calculate the square root of the number of people, I would reply that I merely use that number here as an example; that the relationships of which I speak are not measured solely by the number of men, but in general by the quantity of action, which is itself the combined result of a multitude of causes; and moreover that if I momentarily borrow the vocabulary of geometry in order to express myself in fewer words, I am nevertheless not unaware that geometric precision does not exist in moral quantities.

The government is on a small scale what the body politic that contains it is on a large scale. It is a moral person, endowed with certain faculties; active like the sovereign, passive like the State; and that can be broken down into other similar relationships from which a new proportion consequently arises, and still another within this one according to the order of tribunals, until an indivisible middle term is reached; that is, a single leader or supreme magistrate, who can be considered, in the middle of this progression, as the unity between the series of fractions and that of whole numbers.[75]

Without becoming involved in this multiplication of terms, let us be satisfied to consider the government as a new body in the State, distinct from both the people and the sovereign, and intermediate between them.

The essential difference between these two bodies is that the State exists by itself, but the government exists only through the sovereign. Thus the dominant will of the prince is not or should not be anything except the general will or the law; his force is only the public force concentrated in him. As soon as he wants to derive from himself some absolute and independent act, the bond tying the whole together begins to loosen. If it finally came about that the prince had a private will more active than that of the sovereign, and that he used some of the public force at his discretion to obey that private will, so that there were, so to speak, two sovereigns—one by right, the other in fact—at that moment the social union would vanish and the body politic would be dissolved.[76]

However, in order for the body of the government to exist, to have a real life that distinguishes it from the body of the State, and for all its members to be able to act in concert and fulfill the purpose for which it is instituted, it must have a separate *self*, a sensibility shared by its members, a force or will of its own that leads to its preservation. This separate existence supposes assemblies, councils, power to deliberate and decide, rights, titles, privileges that belong exclusively to the prince and that make the magistrate's status more honorable in proportion as it is more laborious. The difficulties lie in organizing this subordinate whole within the whole in such a way that it does not change the general constitution by strengthening its own; that it always distinguishes between its separate force intended for its own preservation and the public force intended for the preservation of the State; and in short that it is ever ready to sacrifice the government to the people and not the people to the government.

Besides, although the artificial body of the government is the product of another artificial body and has, in a sense, only a borrowed and subordinate life, this does not prevent it from acting with more or less vigor or speed, or from enjoying a more or less robust state of health, so to speak. Finally, without directly departing from the goal of its institution, it can deviate from that goal to a greater or lesser extent according to the way in which it is constituted.

From all these differences arise the various relationships the government ought to have with the body of the State, according to the accidental and particular relationships that modify a given State. For often the government that is in itself the best will become the worst if its relationships are not modified according to the defects of the body politic to which it belongs.

Chapter II: On the Principle that Constitutes the Various Forms of the Government

In order to present the general cause of these differences, it is necessary here to distinguish between the prince and the government, as I have already distinguished between the State and the sovereign.

The body of the magistracy can be composed of a larger or smaller number of members. We have said that the ratio of the sovereign to the subjects was greater as the people was more numerous, and by an obvious analogy we can say the same about the government with reference to the magistrates.

Now the total force of the government, being always that of the State, does not vary; from which it follows that the more of this force the government uses on its own members, the less is left for acting upon the entire people.

Therefore, the more numerous the magistrates, the weaker the government. Since this maxim is fundamental, let us try to explain it more clearly.

We can distinguish three essentially different wills in the person of the magistrate. First, the individual's own will, which tends only toward his private advantage. Second, the common will of the magistrates, which relates uniquely to the advantage of the prince; which may be called the corporate will, and is general in relation to the government and private in relation to the State, of which the government is a part. Third, the will of the people or the sovereign will, which is general both in relation to the State considered as the whole and in relation to the government considered as part of that whole.[77]

In perfect legislation, the private or individual will should be null; the corporate will of the government very subordinate; and consequently the general or sovereign will always dominant and the unique rule of all the others.

According to the natural order, on the contrary, these different wills become more active as they are more concentrated. Thus the general will is always the weakest, the corporate will has second place, and the private will is the first of all. So that each member of the government is first himself, and then magistrate, and then citizen—a gradation that is exactly opposite to the one required by the social order.

Given the above, suppose that the entire government is in the hands of one man. Then the private will and the corporate will are perfectly combined, and consequently the latter attains the highest possible degree of intensity. Now as the use of force is dependent on the degree of will, and as the absolute force of the government does not vary, it follows that the most active of governments is that of one man.

On the contrary, let us combine the government with the legislative authority; let us make the prince out of the sovereign and all of the citizens into as many magistrates. Then the corporate will has no more activity than the general will with which it is combined, and leaves to the particular will its full force. Thus the government, always with the same absolute force, will have the minimum relative force or activity.

These relationships are incontestable and are further confirmed by other considerations. It is apparent, for example, that each magistrate is more active in his group than each citizen in his, and consequently that the private will has much more influence on acts of the government than on those of the sovereign. For each magistrate is almost always responsible for some function of the government, whereas each citizen, taken separately, performs no function of sovereignty. Besides, the more the State expands, the more its real force increases, although not in proportion to its size. But if the State stays the same, increasing the number of magistrates is useless; the government does not thereby acquire greater real force, because this force is that of the State, whose size is unchanged. Thus the relative force or the activity of the government diminishes, while its absolute or real force cannot increase.

It is also certain that business is expedited more slowly in proportion as more people are responsible for it; that by overestimating prudence, chance is underestimated, opportunity escapes, and by dint of deliberating, the fruits of deliberation are often lost.

I have just proved that the government becomes slack in proportion as the magistrates multiply, and I have proved earlier that the more numerous the people, the greater the increase in repressive force should be. From which it follows that the ratio of magistrates to government should be the inverse of the ratio of subjects to sovereign, which means that the more the State grows, the more the government should shrink, so that the number of leaders diminishes in proportion to the increase of people.[78]

However, I refer here only to the relative force of the government, and not to its rectitude. For on the contrary, the more numerous the body of magistrates, the closer the corporate will is to the general will, whereas under a unique magistrate, this same corporate will, as I have said, is merely a private will. Thus what can be gained on one side is lost on the other, and the legislator's art is knowing how to find the point at which the government's force and will, always in a reciprocal proportion, are combined in the relationship most advantageous to the State.

Chapter III: Classification of Governments

In the preceding chapter, we have seen why the various kinds or forms of governments are distinguished by the number of members composing them. It remains to be seen in this chapter how this classification is made.

The sovereign can, in the first place, entrust the government to the entire people or to the majority of people, so that there are more citizens who are magistrates than citizens who are simply private individuals. This form of government is given the name *democracy.*

Or else it can restrict the government to the hands of a small number, so that there are more simple citizens than magistrates; and this form bears the name *aristocracy.*

Finally, it can concentrate the whole government in the hands of a single magistrate from whom all the others derive their power. This third form is the most common, and is called *monarchy* or royal government.[79]

It should be noted that all these forms, or at least the first two, admit different degrees, and even have a rather broad range. For democracy can include all the people, or be restricted to half. In turn, aristocracy can be indeterminately restricted from half the people down to the smallest number. Even royalty admits some division. Sparta constantly had two kings as provided by its constitution; and in the Roman Empire there were as many as eight emperors at a time, yet one couldn't say that the Empire was divided. Thus there is a point at which each form of government is indistinguishable from the next, and it is apparent that under these three names, government really admits as many diverse forms as there are citizens in the State.

Furthermore, since this same government can, in certain respects, be subdivided into other segments, one administered in one way, the other in another, the combination of these three forms can produce a multitude of mixed forms, each of which can be multiplied by all the simple forms.

People have always argued a great deal over the best form of government, without considering that each of them is the best in certain cases, and the worst in others.

If the number of supreme magistrates in different States ought to be in inverse proportion to the number of citizens, it follows that in general democratic government is suited to small States, aristocratic to medium-sized ones, and monarchical to large ones. This rule is derived directly from the principle; but countless circumstances can furnish exceptions.

Chapter IV: On Democracy

He who makes the law knows better than anyone else how it ought to be executed and interpreted. It therefore seems that there could be no better constitution than one in which the executive power is combined with the legislative. But it is this very thing that makes such a government inadequate in certain respects, because the things that ought to be distinguished are not, and the prince and the sovereign, being nothing but the same person, form so to speak only a government without a government.

It is not good for him who makes the laws to execute them, nor for the body of people to turn its attention away from general considerations to particular objects. Nothing is more dangerous than the influence of private interests on public affairs; and the abuse of laws by the government is a lesser evil than the corruption of the legislator, which is the inevitable consequence of private considerations. Then, the substance of the State being changed, all reform becomes impossible. A people who would never take advantage of government would never take advantage of independence either. A people who would always govern well would not need to be governed.

In the strict sense of the term, a true democracy has never existed and never will exist. It is contrary to the natural order that the majority govern and the minority be governed. It is unimaginable that the people remain constantly assembled to attend to public affairs, and it is obvious that it could not establish commissions to do so without changing the form of administration.

Indeed, I believe it can be stated as a principle that when the functions of the government are divided among several tribunals, those with the fewest members sooner or later acquire the greatest authority, if only because of the facility in expediting business which brings this about naturally.

Besides, consider how many things that are hard to combine are presupposed by this form of government. First, a very small State where the people is easily assembled and where each citizen can easily know all the others. Second, great simplicity of mores, which prevents a multitude of business and knotty discussions. Next, a great equality of ranks and of fortunes, without which equality of rights and authority could not subsist for long. Finally, little or no luxury, because either luxury is the result of wealth, or it makes wealth necessary. It corrupts both rich and poor, the one by possessing, the other by coveting. It sells out the homeland to indolence and vanity; it deprives the State of all of its citizens by enslaving some of them to others and all of them to opinion.

That is why a famous author named virtue as the principle of a republic. For all these conditions could not subsist without virtue. But because he failed to make the necessary distinctions, this noble genius often lacked precision, sometimes clarity; and he did not see that since the sovereign authority is everywhere the same, the same principle ought to apply to every well-constituted State, albeit to a greater or lesser degree according to the form of government.[80]

Let us add that there is no government so subject to civil wars and internal agitations as the democratic or popular one, because there is none that tends so strongly and constantly to change its form, nor that demands more vigilance and courage to be maintained in its own form. It is above all under this constitution that the citizen ought to arm himself with force and constancy, and repeat every day of his life from the bottom of his heart what a virtuous Palatine* said in the Diet of Poland: *Malo periculosam libertatem quam quietum servitium.*[81]

If there were a people of Gods, it would govern itself democratically. Such a perfect government is not suited to men.

*The Palatine of Posen, father of the King of Poland, Duke of Lorraine.

Chapter V: On Aristocracy

We have here two quite distinct moral persons, namely the government and the sovereign; and consequently two general wills, one relative to all the citizens, the other solely for the members of the administration. Thus, although the government can regulate its internal policy in whatever way it pleases, it can never speak to the people except in the name of the sovereign, that is in the name of the people itself. This must never be forgotten.

The first societies governed themselves aristocratically. The heads of families deliberated among themselves about public affairs. Young people demurred without difficulty to the authority of experience. This is the source of the names *priests, ancients, senate, elders*. The savages of North America still govern themselves in this manner, and are very well governed.

But as instituted inequality came to predominate over natural inequality, wealth or power* was preferred to age, and aristocracy became elective. Finally, when power was passed on together with goods from father to children, creating patrician families, the government was made hereditary, and there were senators only twenty years old.

There are, therefore, three kinds of aristocracy: natural, elective, and hereditary. The first is suited only to simple peoples. The third is the worst of all governments. The second is the best; it is aristocracy properly so-called.[83]

Besides the advantage of distinguishing between the two powers, aristocracy has that of the choice of its members. For in popular government all the citizens are born magistrates, whereas this type limits them to a small number, and they become magistrates only through election,** a means by which probity, enlightenment, experience, and all the other reasons for public preference and esteem become so many new guarantees of being well governed.

Moreover, assemblies are more conveniently held, business is better discussed and acted upon in a more orderly and diligent manner, the prestige of the State is better sustained in foreign countries by venerable senators than by an unknown or scorned multitude.

In short, it is the best and most natural order for the wisest to govern the multitude, as long as it is certain that they govern for its benefit and not for their own. Devices must not be multiplied uselessly, nor must twenty thousand men do what one hundred well-chosen men can do still better. But it must be noted that here the corporate interest begins to direct the public force in accordance with the rule of the general will to a lesser degree, and

---

*It is clear that among ancient peoples the word *optimates* does not mean the best, but the most powerful.[82]

**It is extremely important to regulate by laws the form of the election of magistrates. Because if it is left up to the will of the prince, the government unavoidably falls into a hereditary aristocracy, as happened in the Republics of Venice and Bern. So it is that the former has long been a dissolute State, whereas the latter has maintained itself through the extreme wisdom of its senate. It is a very honorable and very dangerous exception.

that another unavoidable tendency exempts from the laws a part of the executive power.

With regard to particular matters of expediency, a State must not be so small, nor a people so simple and upright, that the execution of laws follows immediately from the public will, as is the case in a good democracy. Nor must a nation be so large that the leaders, dispersed to govern it, can each make decisions for the sovereign in his own department, and begin by making themselves independent in order to become masters in the long run.

But if aristocracy requires somewhat fewer virtues than popular government, it also requires others which are specific to it, such as moderation among the rich and contentment among the poor. For it seems that rigorous equality would be misplaced in an aristocracy. It was not even adhered to in Sparta.

Besides, if this form includes some inequality of wealth, it is simply in order for the administration of public affairs to be generally confided to those who can best devote all their time to it; but not, as Aristotle claims, for the rich to be always given preference.[84] On the contrary, it is important that an opposite choice should occasionally teach the people that personal merit offers more important reasons for preference than does riches.

Chapter VI: On Monarchy

Up to this point, we have considered the prince as a moral and collective person, united by the force of laws and entrusted with the executive power in the State. Now we have to consider this power brought together in the hands of a natural person, a real man, who alone has the right to dispose of it according to the laws. He is what is called a monarch or a king.

Completely to the contrary of the other administrations, where a collective being represents an individual, in this one an individual represents a collective being; so that the moral unity which constitutes the prince is at the same time a physical unity, in which all the faculties combined with such difficulty by law in the other administrations are combined naturally.

Thus the will of the people and the will of the prince, and the public force of the State and the particular force of the government, all respond to the same motivation; all the mechanisms of the machine are in the same hands; everything moves toward the same goal; there are no opposing movements that are mutually destructive; and there is no constitution imaginable in which a lesser effort produces a greater action. Archimedes sitting tranquilly on the shore and effortlessly pulling a huge vessel over the waves is my image of a skillful monarch governing his vast states from his study, and setting everything in motion while appearing immobile himself.

But if no other government has more vigor, there is none where the private will has greater sway and more easily dominates the others. Everything moves toward the same goal, it is true, but this goal is not that of public felicity, and the very force of the administration is constantly detrimental to the State.

Kings want to be absolute, and from afar one cries out to them that the best way to be so is to make themselves loved by their peoples. This maxim is very fine and even very true in certain respects. Unfortunately, it will always be ridiculed in royal courts. The power that comes from the peoples' love is doubtless the greatest, but it is precarious and conditional. Princes will never be satisfied with it. The best kings want to be able to be wicked if it so pleases them, without ceasing to be the masters. A political sermonizer tells them in vain that since the force of the people is their own, their greatest interest is that the people should be flourishing, numerous, formidable. They know very well this is not true. Their personal interest is first of all that the people should be weak, miserable, and unable ever to offer any resistance to them. I admit that, assuming the subjects were always perfectly submissive, the prince's interest would then be for the people to be powerful, so that this power, being his, would make him formidable in the eyes of his neighbors. But as this interest is only secondary and subordinate, and as the two assumptions are incompatible, it is natural that princes should always prefer the maxim that is the more immediately useful to them. This is what Samuel so strongly pointed out to the Hebrews; and what Machiavelli showed with clarity. While pretending to give lessons to kings, he gave great ones to the people. Machiavelli's *The Prince* is the book of republicans. *

We found, through general relationships, that monarchy is suited only to large States, and we find this again in examining monarchy itself. The more numerous the public administration, the more the ratio of the prince to the subjects decreases and approaches equality, so that this ratio is one to one, or equality itself, in a democracy. This same ratio increases in proportion as the government is more restricted, and it is at its maximum when the government is in the hands of one man. The distance between the prince and the people is then too great, and the State lacks cohesion. In order to create this, therefore, there must be intermediate orders; there must be princes, grandees, and nobility to fill them. Now none of that is suited to a small State, which is ruined by all these distinctions.

But if it is difficult for a large State to be well governed it is even more so for it to be well governed by one man alone, and everyone knows what happens when the king appoints agents.

*Machiavelli was an honorable man and a good citizen; but being attached to the Medici household, he was forced, during the oppression of his homeland, to disguise his love of freedom. The choice of his execrable hero is in itself enough to make manifest his hidden intention; and the contrast between the maxims of his book *The Prince* and those of his *Discourses on Titus Livy* and of his *History of Florence* shows that this profound political theorist has had only superficial or corrupt readers until now. The court of Rome has severely forbidden his book. I can well believe it; it is the court that he most clearly depicts.[85]

An essential and inevitable defect, which will always place monarchical government below republican, is that in the latter the public voice almost never raises to high positions any but enlightened, capable men, who fulfill them with honor; whereas those who attain them in monarchies are most often merely petty troublemakers, petty rascals, petty intriguers, whose petty talents—which lead to high positions in royal courts—serve only to reveal their ineptitude to the people as soon as these men are in place. The people makes a mistake in its choice much less often than the prince, and a man of real merit is nearly as rare in a ministry as a fool at the head of a republican government. So it is that when, by some lucky chance, one of those men who are born to govern takes control of public affairs in a monarchy that has almost been wrecked by this bunch of fine managers, people are all amazed at the resources he finds, and it is epoch-making for the whole country.[86]

For a monarchical State to be well governed, its size or extent would have to be measured by the capabilities of the one who governs. It is easier to conquer than to administer. With a big enough lever, it is possible to move the world with one finger, but holding it up requires the shoulders of Hercules. If the State is the least bit large, the prince is almost always too small. When, on the contrary, it happens that the State is too small for its leader, which is very rare, it is still badly governed, because the leader, always pursuing his grandiose views, forgets the peoples' interests and by misusing his excessive talents, makes them no less unhappy than does a stupid leader who is limited by his lack of talents. The kingdom would, so to speak, have to expand or shrink with each reign depending on the competence of the prince. In contrast, because the talents of a senate are more stable, the State can have invariable boundaries and the administration be no less well run.

The most evident drawback of the government of one man is the lack of continuous successions which, in the two others, form an unbroken bond. When one king dies, another is needed. Elections leave dangerous intervals; they are stormy, and unless the citizens have a disinterestedness and integrity rarely found in this form of government, intrigue and corruption are involved. It is difficult for one to whom the State has been sold not to sell it in turn, and compensate at the expense of the poor for the money that has been extorted from him by the powerful. Sooner or later, everything becomes venal under such an administration, and the peace then enjoyed under kings is worse than the disorder of the interregna.

What has been done to prevent these evils? Crowns have been made hereditary in certain families, and an order of succession has been established which prevents all dispute when kings die. Which is to say that by substituting the drawback of regencies for that of elections, apparent tranquillity has been preferred to a wise administration; and that the risk of having children, monsters, or imbeciles for leaders has been preferred to having to argue over the choice of good kings. People have not considered that in being thus exposed to the risks of the alternative, they have almost all the odds against them. Dionysius the Younger answered very sensibly when his father, reproaching him for a shameful action, asked, have I given you such an example? Ah, replied his son, your father wasn't a king.[87]

Everything conspires to deprive of justice and reason a man raised to command others. A great effort is made, it is said, to teach young princes the art of ruling. It does not appear that this education does them any good. It would be better to start by teaching them the art of obeying. The most famous kings in history were not brought up to rule. It is a science that is never less well known than after it has been learned, and that is better acquired by obeying than by commanding. *Nam utilissimus idem ac brevissimus bonarum malarumque rerum delectus, cogitare quid aut nolueris sub alio Principe aut volueris.**[88]

One consequence of this lack of coherence is the instability of a royal form of government which, guided sometimes by one plan and sometimes by another, according to the character of the ruling prince or of those ruling for him, cannot have a fixed object for long, nor a consistent mode of conduct. This variability always causes the State to vacillate from maxim to maxim, from project to project, and does not occur in other governments, where the prince is always the same. It also appears that in general, although there may be more cunning in a royal court, there is more wisdom in a senate; and that republics pursue their goals by means of policies that are more consistent and better followed; whereas each revolution in a royal ministry causes one in the State, given the maxim common to all ministers and almost all kings of doing the reverse of their predecessors in everything.

This same incoherence also provides the answer to a sophism that is habitually used by theorists of royalty. Not only is civil government compared to domestic government, and the prince to the father of a family—an error already refuted—but this magistrate is liberally given all the virtues he might need, and it is always assumed that the prince is what he ought to be. With the help of this assumption, royal government is evidently preferable to any other, because it is incontestably the strongest; and to be the best as well, it lacks only a corporate will more consistent with the general will.

But if according to Plato**, a king by nature is such a rare person, how many times will nature and chance combine to crown him; and if a royal education necessarily corrupts those who receive it, what is to be hoped for from a series of men brought up to rule? It is surely deliberate self-deception, then, to confuse royal government with that of a good king. In order to see what this government is in essence, it must be considered under stupid or wicked princes, for either they are like this when they ascend the throne, or the throne makes them so.

*Tacitus, *Histories*, Book I.
***The Statesman.*[89]

These difficulties have not escaped the notice of our authors, but they have not been troubled by them. The remedy, they say, is to obey without a murmur. God in his anger gives us bad kings, and they must be endured as punishments from heaven. This discourse is doubtless edifying, but I'm not sure whether it would not be better suited to the pulpit than to a book of political theory. What can be said of a doctor who promises miracles, and whose whole art consists of exhorting the sick to be patient? Everyone knows perfectly well that when there is a bad government it must be endured. The question would be to find a good one.

Chapter VII: On Mixed Governments

Properly speaking, there is no simple government. A single leader must have subordinate magistrates; a popular government must have a leader. Thus in the division of the executive power there is always a gradation from the many to the few, with the difference that sometimes the many depend on the few and sometimes the few on the many.

Occasionally there is an equal division; either when the constituent parts are mutually dependent, as in the government of England, or when the authority of each part is independent but incomplete, as in Poland. The latter form is bad, because there is no unity in the government and the State lacks cohesion.

Which is better, a simple or a mixed government? The question is much debated among political theorists, and it requires the same answer that I gave above concerning all forms of government.

Simple government is the best in itself, by the very fact that it is simple. But when the executive power does not depend enough on the legislative power, that is when there is a greater ratio between prince and sovereign than between people and prince, this defect in the proportion must be remedied by dividing the government.[90] For then all of its parts do not have any less authority over the subjects, and their division makes all of them together weaker when opposed to the sovereign.

This same difficulty can also be prevented by establishing intermediate magistrates, who—leaving the government whole—merely serve to balance the two powers and to maintain their respective rights. Then the government is not mixed; it is tempered.

The opposite difficulty can be remedied by similar means, and when the government is too loose, tribunals can be set up to consolidate it. This is done in all democracies. In the first case, the government is divided in order to be weakened; and in the second, to be strengthened. For the *maximum* of force and of weakness are both found in simple governments, whereas mixed forms produce an average force.

Socio–economic side

Chapter VIII: That All Forms of Government Are Not Suited to All Countries

Freedom, not being a fruit of every climate, is not accessible to all peoples. The more one ponders this principle established by Montesquieu, the more one senses its truth.[91] The more it is contested, the more opportunities there are to establish it by new proofs.

In all the governments of the world, the public person consumes, yet produces nothing. What, then, is the source of the substance it consumes? The labor of its members. It is the excess of private individuals that produces what is necessary for the public. It follows from this that the civil state can subsist only as long as the product of men's labor exceeds their needs.

Now this surplus is not the same in all the countries of the world. In several, it is considerable; in others, very minimal; in others, nil; in others, negative. This ratio depends on the fertility of the climate, the kind of labor required by the land, the nature of its products, the force of the inhabitants, the greater or lesser consumption they need, and on several other similar ratios of which it is composed.

Besides, all governments are not of the same nature. They are more or less voracious, and the differences between them are based on the additional principle that the further public contributions travel from their source, the more burdensome they are. This burden must not be measured by the amount of taxes, but by the distance they have to travel to return to the hands they came from. When this circulation is prompt and well established it does not matter whether the people pays a little or a lot. It is always rich and finances are always in good condition. On the contrary, however little the people may give, when this amount does not come back, it is soon exhausted by always giving. The State is never rich, and the people is always destitute.

Tax e It follows that the greater the distance between the people and the government, the more burdensome taxes become. Thus, the people is least burdened in a democracy; more so in an aristocracy; and in a monarchy it bears the greatest weight. Monarchy, then, is only suited to opulent nations; aristocracy to States of average wealth and size; democracy to small and poor States.

In fact, the more one thinks about it, the more this explains the difference between free States and monarchies. In the former, everything is used for the common utility; in the latter, the public and private forces are reciprocal, and one is increased by the weakening of the other. Finally, rather than governing subjects in order to make them happy, despotism makes them miserable in order to govern them.

There are, then, for each climate natural causes on the basis of which it is possible to assign the form of government toward which the force of the climate leads it, and even to say what type of inhabitants it should have. Unproductive and barren places, where the product is worth less than the labor to produce it, should remain uncultivated and deserted, or populated only by savages. Places where the labor of men produces only the bare necessities should be inhabited by barbarous peoples; any polity would be impossible there. Places where the surplus of products over labor is moderate are suited to free peoples. Those where abundant and fertile soil produces a great deal with little labor demand monarchic government, so that the luxuries of the prince consume the excess of the subjects' surplus, because it is better for this excess to be absorbed by the government than dissipated by private individuals. There are exceptions, I know. But these very exceptions prove the rule, in that they sooner or later produce revolutions that bring things back to the order of nature.

Let us always distinguish between general laws and the particular causes that can modify their effect. Even if the entire south were covered with republics and the entire north with despotic regimes, it would be no less true that the effect of climate makes despotism suited to hot countries, barbarism to cold countries, and a good polity to intermediate regions. I see, further, that while granting the principle, there might be dispute over its application. It might be objected that there are very fertile cold countries and very unproductive southern ones. But this is a difficulty only for those who do not examine all the relationships involved. It is necessary, as I have said, to consider those of labor, force, consumption, etc.

Let us assume that given two equal pieces of land, one produces five and the other ten. If the inhabitants of the former consume four, and those of the latter nine, the excess of the first product will be one fifth, and that of the second one tenth. Since the ratio of these two surpluses is therefore the inverse of the ratio of the products, the piece of land that produces only five will provide a surplus that is double that of the land that produces ten.

But it is not a question of a doubled product, and I do not think anyone dares to claim that the fertility of cold countries in general is even equal to that of hot countries. Nevertheless, let us assume this equality. Let us, if you wish, equate England with Sicily, and Poland with Egypt. Farther south, we will find Africa and the Indies; farther north, we will find nothing at all. To achieve this equality of products, what difference is there in cultivation? In Sicily, merely scratching the earth is all that is necessary; in England, what efforts it takes to work it! Now when there must be more hands to yield the same product, the surplus should necessarily be less.

Consider in addition that the same number of men consume much less in hot countries. The climate requires sobriety for good health. Europeans who want to live there in the same style as they do at home all die of dysentary and indigestions. *We are*, says Chardin, *carnivorous beasts, wolves, by comparison with Asians. Some attribute the Persians' sobriety to the fact that their country is less cultivated; but I believe, to the contrary, that their country is less abundant in foodstuffs because the inhabitants need less. If their frugality*, he continues, *were an effect of scarcity in the* country, only the poor would eat little, whereas in general everyone does so; and more or less would be eaten in each province according to the fertility of the countryside, whereas the same sobriety is found everywhere in the kingdom. They praise themselves highly for their way of life, saying one need only look at their complexions to recognize how much better it is than that of Christians. In fact, the complexion of Persians is smooth. They have lovely, delicate, and polished skin, whereas the complexion of their subjects the Armenians, who live in the European manner, is coarse and blotchy, and their bodies are fat and heavy.[92]

The closer one is to the equator, the less peoples live on. They eat almost no meat; rice, maize, couscous, millet, and cassava are their usual foods. In the Indies, there are millions of men whose nourishment costs under one cent a day. In Europe itself we see noticeable differences of appetite between the people of the north and the south. A Spaniard would live for a week on a German's dinner. In countries where men are more voracious, luxury as well turns toward things that are eaten. In England, luxury is shown by tables laden with meats; in Italy, you are treated to sugar and flowers.

Luxury in clothing also offers similar differences. In climates where seasonal changes are abrupt and violent, clothes are better and simpler; in those where dressing is merely for ornamentation, ostentation is more sought after than utility, and clothes themselves are a luxury there. Every day in Naples, you will see men walking along the Posilippo wearing gold-embroidered jackets, but no stockings. The same is true of buildings. Everything is devoted to magnificence when damage from the weather is not a worry. In Paris or London, people want to be lodged warmly and comfortably. In Madrid, there are superb drawing rooms, but not a window that closes; and people sleep in ratholes.

Foods are far more substantial and succulent in hot countries. This is a third difference that cannot fail to influence the second. Why are so many vegetables eaten in Italy? Because they are good, nourishing, and have excellent flavor there. In France, where they are grown only with water, they are not nourishing, and scarcely count at meals. However, they take up no less land, and require at least as much effort to cultivate. It is known from experience that the wheats of Barbary, in other respects inferior to French wheats, yield much more flour, and that those of France, in turn, yield more than the wheats of the north. It can be inferred from this that a similar gradation in the same direction is generally observed from the equator to the north pole. Now isn't it a clear disadvantage to have a lesser quantity of nourishment from equal amounts of produce?

To these different considerations, I can add another that is derived from them and strengthens them. It is that hot countries need fewer inhabitants than cold countries, yet could feed more of them. This produces a double surplus, always to the advantage of despotism. The larger the area occupied by a fixed number of inhabitants, the harder it becomes to revolt, because men cannot take concerted action promptly or secretly, and it is always easy for the government to get wind of the plans and cut off communications. But the closer together a numerous people is, the less the government can usurp from the sovereign. Leaders deliberate as safely in their rooms as the prince in his council, and the crowd assembles as quickly in the public squares as the troops in their quarters. The advantage of a tyrannical government, in this regard, is thus to act over long distances. With the help of the points of support it sets up, its force increases with distance like that of levers.* The people's force, on the contrary, acts only when concentrated; it evaporates and is lost as it spreads, like the effect of gunpowder scattered on the ground, which only ignites grain by grain. The least populous countries are thus the best suited to tyranny. Wild animals reign only in deserts.

Chapter IX: On the Signs of a Good Government

Therefore when the question is asked which is absolutely the best government, one poses a question that is insoluble because it is indeterminate. Or, if you prefer, it has as many correct answers as there are possible combinations in the absolute and relative situations of peoples.[93]

But if one asks by what sign it is possible to know whether a given people is well or badly governed, this is something else again, and the question of fact could be resolved.

However, it is usually not resolved, because each wants to resolve it in his own way. Subjects praise public tranquillity, citizens the freedom of private individuals. One prefers the safety of possessions, the other, that of persons. One claims that the best government is the most severe; the other maintains that it is the mildest. This one wants crimes punished, and that one wants them prevented. One thinks it is fine to be feared by the neighbors; the other prefers to be ignored by them. One is satisfied when money circulates; the other demands that the people have bread. Even if there were agreement on these and other similar points, would a solution be any nearer? Since moral quantities cannot be precisely measured, even if there were agreement about the sign, how could there be about the way to estimate it?

As for me, I am always astounded that one very simple sign is overlooked or not agreed upon out of bad faith. What is the end of the political association? It is the preservation and prosperity of its members. And what is the surest sign that they are preserved and prospering? It is their number and

---

*This does not contradict what I said earlier, in Book II, chapter ix, about the disadvantages of large States. For there it was a question of the authority of the government over its members, and here it is one of its force against the subjects. Its scattered members serve as points of support for acting upon the people from a distance, but it has no support for acting directly on these members themselves. Thus the length of the lever is in one instance the source of its weakness, and in the other of its strength.

their population. Therefore, don't seek this much disputed sign elsewhere. All other things being equal, the government under which—without external aid, without naturalization, without colonies—the citizens populate and multiply the most is infallibly the best. One under which a people grows smaller and dwindles away is the worst. Calculators, it is up to you now. Count, measure, compare.*

Chapter X: On the Abuse of Government and Its Tendency to Degenerate

Just as the private will acts incessantly against the general will, so the government makes a continual effort against sovereignty. The greater this effort becomes, the more the constitution changes, and as there is here no other corporate will which, by resisting the will of the prince, would balance it, sooner or later the prince must finally oppress the sovereign and break the social treaty. That is the inherent and inevitable vice which, from the emergence of the body politic, tends without respite to destroy it, just as old age and death destroy the body of a man.

There are two general routes by which a government degenerates: namely when it shrinks, or when the State dissolves.

The government shrinks when it passes from a large to a small number,

---

*The same principle should be used to judge the centuries that deserve preference in terms of the prosperity of the human race. Those in which letters and arts flourished have been overly admired, without discovering the secret object of their cultivation and without considering its disastrous effect, *idque apud imperitos humanitas vocabatur, cum pars servitutis esset.*[94] Will we never notice in the maxims of books the vulgar interest that prompts the authors to speak? No; whatever they may say, when the population of a country decreases, despite its brilliance it is not true that all goes well; and that one poet has a hundred thousand pounds of income is not enough to make his century the best of all. Less consideration must be given to the apparent calm and to the leaders' tranquillity than to the well-being of entire nations and especially of the most populous social classes. Hail ravages a few cantons, but it rarely creates famine. Riots and civil wars greatly frighten leaders, but they are not the true misfortunes of peoples, who may even have a period of respite while men argue about who will tyrannize over them. It is their permanent condition that gives rise to their true prosperities or calamities. It is when everything remains crushed under a yoke that everything perishes. It is then that leaders destroy them at their pleasure, *ubi solitudinem faciunt, pacem appellant.*[95] When the rivalries of the great agitated the kingdom of France, and the Coadjutor of Paris went to the Parlement carrying a dagger in his pocket, these things did not prevent the French people from living happily and in large numbers in honest and free ease. Long ago, Greece flourished in the midst of the cruelest wars. Blood flowed freely, and the whole country was covered with men. It seemed, says Machiavelli, that in the midst of murders, proscriptions, civil wars, our republic became more powerful; our citizens' virtue, their mores, their independence did more to reinforce it than all the dissensions to weaken it. A little agitation gives vitality to souls, and it is not so much peace as freedom that makes the species truly prosper.[96]

that is from democracy to aristocracy and from aristocracy to royalty. That is its natural tendency.* If it were to go backward from a small number to a large one, it could be said to slacken, but this reverse development is impossible.

Indeed, the government never changes its form except when its worn out mechanism leaves it too weakened to be able to preserve itself. Now if it were to grow still more slack by further extending itself, its force would become entirely null, and it would be even less likely to subsist. The mechanism must therefore be wound up and tightened in proportion as it gives way; otherwise the State it supports would fall into ruins.

The dissolution of the State can come about in two ways.

First, when the prince no longer administers the State in accordance with the laws and usurps the sovereign power. Then a remarkable change takes place, which is that not the government but the State shrinks. I mean that the large State dissolves and another is formed within it that is composed solely of the members of the government and is no longer anything for the

---

*The slow formation and the development of the Republic of Venice in its lagoons offers a notable example of this succession. And it is quite amazing that after more than twelve hundred years, the Venetians seem to be still only at the second stage, which began with the *Serrar di Consiglio* in 1198. As for the ancient dukes who are held against them, whatever the *squitinio della libertà veneta* may say,[97] it has been proved that they were not their sovereigns.

The Roman Republic will not fail to be cited as an objection, for supposedly following a completely opposite development, changing from monarchy to aristocracy and from aristocracy to democracy. I am far from thinking of it in these terms.

The original establishment of Romulus was a mixed government which promptly degenerated into despotism. For some particular reasons, the State perished prematurely, as a newborn dies before reaching manhood. The expulsion of the Tarquins was the true epoch of the birth of the republic. But it did not assume a constant form at first, because by not abolishing the patriciate, only half the work was done. Because the hereditary aristocracy—which is the worst kind of legitimate administration—in this way remained in conflict with the democracy, the form of the government—always uncertain and up in the air—was not settled, as Machiavelli has proved, until the establishment of the tribunes.[98] Only then was there a real government and a true democracy. In fact, the people then was not merely sovereign, but also magistrate and judge; the senate was only a subordinate tribunal to temper and concentrate the government; and the consuls themselves, albeit patricians, first magistrates, and absolute generals in war, were only presiding officers of the people in Rome.

From that time on, the government was seen to follow its natural tendency and lean strongly toward aristocracy. As the patriciate abolished itself in a sense, the aristocracy no longer consisted in the body of patricians as in Venice and Genoa, but in the body of the senate, composed of patricians and plebians, and even in the body of the tribunes when they began to usurp active power. For words do not change things, and when the people has leaders who govern for it, whatever name these leaders may assume, they are always an aristocracy.

The abuse of the aristocracy gave rise to the civil wars and the triumvirate. Sulla, Julius Caesar, Augustus became in fact true monarchs, and finally under the despotism of Tiberius, the State was dissolved. Roman history, then, does not disprove my principle; it confirms it.

Note

rest of the people except its master and tyrant. So that the instant the government usurps sovereignty the social compact is broken, and all the ordinary citizens, by right recovering their natural freedom, are forced but not obligated to obey.

Dissolution also occurs when the members of the government separately usurp the power that they ought only to exercise as a body. This is no less an infraction of the laws, and produces even greater disorder. Then there are, so to speak, as many princes as there are magistrates, and the State—no less divided than the government—perishes or changes its form.

When the State dissolves, the abuse of government of any type whatever takes the general name *anarchy*.[99] To distinguish, democracy degenerates into *ochlocracy;* aristocracy into *oligarchy*. I would add that royalty degenerates into *tyranny,* but this latter term is equivocal and requires explanation.

In the ordinary sense, a tyrant is a king who governs with violence and without regard for justice and the laws. In the precise sense, a tyrant is a private individual who assumes the royal authority without having any right to it. The Greeks understood the word tyrant in this manner, and they gave it indistinguishably to good and bad princes whose authority was not legitimate.* Thus *tyrant* and *usurper* are two words that are exactly synonymous.

In order to give different names to different things, I call the usurper of royal authority a *tyrant* and the usurper of sovereign power a *despot*. The tyrant is one who takes over against the laws in order to govern according to the laws; the despot is one who puts himself above the laws themselves. Thus a tyrant need not be a despot, but a despot is always a tyrant.

Chapter XI: On the Death of the Body Politic

Such is the natural and inevitable tendency of the best constituted governments. If Sparta and Rome perished, what State can hope to endure forever? If we want to form a lasting establishment, let us therefore not hope to make it eternal.[101] To succeed, it is necessary not to attempt the impossible, nor to flatter oneself with giving a solidity to the work of men that human things do not allow.

The body politic, like the human body, begins to die at the moment of its birth, and carries within itself the causes of its destruction. But each can have a constitution that is more or less robust and suited to preserve it for a

*Omnes enim et habentur et dicuntur Tyranni qui potestate utuntur perpetua, in ea Civitate quae libertate usa est. Cornelius Nepos, *Life of Miltiades*.[100] It is true that Aristotle, *Nicomachean Ethics*, Book XVIII, chapter x, distinguishes between tyrant and king by the fact that the former governs for his own utility and the latter solely for the utility of his subjects. But besides the fact that generally all the Greek authors used the term tyrant in another sense, as is best seen in Xenephon's *Hiero*, it would follow from Aristotle's distinction that since the beginning of the world, not a single king would as yet have existed.

longer or shorter time. The constitution of man is the work of nature; that of the State is a work of art. It is not within the power of men to prolong their life; it is within their power to prolong that of the State as far as possible, by giving it the best constitution it can possibly have. Even the best constituted State will come to an end, but later than another, if no unforeseen accident brings about its premature downfall.

The principle of political life lies in the sovereign authority. The legislative power is the heart of the State; the executive power is its brain, giving movement to all its parts. The brain can become paralyzed yet the individual is still alive. A man can remain an imbecile and live. But as soon as the heart has ceased to function, the animal is dead.[102]

It is not through laws that the State subsists, it is through the legislative power. Yesterday's law does not obligate today, but tacit consent is presumed from silence, and the sovereign is assumed to confirm constantly the laws it does not repeal while having the power to do so. Everything the sovereign has once declared it wants, it always wants unless it revoked the declaration.

Why then is so much respect accorded to ancient laws? Because of their very age. People must believe that only the excellence of these ancient expressions of will could have preserved them for so long. If the sovereign had not constantly recognized them as salutary, it would have revoked them a thousand times over. That is why laws, far from weakening, continually acquire new force in every well-constituted State; the prejudice favoring antiquity renders them more venerable each day. In contrast, wherever the laws weaken as they grow older, it is proof that there is no longer any legislative power and that the State is no longer alive.

Chapter XII: How the Sovereign Authority Is Maintained

The sovereign, having no other force than the legislative power, acts only by laws; and since the laws are only authentic acts of the general will, the sovereign can only act when the people is assembled. The people assembled, it will be said, what a chimera! It is a chimera today, but this was not the case two thousand years ago. Have men changed their nature?

The limits of the possible in moral matters are less narrow than we think. It is our weaknesses, our vices, our prejudices that shrink them. Base souls do not believe in great men. Vile slaves smile mockingly at the word freedom.

cf. Barber

Let us consider what can be done on the basis of what has been done. I shall not speak of the ancient republics of Greece; but the Roman Republic, it seems to me, was a large State, and the town of Rome a large town. The last census gave Rome four hundred thousand citizens bearing arms, and the last count of the Empire showed more than four million citizens, not counting subjects, foreigners, women, children, slaves.

One could imagine the difficulties of calling frequent assemblies of the immense population of that capital and its environs. Yet few weeks went by in which the Roman people was not assembled, and even several times. It exercised not only the rights of sovereignty, but a part of those of government as well. It handled certain business matters; it tried certain cases; and at the public assembly, this entire people was nearly as often magistrate as citizen.

By going back to the earliest periods of nations, it would be found that most of the ancient governments, even the monarchical ones like the Macedonians and the Franks, had similar councils. In any case, this one incontestable fact resolves the entire difficulty: the inference from the existent to the possible seems solid to me.

Chapter XIII: Continued

It is not sufficient for an assembled people to have once settled the constitution of the State by sanctioning a body of laws. It is not sufficient for it to have established a perpetual government or provided, once and for all, for the election of magistrates. In addition to extraordinary assemblies that may be required by unforeseen situations, there must be some regular, periodical ones that nothing can abolish or postpone, so that on a designated day the people is legitimately convoked by law, without need of any other formal convocation.[103]

But except for these assemblies, lawful by their date alone, every assembly of the people that has not been called by the magistrates appointed for that purpose and in accordance with the prescribed forms ought to be considered as illegitimate and everything done at it as null; because the order to assemble should itself emanate from the law.

As for the frequency of legitimate assemblies, this depends on so many considerations that no precise rules can be given about it. One can only say in general that the more force the government has, the more frequently the sovereign ought to present itself.

It will be said to me that this may be well and good for a single town, but what is to be done when the State includes several? Will the sovereign authority be divided, or will it be concentrated in a single town and all the others made subject?

I reply that neither should be done. First, the sovereign authority is single and unique, and cannot be divided without being destroyed. In the second place, a town, like a nation, cannot legitimately be the subject of another, because the essence of the body politic lies in the harmony of obedience and freedom, and the words *subject* and *sovereign* are identical correlatives, whose meaning is combined in the single word citizen.

I reply further that it is always an evil to unite several towns in a single City, and that anyone who wants to create such a union should not imagine that its natural drawbacks can be avoided. The abuses of large States must not be raised as an objection to someone who wants only small ones. But how can small States be given enough force to resist large ones? In the same way that the Greek Towns resisted the great king long ago, and Holland and Switzerland more recently resisted the house of Austria.

However, if the State cannot be reduced to a proper size, there is still one remaining expedient. It is not to tolerate a capital, to locate the government alternatively in each town, and to convene the assemblies of the country in each of them by turn.[104]

Populate the territory evenly, extend the same rights everywhere, spread abundance and life everywhere. In this way the State will become, simultaneously the strongest and the best governed possible. Remember that the walls of towns are only made out of the debris of farmhouses. At the sight of each palace that I see built in the capital, I imagine a whole countryside being reduced to hovels.

Chapter XIV: Continued

The instant the people is legitimately assembled as a sovereign body, all jurisdiction of the government ceases, the executive power is suspended, and the person of the humblest citizen is as sacred and inviolable as that of the first magistrate; because where the represented person is, there is no longer any representative. Most of the tumults that arose in Rome at the comitia came from ignoring or neglecting this rule. On those occasions the consuls were merely presiding officers of the people; the tribunes, simple speakers;* the senate, nothing at all.

These intervals of suspension, during which the prince recognizes or ought to recognize an actual superior, have always terrified it; and these assemblies of the people, which are the aegis of the body politic and the restraint on government, have been viewed with horror by the leaders of all times. Thus they never spare efforts, nor objections, nor obstacles, nor promises to discourage the citizens from holding them. When the latter are greedy, cowardly, pusillanimous, fonder of repose than of freedom, they don't hold out long against the redoubled efforts of the government. So it is that with the force of resistance constantly increasing, the sovereign authority finally vanishes, and most Cities fall and perish prematurely.

But between sovereign authority and arbitrary government there is sometimes introduced an intermediate power that must be discussed.

Chapter XV: On Deputies or Representatives

As soon as public service ceases to be the main business of the citizens, and they prefer to serve with their pocketbooks rather than with their persons, the State is already close to its ruin. Is it necessary to march to battle? They pay troops and stay home. Is it necessary to attend the council?

---

*In approximately the sense given to the word speaker in the English Parliament. The similarity between these functions would have created conflict between the consuls and the tribunes even if all jurisdiction had been suspended.

They name deputies and stay home. By dint of laziness and money, they finally have soldiers to enslave the country and representatives to sell it.

It is involvement in commerce and the arts, avid interest in profits, softness and love of comforts that replace personal services by money. One gives up part of his profit in order to increase it at leisure. Give money and you will soon have chains. The word finance is a slave's word. It is unknown in the City. In a truly free State the citizens do everything with their hands and nothing with money. Far from paying to be exempted from their duties, they would pay to fulfill them personally. I am very far from commonly held ideas; I believe that corvées are less contrary to freedom than taxes.

The better constituted the State, the more public affairs dominate private ones in the minds of the citizens. There is even less private business, because since the sum of common happiness furnishes a larger portion of each individual's happiness, the individual has less to seek through private efforts. In a well-run City, everyone rushes to assemblies. Under a bad government, no one likes to take even a step to go to them, because no one takes an interest in what is done there, because it is predictable that the general will won't predominate, and finally because domestic concerns absorb everything. Good laws lead to the making of better ones; bad ones bring about worse ones. As soon as someone says *what do I care?* about the affairs of the State, the State should be considered lost.

The waning of patriotism, the activity of private interest, the immenseness of States, conquests, the abuse of the government have led to the invention of using deputies or representatives of the people in the nation's assemblies. It is what people in certain countries call the third estate. Thus the private interest of two orders is ranked first and second; the public interest is merely third.

Sovereignty cannot be represented for the same reason it cannot be alienated. It consists essentially in the general will, and the will cannot be represented. Either it is itself or it is something else; there is no middle ground. The deputies of the people, therefore, are not nor can they be its representatives; they are merely its agents. They cannot conclude anything definitively. Any law that the people in person has not ratified is null; it is not a law. The English people thinks it is free. It greatly deceives itself; it is free only during the election of the members of Parliament. As soon as they are elected, it is a slave, it is nothing. Given the use made of these brief moments of freedom, the people certainly deserves to lose it.[105]

The idea of representatives is modern. We get it from feudal government, that wicked and absurd government in which the human species is degraded and the name of man is dishonored. In the ancient republics and even in monarchies, the people never had representatives. The word itself was unknown. It is very noteworthy that in Rome, where the tribunes were so sacred, it was never even imagined that they could usurp the functions of the people, and that in the midst of such a great multitude, they never tried to pass a single plebiscite on their authority alone. Yet the difficulties some-times caused by the multitude can be judged by what happened in the time of the Gracchi, when part of the citizenry voted from the rooftops.

Where right and freedom are everything, inconveniences do not matter. Among this wise people, everything was correctly judged. It allowed its lic-tors to do what its tribunes would not have dared to do. It was not worried that its lictors would want to represent it.

However, to explain how the tribunes sometimes represented it, all that is needed is a conception of how the government represents the sovereign. Since the law is only the declaration of the general will, it is clear that the people cannot be represented in the legislative power. But it can and should be in the executive power, which is only force applied to the law. This shows that very few nations, on careful examination, would be found to have laws. However that may be, it is certain that the tribunes, having no part of the executive power, could never represent the Roman people under the rights of their office, but only by usurping those of the senate.

Among the Greeks, everything the people had to do, it did by itself. It was constantly assembled at the public square. It inhabited a mild climate; it wasn't greedy; slaves did its work; its most important business was its freedom. No longer having the same advantages, how can the same rights be preserved? Your more severe climates increase your needs;* during six months of the year, it is impossible to stay out in the public square; your in-distinct languages cannot be heard outdoors; you are more concerned about your profit than your freedom; and you fear slavery far less than poverty.

What! Freedom can only be maintained with the support of servitude? Perhaps. The two extremes meet. Everything that is not in nature has its pro-blems, and civil society more than all the rest. There are some unfortunate situations when one cannot preserve one's freedom except at the expense of others, and when the citizen can only be perfectly free if the slave is com-pletely enslaved. Such was Sparta's situation. As for you, modern peoples, you have no slaves, but you are slaves. You pay for their freedom with your own. You boast of that preference in vain; I find it more cowardly than hu-mane.

I do not mean by all this that it is necessary to have slaves, nor that the right of slavery is legitimate, since I have proved the opposite. I only state the reasons why the modern peoples who believe they are free have representa-tives, and why the ancient people did not have them. However this may be, the instant a people chooses representatives, it is no longer free; it no longer exists.

All things considered, I do not see that it is henceforth possible for the sovereign to preserve the exercise of its rights among us unless the City is

---

*In cold countries, to adopt the luxury and softness of the orientals is to want to be given their chains; it is submitting to these even more necessarily than they did.

very small. But if it is very small, will it be subjugated? No. I shall show later*
how it is possible to combine the external power of a great people with the
ease of regulation and good order of a small State.

Chapter XVI: That the Institution of the Government Is Not a Contract

Once the legislative power has been well established, the problem is to
establish the executive power in the same way.[107] For the latter, which only
operates by means of particular acts, is essentially different from the former
and hence is naturally separate from it. If it were possible for the sovereign,
considered as such, to have the executive power, right and fact would be so
completely confounded that one would no longer know what is law and what
isn't; and the body politic, thereby denatured, would soon fall prey to the violence against which it was instituted.

Since the citizens are all equal by the social contract, what everyone
ought to do can be prescribed by everyone, whereas no one has the right to
require another to do what he himself does not do. Now it is precisely this
right, indispensable for giving life and motion to the body politic, that the
sovereign gives to the prince by instituting the government.

Some have claimed that this act of establishment was a contract
between the people and the leaders it chooses, a contract by which the two
parties stipulated the conditions under which one assumed the obligation to
command and the other to obey. It will be agreed, I am sure, that that is
indeed a strange way to make a contract! But let us see whether this opinion
is tenable.

First, the supreme authority cannot be modified any more than it can be
alienated; to limit it is to destroy it. It is absurd and contradictory for the
sovereign to choose a superior; to obligate oneself to obey a master is to
return to one's full freedom.

Furthermore, it is evident that this contract between the people and
specific persons would be a particular act. From which it follows that this
contract could not be a law or an act of sovereignty, and that consequently it
would be illegitimate.

It can also be seen that in relation to each other the contracting parties
would be under the law of nature alone, and without any guarantee of their
reciprocal engagements, which is contrary in all ways to the civil state. Since
the one who has force available is always master of the outcome, it would be
as sensible to give the name contract to the act of a man who would say to

---

*This is what I had thought of doing in the sequel to this work, when in dealing with
foreign relations, I would have discussed confederations. This subject is altogether
new, and its principles have yet to be established.[106]

another, "I give you all my goods, on condition that you will give back whatever you please."

There is only one contract in the State, that of the association; and that one alone excludes all others. It is impossible to imagine any public contract that was not a violation of the first one.

Chapter XVII: On the Institution of the Government

In what terms, therefore, must the act by which the government is instituted be conceived? I shall begin by noting that this act is complex, or composed of two others, namely the establishment of the law and the execution of the law.

By the first, the sovereign enacts that there will be a governmental body established under a specific form. And it is clear that this act is a law.

By the second, the people appoints the leaders who will be put in charge of the established government. Now since this nomination is a particular act, it is not a second law, but solely a consequence of the first and a governmental function.

The difficulty lies in understanding how there can be an act of government before the government exists, and how the people, which is only sovereign or subject, can become prince or magistrate in certain circumstances.

Here, again, is revealed one of those amazing properties of the body politic, by which it reconciles apparently contradictory operations. For in this case, the operation is accomplished by a sudden conversion of sovereignty into democracy, so that without any noticeable change, and solely by a new relation of all to all, the citizens, having become magistrates, pass from general to particular acts, and from the law to its execution.

This change of relation is no speculative subtlety without practical examples. It occurs daily in the English Parliament, where the lower house on certain occasions turns itself into a committee of the whole to discuss business better, and in so doing becomes a simple commission rather than the sovereign court of the preceding instant. It then reports to itself, as the House of Commons, on what it has just settled as a committee of the whole, and it deliberates once again under one title over what it had already decided under another.

The peculiar advantage of democratic government is that it can be established in reality by a simple act of the general will. After this, the provisional government remains in office, if such is the form adopted, or establishes in the name of the sovereign the government prescribed by law; and thus everything is according to rule. It is not possible to institute the government in any other legitimate way without renouncing the principles established above.

Chapter XVIII: The Way to Prevent
Usurpations by the Government

From these clarifications, it follows, in confirmation of chapter xvi, that the act that institutes the government is not a contract but a law; that the trustees of the executive power are not the masters of the people, but its officers; that the people can establish and depose them when it pleases; that there is no question of their contracting, but rather of obeying; and that in assuming the functions imposed on them by the State, they merely fulfill their duty as citizens, without in any way having the right to argue over the conditions.

Therefore, when it happens that the people institutes a hereditary government, whether it is a monarchy within one family or an aristocracy within one class of citizens, this is not an engagement it undertakes. It is a provisional form it gives to the administration until it wishes to organize things differently.[108]

It is true that these changes are always dangerous, and that the established government must never be touched until it becomes incompatible with the public good. But this circumspection is a maxim of politics and not a rule of right, and the State is no more compelled to leave civil authority to its leaders than military authority to its generals.

It is also true that in such cases it is impossible to be too careful about observing all the requisite formalities, in order to distinguish a regular, legitimate act from a seditious tumult, and the will of an entire people from the clamors of one faction. It is above all in these dangerous cases[109] that demands must not be conceded except insofar as they cannot be denied by the full rigor of the law; and it is also from this obligation that the prince derives a great advantage for preserving his power in spite of the people, without it being possible to say that he has usurped it. For while apparently only using his rights, it is very easy for him to extend them, and under the pretext of public peace to prevent the holding of assemblies destined to reestablish good order. So that he takes advantage of a silence which he keeps from being broken, or of irregularities he himself has committed, to assume that the attitudes of those who are silenced by fear are in his favor, and to punish those who dare to talk. In this way, the decemvirs, at first elected for one year and then continued for another, tried to retain their power in perpetuity, by no longer allowing the comitia to assemble. And it is by this simple means that all the governments of the world, once they are invested with the public force, sooner or later usurp the sovereign authority.

The periodic assemblies I spoke of earlier are suited to prevent or postpone this misfortune, above all when they do not need formal convocation. For then the prince could not prevent them without openly declaring himself a violator of the laws and an enemy of the State.

These assemblies, whose only object is the maintenance of the social treaty, should always be opened by two propositions that can never be omitted and that are voted on separately:

The first: *Does it please the sovereign to preserve the present form of government.*

The second: *Does it please the people to leave the administration in the hands of those who are currently responsible for it.*

Here, I assume what I believe I have demonstrated, namely that in the State there is no fundamental law that cannot be revoked, not even the social compact. For if all the citizens were to assemble in order to break this compact by common agreement, there is no doubt that it would be very legitimately broken. Grotius even thinks that each person can renounce the State of which he is a member and recover his natural freedom and his goods by leaving the country.* Now it would be absurd for all the citizens together to be unable to do what each of them can do separately.

END OF THE THIRD BOOK

---

*On the understanding that the reason for leaving is not to evade one's duty and avoid serving the homeland at the moment it needs us. In such a case, fleeing would be criminal and punishable; it would no longer be withdrawal, but desertion.[110]

BOOK IV

Chapter I: That the General Will Is Indestructible

As long as several men together consider themselves to be a single body, they have only a single will, which relates to their common preservation and the general welfare. Then all the mechanisms of the State are vigorous and simple, its maxims are clear and luminous, it has no tangled, contradictory interests; the common good is clearly apparent everywhere, and requires only good sense to be perceived. Peace, union, and equality are enemies of political subtleties. Upright and simple men are hard to fool because of their simplicity; traps and refined pretexts do not deceive them. They are not even clever enough to be duped. When, among the happiest people in the world, groups of peasants are seen deciding the affairs of State under an oak tree, and always acting wisely, can one help scorning the refinements of other nations, which make themselves illustrious and miserable with so much art and mystery?[111]

A State governed in this way needs very few laws, and to the degree that it becomes necessary to promulgate new ones, this necessity is universally seen. The first to propose them merely states what everyone has already felt, and there is no question of intrigues nor of eloquence to pass into law what each has already resolved to do as soon as he is sure that others will do likewise.

What misleads reasoners, who only see States that have been badly constituted from the beginning, is that they are struck by the impossibility of maintaining similar order in such States. They laugh when they imagine all the nonsense that a clever swindler or an insinuating talker could put over on the people of Paris or London. They don't know that Cromwell would have been condemned to hard labor by the people of Berne, and the Duc de Beaufort sentenced to the reformatory by the Genevans.

But when the social tie begins to slacken and the State to grow weak; when private interests start to make themselves felt and small societies to influence the large one, the common interest changes and is faced with opponents; unanimity no longer prevails in the votes; the general will is no longer the will of all; contradictions and debates arise and the best advice is not accepted without disputes.

Finally, when the State, close to its ruin, continues to subsist only in an illusory and ineffectual form; when the social bond is broken in all hearts;

when the basest interest brazenly adopts the sacred name of the public good, then the general will becomes mute; all—guided by secret motives—are no more citizens in offering their opinions than if the State had never existed, and iniquitous decrees whose only goal is the private interest are falsely passed under the name of laws.

Does it follow from this that the general will is annihilated or corrupted? No, it is always constant, unalterable, and pure. But it is subordinate to others that prevail over it. Each person, detaching his interest from the common interest, sees perfectly well that he cannot completely separate himself from it; but his share of the public misfortune seems like nothing to him compared to the exclusive good that he claims he is getting. With the exception of this private good, he wants the general good in his own interest just as vigorously as anyone else. Even in selling his vote for money, he doesn't extinguish the general will within himself, he evades it. The mistake he makes is to change the state of the question and to answer something other than what he is asked. So that rather than saying through his vote *it is advantageous to the State*, he says *it is advantageous to a given man or to a given party for a given motion to pass*. Thus the law of public order in assemblies is not so much to maintain the general will therein as it is to be sure that it is always questioned and that it always answers.

I could make many comments here about the simple right to vote in every act of sovereignty—a right that nothing can take away from the citizens; and on the right to give an opinion, to make propositions, to analyze, to discuss, which the government is always very careful to allow only to its members.[112] But this important subject would require a separate treatise, and I cannot say everything in this one.

Chapter II: On Voting

It can be seen from the preceding chapter that the way in which general matters are handled can provide a rather precise indication of the current state of the mores and health of the body politic. The more harmony there is in the assemblies, that is, the closer opinions come to obtaining unanimous support, the more dominant as well is the general will. But long debates, dissensions, and tumult indicate the ascendance of private interests and the decline of the State.

This appears less evident when two or more orders are part of the constitution, like the patricians and plebeians in Rome, whose quarrels often disturbed the comitia even in the finest period of the Republic. But this exception is more apparent than real; for then, by the vice inherent in the body politic, there are so to speak two States in one. What is not true of the two together is true of each of them separately. And in fact even in the stormiest times, the plebiscites of the people, when the senate did not interfere with them, always passed calmly and by a large majority of votes. Since the citizens had only one interest, the people had only one will.

At the other extreme, unanimity returns. That is when the citizens, fallen into servitude, no longer have either freedom or will. Then fear and flattery turn voting into acclamations. Men no longer deliberate; they adore or they curse. Such was the abject manner in which the senate expressed its opinions under the emperors. Sometimes this was done with ridiculous precautions. Tacitus notes that under Otho, the senators, while violently denouncing Vitellius, took pains to make a terrific noise at the same time, so that if by chance he became the master, he would be unable to know what each of them had said.[113]

From these various considerations arise the maxims that should regulate how votes are counted and opinions compared, depending on whether the general will is more or less easy to know and the State more or less declining.

There is only one law that, by its nature, requires unanimous consent. That is the social compact. For civil association is the most voluntary act in the world. Since every man is born free and master of himself,[114] no one, under any pretext whatever, can subject him without his consent. To decide that the son of a slave is born a slave is to decide that he is not born a man.

If, therefore, at the time of the social compact, some are opposed to it, their opposition does not invalidate the contract; it merely prevents them from being included within it. They are foreigners among the citizens. Once the State is instituted, consent is implied by residence. To inhabit the territory means to submit oneself to sovereignty.*

Except for this primitive contract, the vote of the majority always obligates all the others. This is a consequence of the contract itself. But it is asked how a man can be free and forced to conform to wills that are not his own. How can the opponents be free yet subject to laws to which they have not consented?

I reply that the question is badly put. The citizen consents to all the laws, even to those passed against his will, and even to those that punish him when he dares to violate one of them. The constant will of all the members of the State is the general will, which makes them citizens and free.** When a law is proposed in the assembly of the people, what they are being asked is not precisely whether they approve or reject the proposal, but whether it does

---

*This should always be understood to refer to a free State, because elsewhere an inhabitant can be kept in the country against his will by family, goods, the lack of a place of refuge, necessity, or violence; and then his sojourn alone no longer presupposes his consent to the contract or to the violation of the contract.

**In Genoa, the word *libertas* can be read on the front of prisons and on convicts' chains in galleys. This application of the motto is noble and just. Indeed, it is only evildoers of all classes who prevent the citizen from being free. In a country where all such men were in galleys, the most perfect freedom would be enjoyed.

1-c. To a universalizable rule

or does not conform to the general will that is theirs. Each one expresses his opinion on this by voting, and the declaration of the general will is drawn from the counting of the votes. Therefore when the opinion contrary to mine prevails, that proves nothing except that I was mistaken, and what I thought to be the general will was not. If my private will had prevailed, I would have done something other than what I wanted. It is then that I would not have been free.[115]

This presupposes, it is true, that all the characteristics of the general will are still in the majority. When they cease to be, there is no longer any freedom regardless of the side one takes. *Note*

In showing earlier how private wills were substituted for the general will in public deliberations, I have sufficiently indicated the feasible means of preventing this abuse. I shall discuss this again later.[116] With regard to the proportion of votes needed to declare this will, I have also given the principles on which it can be determined. The difference of a single vote breaks a tie; a single opponent destroys unanimity. But between unanimity and a tie there are several qualified majorities, at any of which the proportion can be established, according to the condition and needs of the body politic.

Two general maxims can serve to regulate these ratios. One, that the more important and serious the deliberations, the closer the winning opinion should be to unanimity. The other, that the more speed the business at hand requires, the smaller the prescribed difference in the division of opinions should be. In deliberations that must be finished on the spot, a majority of a single vote should suffice. The first of these maxims appears more suited to laws; the second, to business matters. However that may be, it is a combination of the two that establishes the proper ratio of the deciding majority.

Chapter III: On Elections

With regard to the elections of the prince and the magistrates, which are, as I have said, complex acts, there are two ways to proceed, namely by choice and by drawing lots. Both of these have been used in various republics, and a very complicated mixture of the two is still seen in our times in the election of the Doge of Venice.

Voting by lot, says Montesquieu, *is in the nature of democracy.* I agree, but why is this so? *The lot,* he continues, *is a way of electing that offends no one; it provides each citizen with a reasonable hope of serving the homeland.*[117] Those are not reasons.

If it is carefully noted that the election of leaders is a function of government, and not of sovereignty, it will be seen why the drawing of lots is more in the nature of democracy, in which the administration is better to the extent that its acts are fewer in number.

In every true democracy, the magistracy is not an advantage but a burdensome responsibility, which cannot fairly be placed on one private individual rather than another. The law alone can impose this responsibility on the one to whom it falls by lot. For then, as the condition is equal for all, and the choice is not dependent on any human will, there is no particular application that alters the universality of the law.

In an aristocracy, the prince chooses the prince; the government preserves itself, and it is there that voting is appropriate.

The example of the election of the Doge of Venice confirms, rather than destroys, this distinction. This combined form is suited to a mixed government. For it is an error to mistake the government of Venice for a true aristocracy. Although the people there has no part in the government, the nobility itself is like the people. A multitude of poor Barnabites[118] never came close to any magistracy, and all they get out of their nobility is the empty title Excellence and the right to attend the grand council. Since this grand council is as numerous as our general council in Geneva, its illustrious members have no more privileges than our simple citizens. It is certain, discounting the extreme disparity of the two republics, that the Genevan bourgeoisie is exactly equivalent to the Venetian patriciate; our natives and inhabitants are equivalent to the bourgeois and people of Venice; our peasants are equivalent to the subjects on the mainland. Finally, apart from its size, however that republic is considered, its government is no more aristocratic than ours. The entire difference is that since we have no leader for life, we do not have the same need to draw lots.

Elections by lot would not have many drawbacks in a true democracy, in which the choice would become almost indifferent, since everything is equal in mores and talents as well as in maxims and fortunes. But I have already said that there is no true democracy.

When choice and lot are combined, the former should fill the positions that require special talents, such as military functions. The latter is suited to those for which good sense, justice, and integrity suffice, such as judicial responsibilities; because in a well-constituted State, these qualities are common to all the citizens.

Neither lot nor voting has any place in a monarchical government. Since the monarch is by right the sole prince and unique magistrate, the choice of his lieutenants is his alone. When the Abbé de St. Pierre suggested multiplying the councils of the king of France and electing the members by ballot, he did not realize that he was proposing to change the form of the government.[119]

It remains for me to discuss the manner in which the votes are cast and collected in the assembly of the people. But perhaps the history of the Roman regulations in this regard will explain more graphically all the maxims I could establish. It is not beneath the dignity of a judicious reader to consider in some detail how public and private affairs were handled in a council of two hundred thousand men.[120]

Chapter IV: On the Roman Comitia

We have no very reliable remains of the earliest period of Rome. It is even highly probably that most of what is related about it are fables.* And in general the most instructive part of the annals of peoples, which is the history of their establishment, is the part that we know least about. Experience teaches us daily the causes that give rise to the revolutions of empires. But since no more peoples are being formed, we have scarcely anything but conjectures to explain how they were formed.

The practices that are found established are at least evidence that these practices had an origin. Traditions that go back to these origins, those supported by the greatest authorities and confirmed by the strongest reasons, should be accepted as the most certain. These are the maxims I have tried to follow in seeking how the freest and most powerful people on earth exercised its supreme power.

After the foundation of Rome, the emerging republic—that is, the army of the founder, composed of Albans, Sabines, and foreigners—was divided into three classes, which on the basis of this division took the name *tribes*. Each of these tribes was subdivided into ten curiae, and each curia into decuries, at the head of which were placed leaders called *curions* and *decurions*.

In addition to that, a body of one hundred horsemen or knights, called a century, were drawn from each tribe. It can be seen from this that these divisions, hardly necessary in a market-town, were merely military at first. But it seems that an instinct for greatness caused the little town of Rome to furnish itself in advance with regulations suited to the capital of the world.

This initial division soon gave rise to a drawback. The tribes of the Albans** and of the Sabines*** always remained constant, while that of the foreigners**** grew continually due to the perpetual influx of new members, so that it soon grew larger than the other two. The remedy Servius found for this danger was to change the division, and to substitute for the one based on races, which he abolished, another drawn from the location in the city occupied by each tribe. Instead of three tribes, he made four. Each of them occupied one of the hills of Rome and bore its name. Thus, while remedying the existing inequality, he prevented its recurrence in the future. And so that this division was not merely one of location but also of men, he forbade the

---

*The name *Rome*, which supposedly comes from Romulus, is Greek, and means *force*. The name *Numa* is Greek too, and means *law*. How likely is it that the first two kings of that city had in advance names so highly relevant to what they did?[121]
**Ramnenses
***Tatienses
****Luceres

inhabitants of one quarter to move into another, which prevented the races from mixing together.

He also doubled the three ancient centuries of horsemen, and added twelve others to them, but still under the old names, a simple and judicious way by which he succeeded in distinguishing the body of knights from that of the people without creating discontent among the latter.

To the four urban tribes, Servius added fifteen others called rustic tribes, because they were composed of rural inhabitants who were divided into the same number of cantons. Later, the same number of new ones were created, and the Roman people was finally divided into thirty-five tribes, the number at which they remained until the end of the Republic.

This distinction between town tribes and rural tribes produced an effect worthy of note, because there is no other example of it and because Rome owed to it both the preservation of its mores and the growth of its empire. It might be thought that the urban tribes soon arrogated the power and honors to themselves and did not delay in degrading the rustic tribes. The very opposite happened. The early Romans' taste for country life is well known. They derived it from the wise founder who combined rustic and military labors with freedom, and so to speak relegated to the town arts, crafts, intrigue, fortune, and slavery.

Thus, since all who were most illustrious in Rome lived in the country and tilled the soil, it became customary to seek the mainstays of the Republic only there. Since this condition was that of the worthiest patricians, it was honored by everyone. The simple and hardworking life of village people was preferred to the idle and lax life of the bourgeois in Rome. And someone who would have been nothing but a wretched proletarian in the town, became a respected citizen as a farmer in the fields. It was not without reason, said Varro, that our magnanimous ancestors established villages as the nursery of those robust and valiant men who defended them in time of war and nourished them in time of peace. Pliny says positively that the rural tribes were honored because of the men who composed them, whereas cowards who were to be degraded were transferred in dishonor to tribes of the town.[122] When the Sabine Appius Claudius came to settle in Rome, he was showered with honors there and inscribed in a rustic tribe which afterward assumed the name of his family. Finally, freedmen all entered urban tribes, never rural ones. And during the entire Republic, there is not a single example of those freedmen achieving any magistracy, even though they had become citizens.

This maxim was excellent, but it was pushed so far that it finally resulted in a change and certainly an abuse in the regulations.

First, the censors, after having long arrogated to themselves the right to transfer citizens arbitrarily from one tribe to another, allowed most of them to be inscribed in whichever one they pleased. This permission surely served no good purpose, and removed one of the crucial mechanisms of censorship.

Furthermore, since the upper classes and those with power all had themselves inscribed in rural tribes, and since freedmen who had become citizens remained with the populace in town tribes, the tribes in general no longer had either location or territory. Instead, they became so intermingled that it was no longer possible to discern the members of each except by the registers; so that the idea of the word *tribe* shifted from property to persons, or rather became almost a myth.

It happened, further, that the town tribes, being closer at hand, were often the strongest in the comitia, and sold the State to those who stooped to buying the votes of the rabble who composed them.

With regard to the curiae, since the founder had created ten of these in each tribe, the entire Roman people at that point enclosed within the town walls was composed of thirty curiae, each of which had its temples, its Gods, its officers, its priests, and its festivals called *compitalia*, similar to the *paganalia* which the rustic tribes had subsequently.

When Servius created the new division, this number thirty could not be divided up equally among the four tribes; he did not want to alter it, so the curiae, independent of the tribes, became a separate division of the inhabitants of Rome. But there was no question of curiae either within the rustic tribes or among the people composing them, because the tribes had become a purely civil establishment and another regulation had been introduced for the raising of troops, so that the military divisions of Romulus were found to be superfluous. Thus although every citizen was inscribed in a tribe, nowhere near everyone was inscribed in a curia.

Servius created yet a third division which had no relationship to the two preceding ones, and which, through its effects, became the most important of all. He divided the entire Roman people into six classes, which he distinguished neither by location nor by personal attributes, but by wealth. So that the first classes were filled by the rich, the last by the poor, and the middle ones by those who enjoyed a moderate fortune. These six classes were subdivided into 193 other bodies called centuries, and these bodies were so distributed that the first class alone comprised more than half of them, and the last only one. Thus it was that the class that was least numerous in men was most numerous in centuries, and the entire last class counted only as one subdivision even though alone it contained more than half the inhabitants of Rome.

In order that the people would have less understanding of the consequences of this last division, Servius pretended to give it a military appearance. He inserted two centuries of armorers into the second class and two centuries of instruments of war into the fourth. In each class, except the last, he distinguished the young from the old, that is those who were obligated to carry arms from those whose age exempted them by law—a distinction which, even more than that of wealth, produced the necessity of frequently redoing the census or enumeration. Finally, Servius wanted the assembly to be held at the Campus Martius and all those of military age to come there with their arms.

The reason he did not follow this same division of young and old in the last class is that the populace of which it was composed was not accorded the honor of bearing arms for the homeland. It was necessary to have homes in order to obtain the right to defend them; and of those countless troops of beggars who today adorn the armies of kings, there would not have been one, perhaps, who would not have been disdainfully run out of a Roman cohort when soldiers were the defenders of freedom.

However there was still one distinction made in the last class, between the *proletarians* and those called *capite censi*. The former, not completely destitute, at least gave the State citizens, and sometimes even soldiers when needs were pressing. As for those who had nothing whatever, and who could be counted only by their heads, they were regarded as completely worthless, and Marius was the first who deigned to enroll them.

Without deciding here if this third type of enumeration was good or bad in itself, I think I can assert that it was only made practicable by the simple mores of the early Romans, their disinterestedness, their taste for agriculture, their disdain for commerce and for the desire for profit. Where is the modern people whose devouring greed, uneasiness of mind, intrigue, continual moving about, and perpetual revolutions in fortunes would allow such an establishment to last for twenty years without overturning the whole State? It must also be carefully noted that mores and censorship, which were stronger than this institution, corrected its vices in Rome, and that a given rich man could find himself relegated to the class of the poor if he made too great a display of his wealth.

From all this, it is easy to understand why mention is almost never made of more than five classes, even though there were really six. The sixth, since it furnished neither soldiers for the army nor voters at the Campus Martius,* and was of almost no use in the Republic, was rarely counted for anything.

Such were the different divisions of the Roman people. Now let us see what effect these divisions produced on the assemblies. These assemblies, when legitimately convoked, were called *comitia*. They were usually held in the Roman forum or at the Campus Martius, and were either comitia by curiae, comitia by centuries, or comitia by tribes, according to which of these three divisions was the basis of organization. The comitia by curiae were derived from the institution of Romulus, those by centuries from that of Servius, and those by tribes from that of the tribunes of the people. No law received sanction, no magistrate was elected except in the comitia. And since there was no citizen who was not inscribed in a curia, in a century, or in a

---

*I say *Campus Martius* because it was there that the comitia were assembled by centuries. In the other two forms, the people assembled at the *forum* or elsewhere, and then the *capite censi* had as much influence and authority as the first citizens.

tribe, it follows that no citizen was excluded from the right to vote, and that the Roman people was truly sovereign by right and in fact.

Three conditions had to be met in order for the comitia to be legitimately assembled and for what they did to have the force of law. First, the body or magistrate who convoked them had to be invested with the necessary authority to do so. Second, the assembly had to be held on one of the days sanctioned by law. Third, the auguries had to be favorable.

The reason for the first rule needs no explanation. The second is an administrative matter. Thus it was not allowed to hold comitia on holidays and market days, when the people from the countryside, coming to Rome for business, did not have time to spend the day in the forum. By means of the third rule, the senate held in check a proud and restless people, and appropriately tempered the ardor of seditious tribunes, who nonetheless found more than one way to circumvent this constraint.

The laws and the election of leaders were not the only issues submitted to the judgment of the comitia. Since the Roman people had usurped the most important functions of government, it can be said that the fate of Europe was decided in its assemblies. This variety of objects gave rise to the different forms these assemblies assumed according to the matters to be decided.

To judge these different forms, it suffices to compare them. In instituting the curiae, Romulus's purpose was to restrain the senate by the people and the people by the senate, while he dominated both equally. He therefore gave the people, through the curiae, all the authority of number to balance that of power and wealth which he left to the patricians. But in keeping with the spirit of monarchy, he nevertheless left a greater advantage with the patricians through the influence of their clients on the majority of the votes. This admirable institution of patrons and clients was a masterpiece of politics and humanity, without which the patriciate, so contrary to the spirit of the Republic, could not have survived. Rome alone had the honor of giving the world this fine example, which never led to any abuse, yet which has never been followed.

Since this same form of curiae survived under the kings until Servius, and since the reign of the last Tarquin was not considered legitimate, the royal laws were generally distinguished by the name *leges curiatae*.

Under the Republic, the curiae, which were always limited to the four urban tribes and no longer included anyone but the populace of Rome, were no longer suited either to the senate, which was at the head of the patricians, or to the tribunes, who, although plebeians, were at the head of the well-to-do citizens. Therefore the curiae became discredited, and they were so degraded that an assembly of their thirty lictors did what the comitia by curiae ought to have done.

The division into centuries was so favorable to aristocracy that it is not at first apparent why the senate did not always prevail in the comitia of that name and by which the consuls, censors, and other curule magistrates were elected. Indeed, of the one hundred ninety-three centuries that constituted the six classes of the entire Roman people, since the first class included ninety-eight, and since the votes were only counted by centuries, this first class alone prevailed over all the others by the number of its votes. When all of its centuries were in agreement, they did not even continue to collect the votes. What the smallest number decided was taken as a decision of the multitude; and it can be said that in the comitia by centuries matters were more often settled by a majority of money than by one of votes.[123]

But this extreme authority was tempered in two ways. First, since usually the tribunes—and always a large number of plebeians—were in the class of the rich, they balanced the credit of the patricians in this first class.

The second way was as follows. Rather than to have the centuries start to vote according to their order, which would have meant that the first always began, one century was drawn by lot, and that one* alone proceeded with the election. After this, all the centuries were called on another day according to their rank, repeated the same election, and usually confirmed it. Thus the authority of example was taken away from rank and given to lot, in accordance with the principle of democracy.

This practice produced still another advantage, which was that the citizens from the country had time between the two elections to inform themselves of the merit of the provisionally named candidate, so that they could vote knowledgeably. But on the pretext of speed, this practice was finally abolished and the two elections were held on the same day.

The comitia by tribes were really the council of the Roman people. They were convoked only by the tribunes. The tribunes were elected and had their plebiscites passed in them. Not only did the senate have no rank in them, but it did not even have the right to attend them; and since the senators were forced to obey laws on which they could not vote, they were less free in this regard than the last citizens. This injustice was a complete mistake, and alone was enough to invalidate the decrees of a body to which all the members were not admitted. If all the patricians had attended these comitia in accordance with their rights as citizens, since they would then have become simple private individuals, they could hardly have influenced a form of voting based on counting heads, and in which the humblest proletarian carried as much weight as the prince of the senate.

Thus it can be seen that apart from the effect of these various divisions on the way the votes of such a large people were collected, these divisions cannot be dismissed as in themselves indifferent, because each one had effects related to the attitudes that favored it.

---

*The century drawn by lot in this way was called *prærogativa*, because it was the first to be asked for its vote; and that is the origin of the word *prerogative*.

Without going into greater detail about this, the foregoing clarifications indicate that the comitia by tribes were the most favorable to popular government, and the comitia by centuries to aristocracy. With regard to the comitia by curiae, where the populace of Rome alone formed the majority, since these were only good for favoring tyranny and evil schemes, they inevitably fell into disrepute, and the seditious themselves abstained from a means that overly exposed their projects. It is certain that all the majesty of the Roman people was found only in the comitia by centuries, which alone were complete, since the comitia by curiae lacked the rustic tribes and the comitia by tribes lacked the senate and the patricians.

As for the manner of collecting the votes, among the early Romans it was as simple as their mores, although less simple than in Sparta. Each person voted aloud; a registrar wrote down the votes as they were given. A majority of votes within each tribe determined the vote of the tribe; a majority of votes among the tribes determined the vote of the people; and the same was true for the curiae and centuries. This practice was good as long as honesty prevailed among the citizens and each was ashamed to vote publicly for an unjust opinion or an unworthy subject. But when the people became corrupt and votes were bought, it was agreed that voting should be done in secret in order to restrain buyers by distrust and provide scoundrels with the means not to be traitors.

I know that Cicero blames this change and attributes to it in part the ruin of the Republic.[124] But although I am aware of the weight Cicero's authority should carry on this point, I cannot share his opinion. I think, on the contrary, that the downfall of the State was hastened because more changes of this sort were not made. Just as the regimen of healthy people is not suited to the sick, one must not want to govern a corrupt people by the same laws that are suited to a good people. Nothing proves this maxim better than the duration of the Republic of Venice, the semblance of which still exists uniquely because its laws are only suited to wicked men.

Thus ballots were distributed to the citizens on which each one could vote without others knowing his opinion. New formalities were also established for collecting the ballots, counting the votes, comparing the numbers, etc.; all of which did not prevent the fidelity of the officers in charge of these functions* from often being suspected. Finally, in order to prevent intrigue and the buying of votes, edicts were passed, whose number demonstrates their uselessness.

Toward the end, it was often necessary to have recourse to extraordinary expedients to bolster up the inadequacy of the laws. Sometimes miracles were invented; but this means, which could fool the people, could not fool those who governed it. Sometimes an assembly was convoked suddenly, before the candidates had time to arrange their intrigues. Sometimes an entire session was consumed by talk, when it was seen that the people was

---

Custodes, Diribitores, Rogatores suffragiorum.

won over and ready to make a bad choice. But finally ambition eluded everything. And what is unbelievable is that in the midst of so many abuses, by virtue of its ancient regulations this immense people did not cease to elect its magistrates, pass laws, try cases, and expedite public or private affairs almost as smoothly as the senate itself might have done.

Chapter V: On the Tribunate

When an exact proportion cannot be established between the constituent parts of the State, or when indestructible causes constantly alter the relationships between them, a special magistracy is then instituted which is not a part of the others; which places each term back in its true relationship; and which creates a link or middle term either between the prince and the people or between the prince and the sovereign, or on both sides at once if necessary.

This body, which I shall call the *tribunate*, is the preserver of the laws and of the legislative power. Sometimes it serves to protect the sovereign against the government, as the tribunes of the people did in Rome; sometimes to sustain the government against the people, as the Council of Ten now does in Venice; and sometimes to maintain a balance on both sides, as the ephors did in Sparta.[125]

The tribunate is not a constituent part of the City, and should not have any portion of the legislative or executive power. But it is for this very reason that its own power is greater, for although it can do nothing, it can prevent everything. It is more sacred and revered as a defender of the laws than the prince who executes them and the sovereign who makes them. This was seen very clearly in Rome when the proud patricians, who always scorned the entire people, were forced to yield before a simple officer of the people, who had neither auspices nor jurisdiction.

A wisely tempered tribunate is the firmest support of a good constitution. But if it has even a little too much force, it upsets everything. Weakness is not in its nature, and provided that the tribunate counts for something, it will never be less than is necessary.

It degenerates into tyranny when it usurps the executive power, of which it is only the moderator, and when it wants to dispense laws, which it should only protect. The vast power of the ephors, which was without danger as long as Sparta preserved its mores, accelerated corruption once it began. The blood of Agis, murdered by these tyrants, was revenged by his successor. The crime and punishment of the ephors equally hastened the downfall of the Republic; and after Cleomenes, Sparta was no longer anything. Rome also perished in the same way, and the excessive power that the tribunes gradually usurped was finally used, with the help of laws made to protect freedom, as a safeguard for the emperors who destroyed it. As for the Council of Ten in Venice, it is a bloody tribunal, equally horrible for the patricians and the people, and which, far from proudly protecting the laws, now only serves after their debasement for striking shady blows that no one dares notice.

The tribunate, like the government, is weakened by the multiplication of its members. When the tribunes of the Roman people, at first two in number, then five, wanted to double this number, the senate allowed them to do so, certain that some would restrain others, which is just what happened.

The best way to prevent usurpations by such a formidable body—one that no government has thought of up to now—would be not to make this body permanent, but to regulate intervals during which it would be suppressed. These intervals, which should not be long enough to give abuses the time to become established, can be fixed by law in such a way that it is easy to cut them short, in case of need, by special commissions.

This method appears to me to present no difficulties because, since the tribunate—as I have said—is not part of the constitution, it can be removed without doing the constitution any harm. And it appears effective to me because a newly established magistrate does not start from the power his predecessor had, but from that given to him by the law.

Chapter VI: On Dictatorship

The inflexibility of laws, which prevents them from adapting to events, can in certain cases make them pernicious, and they can cause the downfall of the State during a crisis.[126] The order and slowness of formalities require a space of time which circumstances sometimes do not permit. A thousand situations for which the legislator has made no provision can arise, and it is a very necessary foresight to realize that one cannot foresee everything.

It is necessary, therefore, not to want to strengthen political institutions to the point of removing the power to suspend their effect. Even Sparta let its laws lie dormant.

But only the greatest dangers can outweigh the danger of altering the public order, and one should never suspend the sacred power of the laws except when it is a matter of the safety of the homeland. In these rare and manifest cases, a special act provides for public security, placing responsibility for it in the worthiest hands. This commission can be given in two ways, according to the type of danger.

If, as a remedy, it suffices to increase the activity of the government, it is concentrated in one or two of its members. Thus it is not the authority of the laws that is altered, but merely the form by which they are administered. If the peril is such that to guard against it, the apparatus of the laws is an obstacle, then a supreme leader is named who silences all the laws and momentarily suspends sovereign authority. In such a case, the general will is not in doubt, and it is evident that the first intention of the people is that the State should not perish. In this manner, the suspension of legislative authority does not abolish it. The magistrate who silences it cannot make it speak; he dominates it without being able to represent it. He can do anything, except make laws.

The first means was used by the Roman senate when it entrusted the consuls, by a consecrated formula, with providing for the safety of the Republic. The second occurred when one of the two consuls named a dictator,* a practice for which Alba set the precedent in Rome.

At the beginnings of the Republic, recourse to dictatorship was taken often, because the State did not yet have a stable enough basis to be able to sustain itself by the force of its constitution. Since the mores of that period made many precautions superfluous that would have been necessary in other times, there was no fear either that a dictator would abuse his authority or that he would try to keep it beyond his term. It seemed, on the contrary, that such a great power was a burden to the one in whom it was vested, so quickly did he hasten to be rid of it, as though an office that took the place of the laws would have been too painful and too dangerous.

Thus it is not the danger of abuse but rather that of debasement which leads me to blame the indiscriminate use of this supreme magistracy in early times. For while it was being squandered on elections, dedications, and pure formalities, it was to be feared that it would become less formidable in time of need, and that people would grow accustomed to consider empty a title that was used only in empty ceremonies.

Toward the end of the Republic, the Romans, having become more circumspect, used the dictatorship sparingly with as little reason as they had formerly squandered it. It was easy to see that their fear was ill-founded, that the weakness of the capital then guaranteed it against the magistrates in its midst; that a dictator could in certain situations defend public freedom without ever being able to threaten it; and that Rome's chains would not be forged in Rome itself, but in its armies. The feeble resistance of Marius against Sulla and of Pompey against Caesar showed clearly what could be expected of internal authority against external force.

This error caused them to make great mistakes. For example, not having named a dictator in the Catiline affair; for since it was only a question of the interior of the town and at most of some province in Italy, with the unlimited authority that the laws gave the dictator he would easily have dissipated the conspiracy, which was suppressed only by a combination of chance factors which human prudence could never have anticipated.

Instead of that, the senate was content to place all its power in the consuls. Because of this, Cicero, in order to act effectively, was constrained to exceed this power in a crucial respect; and although the first explosions of joy gave approval to his conduct, later on he was justly called to account for the blood of citizens spilled against the laws, a reproach that could not have

---

*This nomination was made at night and in secret, as though it were shameful to place a man above the laws.

been made to a dictator. But the consul's eloquence carried the day. And since even he, although a Roman, preferred his glory to his homeland, he did not seek the most legitimate and surest way to save the State so much as the way that would bring him the greatest honor from this affair.* Thus he was justly honored as the liberator of Rome and justly punished as a violator of the laws. However brilliant his recall, it is certain that it was a pardon.

In any event, no matter how this important commission is conferred, it is important for its duration to be fixed at a very short term which can never be prolonged. In the crises that call for its establishment, the State is soon destroyed or saved, and once the urgent need has passed, the dictatorship becomes tyrannical or useless. In Rome, where the dictators were named for only six months, most of them abdicated before this term. If the term had been longer, perhaps they would have been tempted to prolong it further, as did the decemvirs with a term of one year. The dictator had only the time to attend to the need that led to his election; he did not have enough to think up other projects.

Chapter VII: On Censorship

Just as the general will is declared by the law, public judgment is declared by censorship.[127] Public opinion is the kind of law of which the censor is the minister, and which he only applies to particular situations, following the example of the prince.

Therefore the censorial tribunal, far from being the arbiter of the people's opinion, merely declares it, and as soon as this body departs from that opinion, its decisions are useless and ineffective.

There is no use in distinguishing between the mores of a nation and the objects of its esteem,[128] for all of these things stem from the same principle and are necessarily intermingled. Among all the peoples of the world, it is not nature, but opinion that determines the choice of their pleasures. Reform men's opinions and their mores will purify themselves. One always likes what is beautiful or what is thought to be so, but it is this judgment that may be mistaken. Therefore the problem is to regulate this judgment. Whoever judges mores judges honor, and whoever judges honor derives his law from opinion.

A people's opinions arise from its constitution. Although the law does not regulate mores, it is legislation that gives rise to them. When legislation weakens, mores degenerate, but then the judgment of censors will not be able to do what the force of law has not done.

It follows from this that censorship can be useful for preserving mores, but never for reestablishing them. Establish censors when the laws are in

---

*He could not be certain of this in proposing a dictator, since he did not dare name himself, and he could not be sure that his colleague would name him.

full vigor. As soon as the laws have lost it, the situation is desperate; nothing legitimate has force any longer when the laws no longer have any.

Censorship maintains mores by preventing opinions from becoming corrupt; by preserving their rectitude through wise application; sometimes even by determining them when they are still uncertain. The use of seconds in duels, which became a passion in the kingdom of France, was abolished there by the following few words in an edict of the king: *as for those who are so cowardly as to call upon seconds*. This judgment, anticipating that of the public, determined it at once. But when the same edicts tried to proclaim that it was also an act of cowardice to fight duels—which is quite true, but contrary to common opinion—the public scorned this decision, upon which its judgment was already formed.

I have said elsewhere* that since public opinion is not subject to constraint, there must be no vestige of constraint in the tribunal established to represent it. The art with which this mechanism, altogether lost among modern peoples, was set to work among the Romans and better still among the Lacedemonians cannot be sufficiently admired.

When a man of bad morals offered a good opinion in the council of Sparta, the ephors, taking no notice of it, had a virtuous citizen propose the same opinion. What an honor for one, what a shaming for the other, without even having praised or blamed either of the two. Certain drunkards from Samos** defiled the tribunal of the ephors. The following day, a public edict gave the Samians permission to be filthy. A real punishment would have been less severe than such impunity. When Sparta declared what is or is not decent, Greece did not contest its judgments.

Chapter VIII: On Civil Religion

Men at first had no other kings than the Gods, nor any other government than theocracy.[130] They reasoned like Caligula, and then they reasoned correctly. A long period of change in sentiments and ideas was necessary before men could bring themselves to accept a fellow man as a master and flatter themselves that this was a good arrangement.

By the sole fact that God was placed at the head of every political society, it followed that there were as many Gods as there were peoples. Two peoples foreign to each other and nearly always enemies could not recognize the same master for long; two armies battling one another could not obey the same leader. Thus national divisions resulted in polytheism, and beyond that in theological as well as civil intolerance, which are naturally the same thing, as will be stated hereafter.

*In this chapter, I merely indicate what I have treated at greater length in the *Letter to M. d'Alembert*.

**They came from another island which the delicacy of our language forbids me to name in this context.[129]

The whimsical notion of the Greeks to identify the Gods of barbarian peoples with their own Gods came from their other notion that they were the natural sovereigns of these peoples. But in our day, the equation of the Gods of various nations is ridiculous erudition, as if Moloch, Saturn, and Cronus could have been the same God; as if the Phoenicians' Baal, the Greeks' Zeus, and the Romans' Jupiter could have been the same; as if imaginary beings, bearing different names, could have something in common!

The question may be asked why under paganism, when each State had its cult and its Gods, there were no wars of religion. I reply that it was for this very reason that each State, having its own cult as well as its government, did not distinguish between its Gods and its laws. Political war was also theological. The departments of the Gods were, so to speak, fixed by the boundaries of nations. The God of one people had no rights over other peoples. The Gods of the pagans were not jealous Gods. They divided dominion over the world among themselves. Moses himself and the Hebrew people accepted this idea sometimes when speaking of the God of Israel. It is true that they regarded as nothing the Gods of the Canaanites, a proscribed people destined for destruction, and whose land they were to occupy. But notice how they spoke of the divinities of neighboring peoples whom they were forbidden to attack! *Is not the possession of what belongs to Chamos your God,* said Jeptha to the Ammonites, *legitimately yours? By the same token, we possess the lands that our victorious God has acquired.** It seems to me that this was a clear acknowledgment of parity between the right of Chamos and those of the God of Israel.

But when the Jews, subjected to the kings of Babylon and later to the kings of Syria, wanted to remain obstinate in not acknowledging any other God than theirs, this refusal, regarded as rebellion against the victor, brought on them the persecutions of which we read in their history, and of which there are no other examples prior to Christianity.**

Therefore, since each religion was uniquely attached to the laws of the State that prescribed it, there was no other way to convert a people except to subjugate it, nor any missionaries other than conquerors. And as the obligation to change cult was the law of the vanquished, it was necessary to start by winning before talking about it. Far from men fighting for the Gods, it was— as in Homer—the Gods who fought for the men. Each man asked his own God for victory and paid for it with new altars. Before capturing a place, the

---

Nonne ea quae possidet Chamos deus tuus tibi jure debentur? So reads the text of the Vulgate. Father de Carrières has translated it: *Do you not believe you have the right to possess what belongs to Chamos your God?* I am ignorant of the implication of the Hebrew text; but I see that in the Vulgate Jephtha positively acknowledges the right of the God Chamos, and that the French translator weakens this recognition by an *according to you* which is not in the Latin.[131]

**It is perfectly evident that the war of the Phocaeans called the holy war was not a war of religion. Its object was to punish sacrilege, not to subjugate nonbelievers.[132]

Romans called upon its Gods to abandon it; and when they let the people of Tarantum keep their angry Gods, it was because at that point the Romans considered those Gods as subject to their own and forced to pay them homage. They let the vanquished keep their Gods as they let them keep their laws. A crown for the Capitoline Jupiter was often the only tribute they imposed.

Finally the Romans, having spread their cult and their Gods along with their empire, and having themselves often adopted the Gods of the vanquished by granting legal status in the City to them all, the peoples of that vast empire gradually come to have multitudes of Gods and of cults, which were approximately the same everywhere. And that is how paganism in the known world finally became a single, identical religion.

It was under these circumstances that Jesus came to establish a spiritual kingdom on earth. By separating the theological system from the political system, this brought about the end of the unity of the State, and caused the internal divisions that have never ceased to stir up Christian peoples. Now since this new idea of an otherworldly kingdom could never be understood by the pagans, they always regarded the Christians as true rebels who, beneath a hypocritical submissiveness, were only awaiting the moment to become independent and the masters, and to usurp adroitly the authority they pretended to respect out of weakness. This was the cause of the persecutions.[133].

What the pagans feared happened. Then everything took on a different appearance, the humble Christians changed their language, and soon this supposedly otherworldly kingdom was seen to become, under a visible leader, the most violent despotism in this world.

However, since there has always been a prince and civil laws, this double power has resulted in a perpetual conflict of jurisdiction that has made any good polity impossible in Christian States, and no people has ever been able to figure out whom it was obligated to obey, the master or the priest.

Several peoples, however, even in Europe or near it, have wanted to preserve or reestablish the ancient system, but without success. The spirit of Christianity has won over everything. The sacred cult has always remained, or again become independent of the sovereign, and without a necessary bond with the body of the State. Mohammed had very sound views; he tied his political system together well, and as long as the form of this government subsisted under his successors the caliphs, the government was completely unified, and good for that reason. But when the Arabs became prosperous, lettered, polished, soft, and weak, they were subjugated by barbarians. Then the division between the two powers began again. Although it is less apparent among the Mohammedans than among the Christians, it is there nonetheless, especially in the sect of Ali, and there are States, such as Persia, where it is continually felt.

Among us, the kings of England have established themselves as heads of the church, and the czars have done the same thing. But by this title, they have made themselves not so much the masters as the ministers. They have acquired not so much the right to change it as the power to maintain it. They are not its legislators; they are only its princes. Wherever the clergy constitutes a body,* it is master and legislator in its domain. There are, therefore, two powers, two sovereigns, in England and in Russia just as everywhere else.

Of all Christian authors, the philosopher Hobbes is the only one who correctly saw the evil and the remedy, who dared to propose the reunification of the two heads of the eagle, and the complete return to political unity, without which no State or government will ever be well constituted. But he ought to have seen that the dominating spirit of Christianity was incompatible with his system, and that the interest of the priest would always be stronger than that of the State. It is not so much what is horrible and false in his political theory as what is correct and true that has made it odious.**

I believe that by treating the historical facts in this light, one would easily refute the opposing sentiments of Bayle and Warburton, one of whom claims that no religion is useful to the body politic, the other of whom maintains, to the contrary, that Christianity is its firmest support. One would prove to the former that a State has never been founded without religion serving as its base, and to the latter that Christian law is fundamentally more harmful than useful to the strong constitution of a State. To make myself completely understood, it is only necessary to give a little more precision to the overly vague ideas about religion that are relevant to my subject.

Considered in relation to society, which is either general or particular, religion can also be divided into two types, namely the religion of man and that of the citizen.[135] The former, without temples, altars, or rituals, limited to the purely internal cult of the supreme God and to the eternal duties of morality, is the pure and simple religion of the Gospel, true theism, and what may be called natural divine right. The latter, inscribed in a single country, gives it its Gods, its own tutelary patrons. Its dogma, rites, and external cult are prescribed by laws. Outside the single nation that observes it, everything is considered infidel, foreign, barbarous; it only extends the duties and rights

*It must be carefully noted that it is not so much formal assemblies, like those in France, that bind the clergy into a body as it is the communion of churches. Communion and excommunication are the social compact of the clergy, a compact by means of which it will always be master of peoples and kings. All the priests who take communion together are fellow citizens, even though they may come from opposite ends of the earth. This invention is a political masterpiece. The pagan priests had nothing that resembles it, and therefore they never constituted a body of clergymen.

**Consider, among other things, in a letter Grotius wrote to his brother, April 11, 1643, what this learned man approves and what he blames in the book *De Cive*. It is true that, being indulgent, he appears to pardon the author's good points for the sake of his bad ones. But everyone is not so clement.[134]

Rousseau's 1st principle

of man as far as its altars. Such were all the religions of the early peoples, to which the name of civil or positive divine right can be given.

There is a third, more bizarre, type of religion which, by giving men two legislative systems, two leaders, and two homelands, subjects them to contradictory duties, and prevents them from being simultaneously devout men and citizens. The religion of the Lamas is like this, as is that of the Japanese, and Roman Catholicism. It can be called the religion of the priest. It leads to a type of mixed and unsocial right that has no name.

Considered from a political point of view, each of these three types of religion has its faults. The third is so manifestly bad that it is a waste of time to amuse oneself by proving it. Everything that destroys social unity is worthless. All institutions that put man in contradiction with himself are worthless.

The second is good in that it combines the divine cult and love of the laws, and by making the homeland the object of the citizens' prayers, it teaches them that to serve the State is to serve its tutelary God. It is a kind of theocracy in which there ought to be no other pontif than the prince, nor other priests than the magistrates. Then to die for one's country is to be martyred, to violate the laws is to be impious, and to subject a guilty man to public execration is to deliver him to the anger of the Gods: *sacer estod.*[136]

But this religion is bad in that, being based on error and falsehood, it deceives men, makes them credulous, superstitious, and drowns the true cult of divinity in empty ceremonial. It is bad, too, whenever it becomes exclusive and tyrannical and makes a people bloodthirsty and intolerant to the point where it lives only for murder and massacre, and believes it performs a holy act when killing whoever does not accept its Gods. This places such a people in a natural state of war with all others, which is very harmful to its own security.

There remains the religion of man, or Christianity—not that of today, but that of the Gospel, which is totally different from it. Through this saintly, sublime, true religion, men—children of the same God—all acknowledge one another as brothers, and the society that unites them is not even dissolved by death.

But this religion, having no particular relation to the body politic, leaves laws with only their intrinsic force, without adding any other force to them; and because of this, one of the great bonds of particular societies remains without effect. Even worse, far from attaching the citizens' hearts to the State, it detaches them from it as from all worldly things. I know of nothing more contrary to the social spirit.[137]

We are told that a people of true Christians would form the most perfect society that can be imagined. I see only one major difficulty in this assumption, which is that a society of true Christians would no longer be a society of men.

I even say that assuming such a society existed with all its perfection, it

Communitarian

would be neither the strongest nor the most lasting. By dint of being perfect, it would lack cohesion; its destroying vice would lie in its very perfection.

Everyone would fulfill his duty, the people would be subject to the laws, the leaders would be just and moderate, the magistrates honest and incorruptible, the soldiers would scorn death, there would be neither vanity nor luxury. All that is very well, but let us look further.

Christianity is a totally spiritual religion, uniquely concerned with heavenly matters. The Christian's homeland is not of this world. He does his duty, it is true, but he does it with profound indifference for the good or bad outcome of his efforts. As long as he has nothing to reproach himself for, it matters little to him whether things go well or badly here on earth. If the State is flourishing, he barely dares to enjoy the public felicity for fear of becoming proud of his country's glory. If the State declines, he blesses the hand of God that weighs heavily on his people.

In order for the society to be peaceful and for harmony to last, all citizens without exception would have to be equally good Christians. But if unfortunately there is a single ambitious man, a single hypocrite—a Catiline, for example, or a Cromwell—he will very certainly get the better of his pious compatriots. Christian charity makes it hard to think ill of one's neighbor. As soon as he has learned the art of how to trick them through some ruse and seize part of the public authority for himself, he will be a man of constituted dignity; it is God's will to respect him. Soon he is powerful; it is God's will to obey him. Does the depository of this power abuse it? He is the rod with which God punishes His children. It would be against conscience to chase out the usurper, for it would be necessary to disturb the public tranquillity, use violence, shed blood. All of that is inconsistent with the gentleness of a Christian. And after all, what does it matter whether one is free or a serf in this vale of tears? The essential thing is to go to heaven, and resignation is but an additional means of doing so.

What if a foreign war breaks out? The citizens march readily to combat; none among them thinks of fleeing; they do their duty, but without passion for victory. They know how to die rather than to win. What does it matter if they are victors or vanquished? Doesn't providence know better than they what is good for them? Imagine how a proud, impetuous, passionate enemy can take advantage of their stoicism! Confront them with those generous and proud peoples consumed by a burning love of glory and homeland; suppose that your Christian republic is face to face with Sparta or Rome. The pious Christians will be beaten, crushed, destroyed before they have had time to look around, or they will owe their salvation only to the scorn their enemies will conceive for them. The oath taken by the soldiers of Fabius was a fine one to my mind. They did not swear to die or to win; they swore to return as victors, and they kept their promise. Christians would never have made such a promise; they would have believed they were tempting God.

cf. Nietzsche

But I am mistaken when I speak of a Christian republic; these two words are mutually exclusive. Christianity preaches nothing but servitude and dependence. Its spirit is so favorable to tyranny that tyranny always profits from it. True Christians are made to be slaves.[138] They know it and are scarcely moved thereby; this brief life is of too little worth in their view.

Christian troops are excellent, we are told. I deny this. Let someone show me some. For myself, I don't know of any Christian troops. The crusades will be cited. Without arguing over the valor of the crusaders, I shall note that very far from being Christians, they were soldiers of the priest, they were citizens of the Church; they were fighting for its spiritual country, which the church had made temporal in some unknown way. Properly understood, this amounts to paganism. Since the Gospel does not establish a national religion, a holy war is impossible among Christians.

Under the pagan Emperors, Christian soldiers were brave. All Christian authors assert this, and I believe it. There was a competition for honor against the pagan troops. As soon as the Emperors were Christians, this emulation ceased, and when the cross chased out the eagle, all Roman valor disappeared.

But setting political considerations aside, let us return to right and determine its principles concerning this important point. The right that the social compact gives the sovereign over the subjects does not exceed, as I have said, the limits of public utility.* The subjects, therefore, do not have to account for their opinions to the sovereign, except insofar as these opinions matter to the community. Now it matters greatly to the State that each citizen have a religion that causes him to love his duties; but the dogmas of that religion are of no interest either to the State or to its members; except insofar as these dogmas relate to morality, and to the duties that anyone who professes it is obliged to fulfill toward others. Everyone can have whatever opinions he pleases beyond that, without the sovereign having to know what they are. For since the sovereign has no competence in the other world, whatever the fate of subjects in the life hereafter, it is none of its business, as long as they are good citizens in this one.

There is, therefore, a purely civil profession of faith, the articles of which are for the sovereign to establish, not exactly as religious dogmas, but as sentiments of sociability without which it is impossible to be a good citizen or a faithful subject.** Without being able to obligate anyone to believe them,

---

In the Republic, says the Marquis d'Argenson, *each person is perfectly free with regard to everything that does not harm others.* That is the unvarying limit. It cannot be stated with greater precision. I have not been able to forego the pleasure of citing this manuscript a few times, even though it is unknown to the public, to honor the memory of an illustrious and respectable man, who preserved even in the office of minister the heart of a true citizen, and upright and healthy views about the government of his country.[139]

**In pleading for Catiline, Caesar tried to establish the dogma of the mortality of the

as in Hobbes

the sovereign can banish from the State anyone who does not believe them. The sovereign can banish him not for being impious, but for being unsociable; for being incapable of sincerely loving the laws, justice, and of giving his life, if need be, for his duty. If someone who has publicly acknowledged these same dogmas behaves as though he does not believe them, he should be punished with death. He has committed the greatest of crimes: he lied before the laws.[140]

The dogmas of the civil religion ought to be simple, few in number, stated with precision, without explanations or commentaries. The existence of a powerful, intelligent, beneficent, foresighted, and providential divinity; the afterlife; the happiness of the just; the punishment of the wicked; the sanctity of the social contract and the laws. These are the positive dogmas. As for the negative ones, I limit them to a single one: intolerance. It belongs with the cults we have excluded.[141]

Those who make a distinction between civil and theological intolerance are mistaken, in my opinion. These two intolerances are inseparable. It is impossible to live in peace with people whom one believes are damned. To love them would be to hate God who punishes them. They must absolutely be either brought into the faith or tormented. Wherever theological intolerance exists, it is impossible for it not to have some civil effect;* and as soon as it does, the sovereign is no longer sovereign, even over temporal matters. From then on, priests are the true masters; kings are merely their officers.

Now that there is no longer and can never again be an exclusive national religion, one should tolerate all those religions that tolerate others insofar as their dogmas are in no way contrary to the duties of the citizen. But whoever dares to say *there is no salvation outside of the church* should be chased out

---

soul. To refute him, Cato and Cicero wasted no time philosophizing. They contented themselves with showing that Caesar was speaking as a bad citizen and advancing a doctrine that was pernicious to the State. Indeed, this was what the Roman senate had to judge, and not a question of theology.

*Marriage, for example, being a civil contract, has civil effects without which society could not even subsist.[142] Suppose, then, that a clergy obtains for itself alone the right to pass this act, a right it inevitably usurps in any intolerant religion. Then isn't it clear that by asserting the church's authority in this domain, it will render ineffectual that of the prince, who will have no other subjects than those whom the clergy is willing to give him? As the master of which people can or cannot be married, according to whether they do or do not subscribe to one or another doctrine, whether they accept or reject one or another religious formula, whether they are more or less devout, isn't it clear that by behaving prudently and standing firm, the clergy will have at its sole command inheritances, offices, the citizens, the State itself, which could not subsist if it were composed only of bastards? But, it will be objected, appeal will be made against such abuses; there will be summonses, decrees, seizures of church holdings. What a pity! If the clergy has a little, I won't say courage, but good sense, it will let this happen and go on as usual. It will tranquilly allow the appeals, summonses, decrees, and seizures, and will end up by being the master. It is not, it seems to me, a great sacrifice to abandon a part when one is sure to take possession of the whole.

of the State, unless the State is the church, and the prince is the pontif. Such a dogma is good only in a theocratic government; in any other it is pernicious. The reason for which Henry IV is said to have embraced Roman Catholicism ought to make all honest men—and especially all princes capable of reasoning—leave it.[143]

Chapter IX: Conclusion

After setting forth the true principles of political right and trying to found the State on this basis, what remains to be done is to buttress the State by its foreign relations, which would include international law, commerce, the right of war and conquest, public law, alliances, negotiations, treaties, etc. But all that constitutes a new object, too vast for my limited purview. I should always have set my sights closer to myself.[144]

END

EDITOR'S NOTES

[1] Rousseau carefully chose both his title and subtitle, as is proven by the hesitations on the first draft: see *Geneva Manuscript*, editorial note 1. On the meaning of the terms he finally chose, see Introduction, pp. 13–15; Roger D. Masters, *Political Philosophy of Rousseau* (Princeton, N. J.: Princeton University Press, 1968), pp. 259–293; and Robert Derathé, *Jean-Jacques Rousseau et la Science Politique de Son Temps* (Paris: Presses Universitaires de France, 1950).

[2] Although Rousseau technically lost his citizenship when he converted to Catholicism after running away from Geneva at the age of sixteen, it was officially restored in 1754: *Confessions*, VIII (Pléiade, I, 392–393). Rousseau, however, only added *Citoyen de Genève* to the title pages of those "works that I believe will do honor" to Geneva: *La Nouvelle Héloïse*, Seconde Préface (Pléiade, II, 27).

[3] "In an equitable federation, we will make laws." Virgil, *Aeneid*, xi. 321. Rousseau chose his epigraphs with care because he considered such liminary quotations to symbolize an entire work: *Rousseau Juge de Jean-Jacques*, Dialogue III (Pléiade, I, 941), and Masters, *Political Philosophy of Rousseau*, p. 15, n. 56. In this case, he seems to have chosen a classic example of a social contract, as if according to Virgil's poem Rome was founded by free consent. In context, however, the line comes from a speech by the King of Latium, whose army has just been defeated by the Trojans under Aeneas. A new Trojan attack interrupts the assembly, and the victorious Aeneas founds Rome on the "right of the strongest." Compare *Second Discourse*, Part 2 (ed. Masters, pp. 157–160), *Social Contract*, IV, iv, note, and *Geneva Manuscript*, I,ii: in *fact*, political society rests on violence and deceit, whereas the social contract is a matter of *right*. As Rousseau put it in the *Geneva Manuscript*, I, v: "I seek right and reason, and do not argue over facts."

[4] Rousseau's description of the origin of this project is worth citing at length: "Of the different works I had in progress [in 1756, when Rousseau left Paris to live in the country house of Mme d'Épinay], the one which I had been thinking about for the longest, which occupied me with the greatest pleasure, on which I wanted to work all

my life, and which I thought would put the seal on my reputation was my *Institutions Politiques.* I had conceived the first idea for it thirteen or fourteen years earlier, when—being in Venice [as Secretary to the Comte de Montaigu, French Ambassador, in 1743–1744]—I had some occasion to note the defects of that so highly praised Government. Since then, my perspective had been greatly extended by the historical study of morality. I had seen that everything is basically tied to politics, and that, however one tried, no people would ever be anything except what the nature of its Government would make it be. Thus this noble question of the best possible Government seemed to me to boil down to this: What is the nature of the Government suited to form a people that is the most virtuous, the most enlightened, the wisest, and finally the best, to take this word in its noblest sense. I thought I saw that this question was closely tied to the following one, if indeed it was different from it: What is the Government which by its nature always stays the closest to the law? From that, What is the law? and a series of questions of this importance. I saw that all this led me to great truths, useful to the happiness of the human race, but above all to that of my country." *Confessions,* VIII (Pléiade, I, 404–405). Rousseau goes on to say that "although I had already been working on this project for five or six years, it had hardly gotten ahead" (Ibid.) This corresponds well with Rousseau's letter to Moultou of January 18, 1762: "I should tell you that I am having printed in Holland a small work that is entitled *Du Contrat social* or *Principes du droit politique,* which is extracted from a larger work, entitled *Institutions Politiques,* started ten years ago and abandoned as I cease writing, and in any event an enterprise that was certainly beyond my strength" (cited Pléiade, III, 1431). Rousseau thus started serious work on his *Political Institutions* around 1751, but only made major headway with it after 1756. Despite Rousseau's "Foreword," some fragments presumably from his original project have survived, notably *État de Guerre* ("That the State of War is born from the Social State"— Vaughan I, 293–307 or Pléiade, III, 601–616), "A Comparison between Rome and Sparta" (Vaughan, I, 314–320 or Pléiade, III, 538–543), "On Luxury, Commerce, and the Arts" (Vaughan, I, 341–349 or Pléiade, III, 516–524), "On Laws" (Vaughan, I, 330–334, 355–356 or Pléiade, III, 491–500), and other materials including what appear to have been a list of chapters and a Preface (Vaughan, I, 339, 350–351 or Pléiade, III, 473–474). Some passages from these fragments are translated into English in editorial notes 21, 26, 46, 58, 66, 89. In the account of the *Confessions* cited earlier in this note, the "historical study of morality" may well refer in part to the fragmentary "History of Morals" (Vaughan, I, 334–339 or Pléiade, III, 554–560).

[5]The duality of Rousseau's perception of the problem of political theory deserves emphasis: "men as they are" have concerns of "interest" or "utility" which "prescribe" limits to a solution, whereas "laws as they can be" depend on considerations of "right" and "justice" which "permit"—but only *permit*—of legitimacy. In other words, Rousseau will try to adjust "right" and "justice" to the *necessary* demands of self-interest. Compare *Geneva Manuscript,* I, ii.

[6]This passage is probably a veiled criticism of King Frederick the Great of Prussia, who had published a book entitled *Anti-Machiavel:* see Masters, *Political Philosophy of Rousseau,* pp. 306–309.

[7]Compare *Political Economy,* p. 228. Despite this praise, Rousseau's ambivalent attitude toward his native Geneva has been noted (Introduction, note 27 and references there cited). This ambivalence is not, however, merely a logical contradiction. Since Geneva's republican regime is superior to monarchies, it deserves to be a model for French readers whereas, for Genevan readers, the issue is the extent to which one can slow down the inevitable decline of all governments toward despotism. Compare *Letter to d'Alembert* (ed. Bloom, pp. 17–18, 58–65, 92–123) and *Lettre à Philopolis* (Pléiade, III, 230–236) with *Social Contract,* III, x.

[8]This chapter is a revised version of the first two paragraphs of *Geneva Manuscript*, I, iii (p. 163). For an explanation of the apparently awkward translation of this famous sentence, see Introduction, pp. 10–11. The next sentence deserves particular attention, since it denounces all forms of personal power and authority. As Rousseau says elsewhere: "Freedom *(la liberté)* does not consist as much in acting according to one's own will as in not being subjected to the will of anyone else; it also consists in not subjecting the will of another to our own. Whoever is master cannot be free, and to rule is to obey." *Lettres Écrites de la Montagne*, VIII (Pléiade, III, 841 and 1434). Cf. Hegel's striking analysis of "Lordship and Bondage" in *Phenomenology of Mind* (ed. Baillie [London: George Allen & Unwin, 1931], pp. 229–240). According to one of Rousseau's fragments, in "the relation of master and slave" both participants are "always in a state of war" (Vaughan, I, 310 or Pléiade, III, 615). On the remainder of this paragraph, see also editorial note 15 to the *Geneva Manuscript*.

[9]This chapter was added when Rousseau reorganized Book I, putting his rejection of alternative definitions of the "social bond" *before* his own principles (whereas in the *Geneva Manuscript* most of this material was in I, v—*after* the presentation of the "general will" in I, iii–v). Since the passage of the *Geneva Manuscript*, I, v, which rejects paternal authority as the source of political power had been used in *Political Economy*, presumably Rousseau decided to write a new discussion. The first sentence appears to reflect a shift from the argument of the *Second Discourse*, which treats "the establishment of the family" as the result of a "first revolution" changing man's isolation in the pure state of nature: see Part 1 (ed. Masters, pp. 134–137), Part 2 (pp. 146–147), and note *l* (pp. 213–220). Compare, however, the *Essay on the Origin of Languages*, chap. ix: "In primitive times the sparse human population had no more social structure than the family, no laws but those of nature, no language but that of gesture and some inarticulate sounds. They were not bound by any idea of common brotherhood and, having no rule but that of force, they believed themselves each other's enemies" (ed. Moran and Gode, pp. 31–32). On the status of the family in the state of nature, see Masters, *Political Philosophy of Rousseau*, pp. 125–136.

[10]In the margin of his copy of the *Social Contract*, Voltaire wrote: "But it has to be agreed that this convention is indicated by nature" (ed. Jouvenel, p. 175). Rousseau follows Locke's argument in the *Second Treatise of Civil Government*, chap. vi, especially paragraphs 55, 61–71 (ed. Laslett [Cambridge, Eng.: University Press, 1963], pp. 322–323, 326–332). See also *Second Discourse*, Part 2 (ed. Masters, pp. 165–166) and *Geneva Manuscript*, I, v (pp. 169–171)—used with revisions in *Political Economy* (pp. 209–211). On the relationship between paternal and political authority, compare Plato, *Statesman*, 258e–259c, 276c–e, 287c–291c; Aristotle, *Politics*, I.i.1252a (ed. Barker [Oxford: Clarendon Press, 1952], p. 1); and Jean Bodin, *Six livres de la République*, I, ii (cited Pléiade, III, 1434).

[11]"It is not true, generally and without restriction, that all power is established in favor of those who are governed. There are powers which, by themselves, are established in favor of the one who governs, such as the power of a master over his slave." Grotius, *Droit de la Guerre et de la Paix*, I, iii, § 8 (trad. Barbeyrac—cited in Pléiade, III, 1435). Compare the dialogue between Thrasymachus and Socrates in Plato's *Republic*, I.338a–354c (ed. Bloom [New York: Basic Books, 1968], pp. 15–34).

[12]In the first edition, the author was indicated only by the initials "M.L.M. d'A." This treatise, which Rousseau cited in 1762 from a manuscript, was subsequently published by Rey in 1764 under the title *Considérations sur le Gouvernement Ancien et Présent de la France;* in the 1782 edition of the *Social Contract*, based on Rousseau's emendations, d'Argenson's name is spelled out. On the possible significance of this work, see Rousseau's fifth note to Book IV, chap. viii and Masters, *Political Philosophy of Rousseau*, pp. 307–309. Note that whereas Grotius supposedly

tries to "establish right by fact," for Rousseau the necessary procedure is to "test facts by right": *Second Discourse*, Part 2 (ed. Masters, p. 166). "Let the reader remember that here it is less a question of history and facts than of right and justice." *État de Guerre* (Pléiade, III, 603).

[13]Rousseau seems to refer to Hobbes's argument that "whatsoever he [the sovereign] doth, it can be no injury to any of his subjects; nor ought he to be by any of them accused of injustice." Thomas Hobbes, *Leviathan*, Part 2, chap. 18 (ed. Oakeshott [Oxford: Blackwell, 1960], p. 115). For the origin of the comparison between a leader and a shepherd, see Thrasymachus' speech in Plato's *Republic*, I, 343a–344c (ed. Bloom, pp. 21–22).

[14]For the source of Rousseau's reference to Philo (*De Legatione ad Caium*), see Pléiade, III, 1435. Aristotle, in *Politics*, I.ii.1252a, argues that "the element which is able, by virtue of its intelligence, to exercise forethought, is naturally a ruling and master element; the element which is able, by virtue of its bodily power, to do what the other element plans, is a ruled element, which is naturally in a state of slavery." (ed. Barker, p. 3). Note, however, that Aristotle—unlike Thrasymachus or Grotius—immediately adds: "and master and slave have accordingly a common interest" (Ibid.) See also *Politics* I.v–vi.1254a–1255b (ed. Barker, pp. 11–17).

[15]This short dialogue in Plutarch's *Moralia* is worth reading: in reply to Ulysses' request that the Greeks turned into animals be released in human form, Circe asks him to persuade one of them, named Gryllus, that this would be desirable. Gryllus then explains why "man is the most miserable and most calamitous animal in the world" whereas "the soul of animals is better disposed and more perfected for producing virtue, since without being forced, or commanded, or taught, . . . it produces and nourishes the virtue which, according to nature, suits each one." Hence, instead of proving that slavery is unnatural—as the text leads one to expect—Plutarch's dialogue suggests that human *civilization* is unnatural and corrupt; indirectly, the citation thus echoes the central theme of the *Second Discourse* (see ed. Masters, editorial note 26). Rousseau probably consulted the French translation by Jacques Amyot: *Oeuvres Morales et Meslées de Plutarque* (Geneva: Jacob Stoer, 1627), pp. 273–276.

[16]Rousseau thus rejects with irony Filmer's argument for "the natural power of kings"; compare Locke, *First Treatise of Government*, especially chap. xi, paragraph 111 (ed. Laslett, pp. 239–240).

[17]Like the preceding chapter, this one was newly written for the final version. Rousseau's insistence that "might does not make right" deserves more emphasis than it is usually given, since it means that "legitimate authority" must be freely accepted "in *conscience*" even by those who are being punished for violating the rules. See editorial note 37. The second sentence contains an untranslatable play on words: when Rousseau speaks of the "right of the strongest" as a right that is "*réellement établi en principe*" he could mean either that this right is "in principle really established" in the works of political theorists like Grotius or Hobbes, or that this right was "really established *in the beginning*" (i.e., that human history was originally based only on the right of the strongest). Compare *Geneva Manuscript*, I, ii; *Essay on the Origin of Language*, chap. ix (ed. Moran and Gode, pp. 33–37); *Second Discourse*, Part 1 (ed. Masters, p. 139), Part 2 (p. 177), and Note *o* (p. 222).

[18]Compare St. Paul's *Letter to the Romans*, xiii.1–2: "You must all obey the governing authorities. Since all government comes from God, the civil authorities are appointed by God, and so anyone who resists authority is rebelling against God's decision, and such an act is bound to be punished." *Jerusalem Bible* (Garden City, N.Y.: Doubleday, 1971), p. 209.

[19]With the exception of the sixth paragraph (largely from *Geneva Manuscript*, I, v),

this chapter was also written anew for the final version. See the fifth fragment at the end of the *Geneva Manuscript,* used in the eleventh paragraph. The argument of the chapter as a whole, however, echoes the fragment originally titled "That the State of War is born from the Social State"—usually called *État de Guerre* (Pléiade, III, 601–612). This fragment is of interest because it is an attack on the "horrible system of Hobbes" (Pléiade, III, 610), whereas the final version of the *Social Contract* criticizes "Grotius and others." Although the shift may be related to Rousseau's qualified praise of Hobbes in Book IV, chap. viii, the central thrust remains hostile to the Hobbesian version of the social compact.

[20]Rousseau paraphrases Grotius, *Droit de la Guerre et de la Paix,* I, iii. § 8 (trans. Barbeyrac), cited in Pléiade, III, 1438.

[21]Homer, *Odyssey,* IX. 216–436. Compare *État de Guerre,* where Rousseau first uses this example: "I open the books on right and morality, I listen to the scholars and jurists and, touched by their insinuating discourses, I admire the peace and justice established by the civil order, I bless the wisdom of public institutions, and I console myself for being a man by seeing myself as a citizen. Well taught concerning my duties and my happiness, I close the book, leave the classroom, and look around me. I see unfortunate peoples groaning under an iron yoke, the human race crushed by a handful of oppressors, a starving crowd worn out by difficulty and hunger whose blood and tears the rich drink in peace, and everywhere the strong armed against the weak with the fearsome power of the laws. All that is done peacefully and without resistance; it is the tranquillity of Ulysses' companions trapped in the Cyclop's cave, waiting to be devoured." (Pléiade, III, 608–609). Rousseau emphatically denies Hobbes's argument that it is rational to abandon one's natural freedom to enter any society as long as it is peaceful and quiet. Compare *Leviathan,* Part 2, chap. 18 (ed. Oakeshott, p. 120) and Locke, *Second Treatise,* chap. xix, paragraph 228 (ed. Laslett, pp. 434–435).

[22]Compare *Second Discourse,* Part 2 (ed. Masters, pp. 165–168). The remainder of this paragraph is taken from *Geneva Manuscript,* I, v, paragraph ten.

[23]For the relevant passages, see Grotius, *Droit de la Guerre et de la Paix,* II, v, § 27, and Pufendorf, *Droit de la nature et des gens* VI, iii, § 5 (cited in Pléiade, III, 1438–1439). See also Hobbes's notion of a "commonwealth by acquisition," *Leviathan,* Part 2, chap. 20 (ed. Oakeshott, especially pp. 132–133).

[24]For the original draft of this paragraph, see *État de Guerre* (Pléiade, III, 602–603). The technical point, as this fragment had stressed, is that a state of war in any juridical or "rational" sense can only exist between "the moral beings" known as States, and not between individuals (as in Hobbes's state of nature). As Rousseau puts it in *Geneva Manuscript,* I, v, the "state of war" presupposes a "free and voluntary convention."

[25]This note was added by Rousseau and first published in the edition of 1782.

[26]For the rest of this paragraph up to the last sentence, see the fifth fragment at the end of the *Geneva Manuscript.* Rousseau's argument rests on what he called "fundamental distinctions" in *État de Guerre:* "If things are only considered according to the strict interpretation of the social pact, the land, money, men, and all that is comprised within the boundaries of the state belong to it without reserve. But since the rights of society, founded on those of nature, cannot annihilate them, all these objects should be considered in a double relationship: namely the soil as public territory and as individuals' patrimony, goods as belonging in one sense to the sovereign and in another to the property owners, the inhabitants as citizens and as men. At bottom, since the body politic is only a moral person, it is only a being of reason. Remove the public convention, at that instant the State is destroyed without the slightest alteration in everything that composes it; and all the conventions of men could never change anything in the

nature of things" (Pléiade, III, 608). Compare Montesquieu, *Esprit des Lois*, X, iii and XV, ii.

[27]Again, this chapter was newly written for the final version; however, compare *Geneva Manuscript*, I, v.

[28]In addition to Grotius (see editorial note 20 above), this passage criticizes Hobbes, who admits that each individual has "tacitly covenanted" to accept a majority vote *before* the assembly "hath by consenting voices declared a sovereign": *Leviathan*, Part 2, chap. 18 (ed. Oakeshott, p. 115). Rousseau insists that the "true basis of society" is Hobbes's "tacit covenant," whereas Hobbes had treated the subsequent election of the sovereign or ruler as the social contract. In other words, Rousseau's definition of the social contract can be treated as the logic which leads any assembly to accept the principle of majority rule.

[29]This chapter is revised from paragraphs two to four of *Geneva Manuscript*, I, iii, which became the first two and last two paragraphs of the final version. Note that from the outset, Rousseau treats the problem of social obligations in the terms of Newtonian mechanics ("forces," "resistance," "obstacles," etc.). Compare the image of the "general will" as a "frictionless surface" in *Geneva Manuscript*, I, iv, and Introduction, p. 20, as well as the repeated references to "springs," "levers," and other mechanistic analogies in the final text.

[30]This paragraph, added in the final version, implies that Rousseau's definition of the social contract is analogous to the law of gravity. "Everywhere the same" even if "never" stated, like Newton's law, Rousseau's principle is also self-enforcing: if "the social contract is violated," it follows immediately that "each man recovers his original rights and resumes his natural freedom." Compare the passage of *État de Guerre* cited in editorial note 26: since the social contract establishes a psychological or rational commitment to live as a community, the sovereign is only a "moral" body and can be destroyed without touching the physical or natural existence of the men and objects comprising it. See also the "important proposition" in the first paragraph of *Geneva Manuscript*, I, iv., and *Social Contract*, editorial notes 35 and 36.

[31]These additions to the first draft emphasize the importance of avoiding any form of *personal* dependence. As Rousseau says in *Émile*, II: "There are two kinds of dependence. That on things is from nature; that on men is from society. Since dependence on things has no morality, it neither hinders freedom nor engenders vice. Since the dependence on men is disordered, it engenders them all, and this is how the master and slave mutually deprave each other. If there is some way to remedy this evil within society, it is to substitute law for men, and to arm the general wills with a real force greater than the activity of any private will. If the laws of nations could have an inflexibility like those of nature, so that no human force could ever overcome them, the dependence on men would then become like that on things, one would unite in the Republic all the advantages of the natural state with those of the civil state, one would combine freedom, which keeps man free from vices, with morality, which raises him to virtue" (Pléiade, IV, 311). That this passage relates to the *Social Contract* is proven by a note appended at the word "disordered": "In my *Principles of Political Right*, it is demonstrated that no private will can be well–ordered in the social system" (Ibid.) For a particularly insightful study of the attitudes which led Rousseau to detest dependence on other individuals, see Judith N. Shklar, "Rousseau's Images of Authority" in *Hobbes and Rousseau*, ed. Maurice Cranston and Ricard S. Peters (Garden City, N.Y.: Anchor Books, 1972), pp. 333–365.

[32]Rousseau refers to the early editions of Bodin's *Les six livres de la République*, I, vi, and to d'Alembert's *Geneva* in Volume VII of the *Encyclopédie* (both cited in Pléiade, III, 1446, 1448). Note that Rousseau's terminology takes the ancient *polis* ("city-

state") as the norm. The resulting rehabilitation of the word "citizen" was to have profound effects during the French Revolution. Compare *Émile*, IV: "As if there were citizens who were not members of the City, and as such did not have a part in the sovereign authority. But the French, having judged it appropriate to usurp this respectable name of Citizens, formerly due to members of the cities of the Gauls, have denatured the idea to the point where one cannot understand anything" (Pléiade, IV, 667, note). Although the word "bourgeois" has taken on a Marxist class connotation not intended by Rousseau, it will be used to translate the French "*bourgeois*."

[33]This chapter is taken over, with some additions and deletions, from *Geneva Manuscript*, I, iii, paragraphs five to seven.

[34]This paragraph, an addition to the first draft, could be read as an assertion of the territorial and social inviolability of the modern nation-state. Compare Alfred Cobban, *Rousseau and the Modern State* (London: George Allen & Unwin, 1934).

[35]These two sentences, added to the first draft, emphasize the extent to which the "body politic" is a "moral person" or "being of reason." See Introduction, pp. 18–20 and *Social Contract*, editorial note 26.

[36]Note that since the State *is* a "moral person" and thus, in a sense, "an imaginary being," Rousseau's principles of political right could increase injustice if they are taught to selfish or corrupted men. "The democratic constitution is certainly the masterpiece of political art: but the more admirable its artifice, the less it belongs to all eyes to penetrate it." *Lettres Écrites de la Montagne*, VIII (Pléiade, III, 838). Compare *First Discourse*, Part 2 (ed. Masters, pp. 49–50).

[37]The last phrase seems a puzzling contradiction in terms, and has led some to call Rousseau a "totalitarian": for example, J. L. Talmon, *The Origins of Totalitarian Democracy* (New York: Praeger, 1960), pp. 38–49; Lester G. Crocker, "Rousseau et la voi du totalitarisme," *Rousseau et la Philosophie Politique* (Paris: Presses Universitaires, 1965), pp. 99–136. In context, however, the sentence concerns the means by which each individual can have an obligation, in *conscience*, to obey the laws he has previously enacted. Rousseau applied precisely this reasoning in defending his works against the charges brought by the Magistrates of Geneva: "an accuser must convince the accused before the judge. To be treated as a wrongdoer, it is necessary that I be convinced of being one." *Lettres Écrites de la Montagne*, I (Pléiade, III, 693). For a brilliant psychological analysis of the phrase "forced to be free," see John Plamenatz, "Ce qui ne signifie autre chose sinon qu'on le forcera d'être libre," in *Hobbes and Rousseau*, ed. Cranston and Peters, pp. 318–332. That the passage concerns the conscience of the individual was made clear by the deleted sentence concerning "the oath" and each man's "inner maxims," which comes after the words "vain formula" in *Geneva Manuscript*, I, iii. See also the third paragraph of *Geneva Manuscript*, I, vii, which reappears in *Political Economy* (p. 214). On Rousseau's definition of freedom, see *Social Contract*, editorial note 8.

[38]The first two paragraphs of this chapter come from *Geneva Manuscript*, I, iii, paragraphs eight and nine. Although Rousseau praises civil society, his pessimistic view of history leads to a strong qualification: "if the abuses of this new condition did not often degrade him beneath the condition from which he emerged." Compare *Second Discourse*, especially note *i* (ed. Masters, pp. 192–203); *Émile*, II (cited in *Social Contract*, editorial note 31), and Introduction, above pp. 7–12. The last paragraph of this chapter, an addition to the first draft, clearly refers to *Émile* as the work in which Rousseau "said too much" about the "philosophic meaning of the word *freedom*."

[39]This chapter is a revised version of the last five paragraphs of *Geneva Manuscript*, I, iii; the second paragraph is added; and the third and fourth come from *Geneva Manuscript*, I, v (paragraphs nine and eight respectively). On the relation of the "right

of the strongest," "the right of the first occupant," and the "right of property," see also *Second Discourse*, Part 2 (ed. Masters, pp. 154–160). Rousseau's principles are quite consciously critical of European colonial policies, as was particularly clear in the first draft; see Rousseau's note to *Geneva MS*, I, v (paragraph eight).

⁴⁰Compare *Emile*, IV: "The universal spirit of the Laws of all countries is always to favor the strong against the weak, and the one who has against the one who has nothing. This inconvenience is inevitable, and it is without exception" (Pléiade, IV, 524, note). On the difference in tone between *Émile* and *Social Contract*, see Introduction, p. 12.

⁴¹The original draft of this chapter—*Geneva Manuscript*, I, iv—was heavily revised when Rousseau reworked it. This sentence shows clearly, however, that the concept of the "general will" was from the first a voluntaristic equivalent of the traditional concept of the "common good." Compare *Geneva Manuscript*, editorial note 22.

⁴²This chapter and the next were added when Rousseau revised the *Geneva Manuscript*. Many commentators have assumed that Rousseau criticizes Montesquieu when arguing that sovereignty is "indivisible," but Derathé suggests that the chapter is a refutation of Hobbes, Pufendorf, Burlamaqui, and other theorists of "political right" (Pléiade, III, 1453). The last sentence of this chapter is a variant of *État de Guerre* (Pléiade, III, 609).

⁴³See *Social Contract*, II, vi. It follows, for Rousseau, that concerns of foreign affairs or "national security" cannot justify violation of the laws. Compare Locke, *Second Treatise*, chap. xii, para. 145–148 and chap. xiv, especially para. 160 (ed. Laslett, pp. 383–384, 393).

⁴⁴Marquis d'Argenson, *Considérations sur le Gouvernement Ancien et Présent de la France*, chap. ii, pp. 26–27 (see editorial note 12). In Rey's edition, d'Argenson's text reads "by *a reason opposed* to the interest" (*par une raison opposée*) whereas Rousseau's citation says "in opposition to the interest" (*par opposition*): Masters, *Political Philosophy of Rousseau*, p. 308, n. 28. The sentence to which this note is appended presumes that in any society, private interests necessarily conflict: "in the social state, the good of one man necessarily produces the ill of another. This relation is in the nature of the thing, and nothing could possibly change it." *Émile*, II (Pléiade, IV, 340, note). In terms of contemporary game theory, Rousseau asserts that private interests represent a "zero-sum" game. Since the "will of all" appears as a synonym for the "general will" in *Geneva Manuscript*, I, vii (p.178)—a passage which reappears in *Political Economy* (p. 214)—Rousseau's distinction between these terms may date from his final revision of the manuscript (compare Masters, *Political Philosophy of Rousseau*, pp. 325–327; *Geneva Manuscript*, I, iv [p. 168]; and *Political Economy*, pp. 213, 216, 217).

⁴⁵"True it is, that some divisions injure republics, while others are beneficial to them. When accompanied by factions and parties they are injurious; but when maintained without them they contribute to their prosperity. The legislator of a republic, since it is impossible to prevent existence of dissensions, must at least take care to prevent the growth of faction." Machiavelli, *History of Florence*, VII, i (New York: Harper Torchbooks, 1960), p. 310. For Rousseau's generally favorable attitude toward Machiavelli, see *Social Contract*, III, vi, especially the first note. Rousseau's citation reinforces the interpretation of the "general will" as an ideal which cannot be perfectly realized in practice; as Machiavelli says in the sentence preceding the quotation: "those who think a republic may be kept in perfect unity of purpose are greatly deceived." It must be added that Machiavelli's text apparently makes a subtle distinction between "*sette*" (perhaps best translated as "sects") and "*partigiani*" ("parties"): whereas "sects" are always harmful, "parties" are harmful if accompanied by "sects," but apparently need not themselves be forbidden by the "legislator of a republic." Com-

pare Machiavelli's *Discourses on Titus Livy*, I, 4 (ed. Crick [Baltimore: Penguin, 1970], pp. 113–115)—according to which the Roman Republic was based on the rivalry between plebs and patricians—with the next editorial note.

[46]This criticism of "partial societies" has often been cited as an indication of Rousseau's hostility to pluralist democracy and political practice; some even speak of "totalitarianism" in this regard (ed. Watkins, p. xxx; Vaughan, I, 60). But in reading this passage, one must take into account Rousseau's definition of a "partial society" as a group with a "corporate will": see the group theory of politics spelled out in *Political Economy*, pp. 212–213 and discussed in the Introduction, pp. 21–23. The right to vote in secret, without others watching how the ballot is marked, is based on reasoning like that of Rousseau; expecting "partial societies" in every community, Rousseau's principles are particularly opposed to a single-party system—and oriented to a multiplicity of groups and/or parties, none of which can claim to rule in its own name. Note that while Sparta was "unique and sublime," it was Rome—whose laws were formed by Numa and revised by Servius—which Rousseau calls "the best government that ever existed." *Lettres Écrites de la Montagne*, VII (Pléiade, III, 809). Indeed, in a fragment comparing Sparta and Rome. Rousseau remarks that the founders of both republics established "many electoral divisions *(Colleges)* and private societies in order to create and excite among the citizens those sweet habits and that innocent and disinterested commerce which forms and nourishes patriotism." *Parallèle entre Sparte et Rome*, Frag. 2 (Pléiade, III, 542).

[47]For the first draft, see *Geneva Manuscript*, I, vi, entitled "On the Respective Rights of the Sovereign and the Citizen." Since this chapter was carried over to the final version with relatively few changes, it would seem to reflect an important statement of Rousseau's principles. For that very reason, the modifications of the text are of exceptional importance.

[48]"I have thought a hundred times when writing that it is impossible in a long work to give the same meanings always to the same words. There is no language rich enough to give as many terms, nuances and phrases as our ideas can have changes. . . . In spite of that, I am persuaded that one can be clear, even in the poverty of our language; not in always giving the same meaning to the same words, but in so doing that each time that every word is used, the meaning one gives it be sufficiently determined by the ideas related to it. . . . " *Émile*, II (Pléiade, IV, 345 note). Compare *First and Second Discourses* (ed. Masters, pp. 25–26).

[49]The last clause was added to the final version. While it appears to be "collectivist" in tone, Rousseau was concerned by the danger of an individual who sought the protection and benefits of civil society without paying his share of the costs. As he put it in *Geneva Manuscript*, I, ii: "private interest and the general good . . . are mutually exclusive in the natural order of things, and social laws are a yoke that each wants to impose on the other without having to bear himself." In the first draft, Rousseau wrote that the "life and *existence*" of citizens as "private persons" are "naturally independent" of the "public person" (p. 175); in the final version, he changed the phrase to read "life and *freedom*" of "private persons," thus emphasizing "the natural rights to which they are entitled as men." Rousseau constantly tries to *balance* the claims of the individual and of society. Compare Rousseau's "fundamental distinctions," cited in *Social Contract*, editorial note 26.

[50]This chapter was added in the final version. Although it could be viewed as a gloss on the famous phrase discussed in editorial note 37, Rousseau also presents a criticism of Hobbesian principles. According to *Leviathan*, Part 1, chap. 14: "a man cannot lay down the right of resisting them, that assault him by force, to take away his life. . . . The same may be said of wounds, and chains, and imprisonment" (ed. Oakeshott, pp. 86–87). As a result, for Hobbes the right of self-preservation is inalienable. "If the

sovereign command a man, though justly condemned, . . . not to resist those who assault him . . . yet hath that man liberty to disobey." Ibid., Part 2, chap. 21 (p. 142).

Moreover, Hobbes's principle gives rise to a possible claim against military service: "Upon this ground, a man that is commanded as a soldier to fight against the enemy, though his sovereign have right enough to punish his refusal with death, may nevertheless in many cases refuse, without injustice" (Ibid.) Since Rousseau seeks to found a rational theory of obedience, he rejects Hobbes's view that an individual could judge of whether or not he has the "liberty to disobey" after having been "justly condemned," or whether he can "refuse, without injustice" to "fight against the enemy." Compare Ibid., Part 2, chap. 29 (p. 211).

51The first paragraph of this chapter is taken from *Geneva Manuscript*, II, i; paragraphs two to eight from *Geneva Manuscript*, II, iv (paragraphs one to three and seven to eleven); and the last paragraph from *Geneva Manuscript*, I, vii (paragraph four). The next to last paragraph, containing the radical equation of "every legitimate government" with a "republic," is the only entirely new text in the chapter. Although this reorganization removes redundancies in the first draft, note the treatment of natural law which was thereby deleted: *Geneva Manuscript*, II, iv (paragraphs twelve to seventeen) and editorial notes 34 and 36 thereto.

52The first draft of this sentence reads: "emanating from reason along *and founded on the simple right of humanity*" (*Geneva Manuscript*, II, iv; p. 189). The italicized words, deleted in the final version, make it clear that Rousseau is speaking about the kind of natural law or "law of reason" which he rejected in *Geneva Manuscript*, I, ii. Although politically impotent, Rousseau never denied the existence of such rational "laws of justice"; far from being ironic, the phrase "all justice comes from God" was meant very seriously. See *Émile*, IV: "Let all other men work for my good at the expense of their own, let everything relate to me alone, let the entire human race die in tribulation and misery, if need be, to spare me a moment of pain or hunger; such is the interior language of every rational nonbeliever. Yes, I will insist all my life: anyone who says in his heart there is no God and speaks otherwise is only a liar or a fool" (Pléiade, IV, 636–637).

53For the first draft of this chapter, see *Geneva Manuscript*, II, ii, paragraphs one to five, seven, and twelve to fifteen. On the role of the legislator in Rousseau's political thought, see Masters, *Political Philosophy of Rousseau*, pp. 354–368.

54The quotation is from Montesquieu's *Considerations on the Causes of the Greatness of the Romans and their Decline*, chap. 1 (ed. Lowenthal [Ithaca, N.Y.: Cornell University Press, 1965], p. 25). For the reference to Caligula, see the passage of Philo mentioned in editorial note 14. On Plato, see *Statesman*, 261d: "the statesman . . . is much more like the man in charge of a whole herd of cows or of a stud of horses" (trans. J. B. Skemp, in *Collected Dialogues*, ed. Hamilton and Cairns [New York: Bollingen, 1961], p. 1025). Compare ibid, 275c (pp. 1040–1041) and *Republic*, I.343a–344c.

55Voltaire wrote in his copy: "Weak praise of a vile sectarian and absurd preacher whom you detest in your heart" (ed. de Jouvenel, p. 229). In effect, Rousseau later wrote: "Calvin was doubtless a great man; but after all he was a man, and what is worse a theologian: he had all the pride of the genius who is aware of his superiority, and who is indignant when anyone disagrees with him. Most of his colleagues were in the same category." *Lettres Écrites de la Montagne*, II (Pléiade, III, 715). In other words, Rousseau treats Calvin as a "great man" and "genius" for his role as a legislator in Geneva rather than as founder of Calvinism; compare editorial note 58.

56Of the Decemvirs, Montesquieu says: "Ten men in the [Roman] Republic had alone all the legislative power, all the executive power, all the power of judging. Rome found itself subjected to a tyranny as cruel as that of Tarquin." *Esprit des Lois,* XI, xv (in *Oeuvres Complètes,* ed. Caillois [Paris: Editions de la Pléiade, 1966], II, 417–418). Compare Machiavelli, *Discourses on Titus Livy,* I, 40 (ed. Crick, pp. 210–216).

[57]"Nor in fact was there ever a legislator who, in introducing extraordinary laws to a people, did not have recourse to God, for otherwise they would not be accepted, since many benefits of which a prudent man is aware, are not so evident to reason that he can convince others of them." Ibid., I, 11 (ed. Crick, p. 141).

[58]This sentence is apparently an indirect criticism of Voltaire, whose play *Mohamet* explicitly treats the "son of Ishmael" as an "impostor" from the beginning (Act I, Scenes 1, 2, 4) to the end (Act V, Scene iv). Compare Masters, *Political Philosophy of Rousseau,* p. 8, n. 23. Rousseau's view of Moses and Mohammed as *legislators* rather than founders of religions follows Machiavelli, *The Prince,* chap. vi. In a fragment, Rousseau imagines Moses joining other famous legislators in the afterlife and saying: "I lived alone on earth, among a numerous people I was alone. Lycurgus, Solon, Numa are my brothers. I have come to rejoin my family. I have come to enjoy finally the sweetness of conversing with my fellows, to speak and be understood." (Pléiade, III, 500).

[59]Rousseau refers to William Warburton, Bishop of Gloucester (1698–1779), and author of *The Alliance between Church and State* (1736) and *Divine Legation of Moses* (1737–1741).

[60]For the first draft of this chapter, see *Geneva Manuscript,* II, iii, paragraphs two to five. In the definitive text, the next to last paragraph is rewritten and the last paragraph new material. As Robert Derathé has noted, the addition of a criticism of Peter the Great is an indirect rejection of Voltaire's highly favorable judgment (Pléiade, III, 1466–1469).

[61]Cf. Aristotle, *Politics,* VII.iv.1325b–1326b. *Geneva Manuscript,* II, iii, paragraphs seven to eleven, has the original version of this chapter. Note that what was the next sentence of the first draft was deleted. One explanation may be that the last paragraph of the chapter seems to refer to Republican Rome, which Montesquieu described as "in an endless and constantly violent war . . . by the very principle of its government." *Considerations on the Greatness of the Romans,* chap. 1 (ed. Lowenthal, p. 27). Given Rousseau's praise of Rome, he may have decided that one could indeed imagine something "more foolish than the maxims of those conquering nations" for whom "the necessity of conquests was part of their constitution" (*Geneva Manuscript,* II, iii, pp. 184, 186).

[62]For the first draft of this chapter, see *Geneva Manuscript,* II, iii, paragraphs fourteen to sixteen and twenty–one. Rousseau's emphasis on the effects of geography, climate, and a host of other factors often ignored by political scientists, contrasts with the image of his political theory as abstract and unrealistic. The last paragraph, added for the final version, led an influential Corsican to ask Rousseau's opinion on a constitution for the island (which had rebelled against Genoa in 1752—but was eventually taken over by France in 1768). See *Constitutional Project for Corsica* (ed. Watkins, pp. 277–330) and Sven Stelling-Michaud's Introduction (Pléiade, III, cxcix–ccxv).

[63]For the first draft, see *Geneva Manuscript,* II, vi. The only notable change is the addition of the footnote, citing d'Argenson's *Considerations* (compare *Social Contract,* editorial note 12 and Vaughan, II, 62).

[64]In the first edition, Rousseau referred to the author only by initials as "M. d'A." (see editorial notes 12, 44, and 139); the name was added throughout in the posthumous edition of 1782. Here, the published text of d'Argenson's work reads: "A branch of commerce, acquired at great expense, only secures a deceptive utility for the kingdom

in general, and enriches only some towns or private individuals that are already living in abundance" (cited by Vaughan, II, 62).

[65]Montesquieu had written: "Although all States have in general the same object, which is to survive, each State nonetheless has one that is particular to itself. Expansion was the object of Rome, war that of Sparta; religion that of the Jewish laws; commerce that of Marseille; public tranquillity that of the laws of China; navigation that of the laws of Rhodes; natural liberty the object of the regulations among savages; in general the delights of the prince that of monarchies; the independence of each private individual is the object of the laws of Poland, and what results from that is the oppression of all." *Esprit des Lois*, XI, v (ed. Caillois p. 396). While a number of previous editors (including Derathé and Grimsley) have noted this parallel, the *differences* between Rousseau and Montesquieu are worth considering—especially with respect to Rome. Compare *Social Contract*, editorial note 61. Note also that Montesquieu goes on, in the immediate sequel, to speak of England as the "one nation in the world that has, as the direct object of its constitution, political liberty." Rousseau's answer is found in Book III, chap. xv.

[66]Rousseau's insistence that nature is "invincible" contrasts sharply with Bacon's notion of a scientific "conquest" of nature. Compare Roger D. Masters, "Human Nature, Nature, and Political Thought," in *Nomos XVII: Human Nature and Politics*, ed. Roland Pennock and John Chapman (New York: Lieber-Atherton, 1976), chap. 3. To be sure, Bacon insists that "Nature to be commanded must be obeyed." *New Organon*, Book I, Aphorism iii, in Francis Bacon, *A Selection of His Works*, ed. Sidney Warhaft [New York: Odyssey, 1965], p. 331). But Bacon's explicit aim is to "extend more widely the limits of the power and greatness of man" (Ibid., Aphorism cxvi [p. 368]). Since his definition of "the work and aim of human power" is "on a given body to generate and superinduce a new nature or new natures" (Ibid., Book II, Aphorism i [p. 376]) it follows that Baconian science is conceived as a means to overcome precisely those natural features which Rousseau here describes as "invincible." Whereas Bacon praises "famous discoveries" or "inventions" as holding "by far the first place among human actions" (Ibid., Book I, Aphorism cxxix [p. 372]), Rousseau is essentially hostile to technological innovation. Hence, one of Rousseau's fragments counsels: "in everything that depends on human industry, one should forbid with care any machine and any invention that can shorten labor, spare manpower, and produce the same effect with less difficulty" (Vaughan, I, 320). In a fundamental sense, Rousseau was the first great critic of industrial society.

[67]This chapter uses *Geneva Manuscript*, II, v, paragraphs one, two, five, six, and seven. In the next sentence, Rousseau refers to Book III, chap. i. As Derathé points out (Pléiade, III, 1471), Rousseau goes on to modify Montesquieu's distinction between "*droit politique*" and "*droit civil*" in *Esprit des Lois*, I, iii. On the importance of "mores"—the French term is *moeurs*, which means the customs, morals, and way of life of a people—which Rousseau emphasizes in the last paragraph of the chapter, see also Book IV, chap. vii (especially editorial note 125), and *Letter to d'Alembert*.

[68]Since the *Geneva Manuscript* breaks off in the middle of the third paragraph of this chapter, for all practical purposes there is no preliminary version of the remainder of the text—except for one paragraph in Book III, chap. vi and the chapter on "Civil Religion" (IV, viii). The importance Rousseau attached to Book III, chap. i, is underlined not only by his warning that the reader be "attentive," but also by the fact that its main point—the distinction between the government and the sovereign—is emphasized so strongly in *Political Economy* (p. 211) and *Lettres Écrites de la Montagne*, V, VI, and VIII (Pléiade, III, 770–771, 808–809, 837–838). In the "extract of the treatise *On the Social Contract*," which Rousseau includes in *Émile*, V, he cites six paragraphs from this chapter (Pléiade, IV, 843–845) as well as six paragraphs each from III, ii, and III,

iii. One could say that the beginning of Book III is the center of Rousseau's political teaching in more ways than one.

[69]The distinction between "physical" *force* (or power) and "moral" *will* (or free choice) is fundamental to the thought of Rousseau. Unlike Hobbes, who treats thought and sensation as the consequence of matter in motion (*Leviathan*, Part 1, chap. 1–3), Rousseau denied that "sensation" and "will" could be explained solely in materialist terms. See *Second Discourse*, part 1 (ed. Masters, pp. 113–114), *Émile*, IV—notes to the "Profession of Faith" (Pléiade, IV, 574, 575, 584–585), and Masters, *Political Philosophy of Rousseau,* pp. 66–74.

[70]Despite the example of Venice, the use of the term "prince" to designate a collective body was highly unusual, and can be taken as another example of Rousseau's radically antimonarchical principles.

[71]A continuous proportion is a geometric progression such that:

$$\frac{A}{B} = \frac{B}{C} = \frac{C}{D} \cdots$$

Hence Rousseau's formulation could be restated algebraically as follows:

$$\frac{\text{Sovereign}}{\text{Government}} = \frac{\text{Government}}{\text{Subjects}} \text{ or}$$

$$(\text{Sovereign})(\text{Subjects}) = (\text{Government})^2$$

On this mathematical formulation and its implications, see Masters, *Political Philosophy of Rousseau,* pp. 340–348, and Marcel Françon, "Le Langage Mathématique de Jean-Jacques Rousseau," *Cahiers pour l'Analyse,* No. 8 (1967), pp. 85–88.

[72]Rousseau says that "the subject always remains one" because the laws, if legitimate, must apply equally—and with full force—on each citizen as subject (compare II, vi). It follows, however, that both the ratio of the sovereign to the State and the ratio of the government to the State must be whole numbers (i.e., the denominator is always one). This detail is crucial if one is to understand Rousseau's reference to "the series . . . of whole numbers" later in this chapter.

[73]Rousseau uses the French word *rapport*, which can mean either a mathematical "ratio" or a "relationship," twice in this sentence. Since Rousseau's play on the ambiguilty of the term is untranslatable, "ratio" is used for "*rapport* in the geometrical sense" and "relationship" for "*rapport* in the ordinary sense."

[74]Rousseau's eighteenth-century mathematical terms should not obscure the basic idea. Starting from the last equation given in editorial note 71, and substituting the value of "subjects" as equal to 1 (editorial note 72), Rousseau indicates that:

$$(\text{Sovereign}) = (\text{Government})^2$$

Calling the expression "(Government)²" a "doubled ratio," Rousseau concludes that the force of the government should vary according to the size of the sovereign. Compare the next paragraph.

[75]At first, this phrase cannot fail to be puzzling. Rousseau seems to say that the government is a "moral person" that "can be broken down into other similar relationships" that constitute "a new proportion" that is "within" the continuous proportion discussed to this point. But if the "supreme magistrate" is an "indivisible middle term" or "unity" ($\frac{1}{1}$), separating "the series of fractions and that of whole numbers," then the ratio of sovereign to government is a "fraction," and the ratio of the government to the State is a "whole number." The latter is clear enough (see editorial note 72). But since a fraction *cannot* equal a whole number, it follows that the continuous

proportion can *never* be perfectly realized in practice. Although the government "should" be subordinate to the sovereign, the "quantity of action" of the people as sovereign is apparently always less than the "quantity of action" of the government. See Introduction, pp. 18–20.

[76]When Rousseau says that "the body politic would be dissolved," he does not mean that the society would automatically fall into anarchy—but merely that subjects no longer have a moral *obligation* or *duty* to obey. Compare I, iii and III, x, first note.

[77]Rousseau here applies, to the "government" as a "corporate" body, the logic that he applies to *all* "partial societies" in *Political Economy*, pp. 212–213. Compare editorial notes 46 and 83.

[78]As Bertrand de Jouvenel has pointed out, when Rousseau says "the government *should* [*doit*] shrink," he uses the word *doit* (should, must, or ought to) in a "scientific" rather than an "ethical" way: "Rousseau is not saying 'It is good that . . . ' but 'It will come about that . . . ' " "Rousseau's Theory of the Forms of Government," in *Hobbes and Rousseau,* ed. Cranston and Peters (pp. 494–495). De Jouvenel's interpretation, in this article and in the introduction to his edition of the *Social Contract,* is extremely illuminating.

[79]Rousseau's use of the tripartite classification of monarchy, aristocracy, and democracy is in keeping with a long tradition in political theory. Aristotle had distinguished forms of government on the basis of two criteria: the number of rulers (one, few, many) and objective of rule (common good versus good of rulers). This produced the famous classification of six types of regime—three good or just (kingship, aristocracy, and 'polity') and three unjust or evil (democracy, oligarchy, tyranny). See Aristotle, *Politics,* III.vi. 1278b–viii. 1280a (ed. Barker, pp. 110–116), and compare Plato, *Statesman,* 300–303b and St. Thomas Aquinas, *On Kingship,* I.xi–xii (*The Political Ideas of St. Thomas Aquinas,* ed. Bigogniari [New York: Hafner, 1957], p. 178). Cicero, however, asserted that what Aristotle had called "bad" regimes are "really no commonwealth at all." *De Re Publica,* III.xxxi.43 (ed. Keyes [London: Loeb Classical Library, 1959], p. 219). Since, for Cicero, *res publica res populi* ("a commonwealth is the property of the people"), there are only three forms of government, each of which is "an assemblage of people in large numbers associated in agreement with respect to justice and a partnership for the common good." Ibid., I.xxv.39 (pp. 64–65). Rousseau basically agrees with Cicero, explicitly rejecting Aristotle's usage—see III, x, note. Compare Machiavelli, *Prince,* chap. 1 (ed. Musa [New York: St. Martin's, 1964], p. 5) and *Discourses,* I, 2 (ed. Crick, pp. 106–111); Hobbes, *Leviathan,* Part 2, chap. 19 (ed. Oakeshott, pp. 121–122) and *De Cive,* ch. vii, paragraphs 1–4 (ed. Gert [Garden City, N.Y.: Doubleday, 1972], pp. 190–194); Locke, *Second Treatise,* chap. x, paragraph 132 (ed. Laslett, p. 372). It follows that Rousseau's usage of the term "democracy" differs from contemporary practice. In a note to his edition of the *Social Contract* (p. 144), Vaughan observes "that a sense unusual in modern times . . . but familiar to the ancients (for example, Plato and Aristotle), is here given to *Democracy;* and that Rousseau's *Aristocracy,* coupled as it is with the 'sovereignty of the people,' corresponds much more closely with the modern conception of democracy." But see editorial note 83.

[80]The "famous author" is Montesquieu, who had said: "Not much honesty is needed for a monarchical or despotic government to survive or support itself. . . . But in a popular state, an additional motivation is necessary, namely VIRTUE." *Esprit des Lois,* III, iii (ed. Caillois, p. 251). Rousseau's criticism of Montesquieu here is similar to a remark in *Émile,* V: "Political right (*le droit politique*) is yet to be born, and it is to be presumed that it never will be. . . . The only modern capable of creating this noble and useless science would have been the illustrious Montesquieu. But he did not

bother to treat the principles of political right; he was content to treat the positive right of established governments, and nothing in the world is more different than these two studies" (Pléiade, IV, 836). For Rousseau, "the same principle" of political right "ought to apply to every well-constituted state" (compare Introduction, pp. 12–20), whereas Montesquieu speaks of the "principle" of each form of government as "that which makes it act . . . the human passions which move it" (*Esprit des Lois*, III, i).

[81]"I prefer dangerous freedom to quiet servitude." Rousseau apparently cites *Observations sur le gouvernement de Pologne* (1749), in which Stanislas Leczinski, titular King of Poland and Duke of Lorraine, attributes this phrase to his father (Vaughan, II, 74).

[82]In the copy of the *Social Contract* given to his friend d'Ivernois, as well as in a manuscript (Neuchâtel 7842, f° 52), Rousseau added the following to this note: "*Dum pauci potentes dominationes affectabant, bonique et mali cives adpellati, non ob merita in Rempublicam, sed uti quisque locupletissimus et injuria validior, quia praesentia defendebat pro bono ducebatur. Sallust. Hist. L. I.*" (Pléiade, III, 1478). "Since a small number of powerful people distributed positions, citizens were called good or bad not on the basis of their merit in the Republic, but on the basis of their wealth and their force in scorning the law, so that an individual's position pleading in his favor, he was considered a good man."

[83]Rousseau's concept of "elective aristocracy" is thus his closest approximation to what has come to be called "representative government." As will be noted, however, Rousseau flatly rejects the concept of "representatives or deputies" (III, xv). In this regard, his distinction between sovereignty and government is crucial. Compare *Lettres Écrites de la Montagne*, VI: "The best of governments is aristocratic; the worst of sovereignties is aristocratic" (Pléiade, III, 809). "The interests of partial societies are no less distinct from those of the State, nor less pernicious to the Republic, than those of private individuals . . . and since what is dishonest in preferring oneself to others disappears in favor of a numerous society of which one is a part, by being a good Senator one finally becomes a bad citizen. This is what makes Aristocracy the worst of sovereignties." *Jugement sur la Polysynodie* (Pléiade, III, 644–645).

[84]Rousseau seems to misrepresent Aristotle flagrantly, as has been noted by many editors (Vaughan, Derathé, Grimsley). According to *Politics*, III.vi–vii.1279a (ed. Barker, pp. 112–114), "aristocracy" is a "right constitution" in which the few rule "with a view to the common interest"; the name aristocracy is "given to this species either because the best (*aristoi*) are the rulers or because its object is what is best (*ariston*) for the state and its members." Hence aristocracy is "a government vested in a number of persons who are all good men." Ibid, III, xv.1286b (p. 143). In contrast, Aristotle is explicit in defining rule by the rich as *oligarchy*: "It is inevitable that any constitution should be an oligarchy if the rulers under it are rulers in virtue of riches, whether they are few or many" Ibid., III. viii, 1279b–1280a (p. 116). The same distinction is found in Aristotle's *Nicomachean Ethics*, VIII.x.1160a–b (ed. Ostwald [Indianapolis, Ind.: Bobbs-Merrill, 1975], pp. 233–234). Rousseau thus applies Aristotle's criterion of a *bad* form of government by a few (oligarchy) to what Aristotle had called a *good* form of government by a few (aristocracy). This is probably not merely a careless slip, since in the note to *Social Contract*, III, x, Rousseau attacks Aristotle's distinction between kingship and tyranny, citing *Nicomachean Ethics*, VIII.x. In other words, Rousseau seems to have consistently blurred Aristotle's distinction between "right" or good regimes and bad or unjust ones. Compare editorial note 79.

[85]This note was added in the edition of 1782. On Rousseau's praise of Machiavelli, see Grimsley's Introduction, pp. 73–77 and Masters, *Political Philosophy of Rousseau*, pp. 364–368. It is particularly instructive to note Rousseau's insistence on reading another "profound political theorist" with an eye to a "hidden intention" that is revealed only to careful readers. Compare the opening passage of III, i.

[86]This paragraph was added while the *Social Contract* was in press, apparently in order to compliment the Duke de Choiseul. Unfortunately, Choiseul—then Prime Minister—took the passage as personal criticism instead of praise: Pléiade, III, 1482; Vaughan, II, 78; and—for Rousseau's own account—*Confessions*, XI (Pléiade, I, 571, 576–577). For the first draft of the next paragraph see *Geneva Manuscript*, II, iii (p. 186).

[87]Plutarch, *Sayings of Kings,*175E in *Moralia*, ed. F. C. Babbitt (London: Loeb Classical Library, 1961), III, 30–31. In the Greek, Dionysius the Younger calls his father a "tyrant" (*tyrannon*) not a "king"; compare Rousseau's second footnote to III, x.

[88]"The most practical and shortest method of distinguishing between good and bad measures is to think what you yourself would or would not like under another emperor." Tacitus, *Histories* I. 16 (in *The Complete Works of Tacitus*, ed. Moses Hadas [New York: Modern Library, 1942], p. 429).

[89]Rousseau again refers to Plato's *Statesman*, especially 297b–c, 300e, 303c, 309d. (Compare editorial note 54.) The frequency of Rousseau's references to the *Statesman*—combined with the surprising absence of references to the *Republic*—deserves comment. Could it be that, like Plato, Rousseau was seeking a "statesman"— not as monarch, but as legislator? Among the fragments presumably intended for Rousseau's projected *Political Institutions* is a list of chapters concluding with "Examination of Plato's Rep[ublic]" (Pléiade, III, 473), and a Preface which says: "I like to flatter myself that one day some statesman will be a citizen, that he will not change things solely to do otherwise than his predecessor, but to act so that they are better, that he will not have the public welfare constantly in his mouth, but that he will have it a little in his heart; that he will not make peoples unhappy to strengthen his authority, but that he will use his authority to establish the happiness of peoples, that by a happy chance he will see this book; that my unformulated ideas will lead him to think of more useful ones; that he will work to make men better or happier; and that I will have contributed something to this effect. This chimera has set me to writing . . . " (Pléiade, III, 474). On Rousseau's longing for "a superhuman genius" who would exercise "creative legislative authority," see Judith Shklar, "Rousseau's Images of Authority," in *Hobbes and Rousseau*, ed. Cranston and Peters, especially pp. 340–347.

[90]If the ratio of the sovereign to the government is a "fraction" whereas that of the government to the state is a "whole number" (III, i and editorial note 75), in practice the ratio of prince to sovereign is always greater than—and the ratio of people to prince less than—unity.

[91]See *Esprit des Lois*, especially Book XVII: "How the Laws of Political Servitude are Related to Climate" (ed. Caillois, pp. 523–530) as well as I, iii; XV, vii; XVI, ii–iv, xi, xii; XIX, iv, xxvii; XXI, i–iv; XXIII, xvi; XXV, xxvi; and *Persian Letters*, cxxxi. For the classic statement of this view, see Aristotle, *Politics*, VII.vii.1327b (ed. Barker, p. 296).

[92]Rousseau's citation is from Chardin's *Voyages en Perse* (4 vols.; Amsterdam, 1735), III, 76, 83–84. The remainder of this chapter relates economics to climate in a way that is strikingly different from most modern economic theories. Compare Locke, *Second Treatise*, chap. v, and Montesquieu, *Esprit des Lois*, Book XVIII and especially part IV, Books XX–XXII.

[93]Compare Aristotle, *Politics*, Books I–II, VII–VIII. On Rousseau's reasons for transforming the ancients' question of the "best regime" into the modern one of "what is law?" (i.e., is there a rational principle of obedience?), see the passage of the *Confessions* cited in editorial note 4. On the argument of the chapter as a whole, compare Montesquieu, *Esprit des Lois*, Book XXIII. Note that over the long run, a "suc-

cessful" government necessarily destroys freedom, since "the larger the State grows, the less freedom there is" (III, i). Compare the next chapter.

⁹⁴"And this in their ignorance, they called civilization, when it was but a part of their servitude." Tacitus, *Agricola*, 21 (ed. Hadas, p. 690). Like Rousseau's preceding note, this one was added when the *Social Contract* was in press (Pléiade, III, 1484–1485).

⁹⁵"They make a solitude and call it peace." Tacitus, *Agricola*, 30 (ed. Hadas, p. 695). On the example in the next sentence, see the passage of the *Memoires* of the Cardinal de Retz—who was Coadjutor of Paris—cited in Pléiade, III, 1485 (n. 5).

⁹⁶Rousseau paraphrases the Introduction of Machiavelli's *History of Florence*. But compare Machiavelli's argument in III, i (New York: Harper Torchbooks, 1960, pp. 108–109) with *Discourses on Titus Livy*, I, 4 (ed. Crick, pp. 113–115). On this note—and Rousseau's argument in the chapter—consider Bertrand de Jouvenel's judgment: "This very criterion of population overthrows Rousseau's entire thesis that civilization is decadent. For, along with commercial growth and the flowering of the arts and sciences which alarmed him, population in his time grew enormously. On this point, he has for him a passage from Tacitus and against him all the statistics. It is true that now population is declining in the most civilized countries, sometimes even rapidly. But nonetheless civilized peoples have larger populations than barbarians" (ed. de Jouvenel, p. 291).

⁹⁷An anonymous work published in 1612, with the objective of legitimizing the sovereignty of the Emperor over the Venetian Republic (Pléiade, III, 1486).

⁹⁸Rousseau apparently has in mind the account of Rome in *Discourses on Titus Livy*, I, 2–4, 17 (ed. Crick, pp. 110–115, 157–158). This reference is nonetheless surprising, since Machiavelli describes "the cycle through which all commonwealths pass" as monarchy, tyranny, aristocracy, oligarchy, democracy, anarchy (Ibid., I, 2; pp. 106–109). Moreover, Machiavelli explicitly applies this view to Rome: "And so favored was it [Rome] by fortune that, though the transition from Monarchy to Aristocracy and thence to Democracy, took place by the very stages and for the very reasons laid down earlier in this discourse, none the less the granting of authority to the aristocracy did not abolish altogether the royal estate, nor was the authority of the aristocracy wholly removed when the populace was granted a share of it. On the contrary, the blending of these estates made a perfect commonwealth . . ." (Ibid., p. 111). Cf. Plato's cycle of regimes: monarchy or aristocracy, timocracy, oligarchy, democracy, and tyranny (*Republic*, Books VIII–IX).

⁹⁹As numerous editors have noted, Rousseau uses "anarchy" to describe the absence of *legitimate* government rather than the chaotic absence of any *effective* government. This usage is consistent with Rousseau's tendency to follow Cicero's classification of regimes rather than that of Aristotle or Plato (compare editorial note 84). The term *ochlocracy* (mob rule) in Rousseau's next sentence was apparently first used by Polybius (Pléiade, III, 1486): see Polybius, *The Histories*, VI.4.7–10 (ed. W. R. Paton [London: Loeb Classical Library, 1960], III, 274–275). Curiously enough, however, in this very passage Polybius contradicts Rousseau's assertion that all government naturally evolves from democracy to monarchy. And Machiavelli seems to have had Polybius in mind when writing *Discourses*, I, 2 (see the preceding editorial note). In other words, Rousseau was fully conversant with the technical usage of ancient and modern political theorists, but he adapts their concepts to his own point of view.

¹⁰⁰"For all those who exercise power for life in a city that has been accustomed to be free are considered and called tyrants." Cornelius Nepos, *Life of Miltiades*, chap. viii (in *Lives of the Excellent Commanders*, ed. John Clarke [London: Hitch and Johnston, 1754], pp. 32–33). On the remainder of this note, compare Aristotle, *Politics*, IV.x.1295a (ed. Barker, pp. 178–179) with editorial note 84. For a very im-

portant analysis of Xenophon's *Hiero*, see Leo Strauss, *On Tyranny*, rev. ed. (Glencoe: Free Press, 1963)—especially p. 126, note 7. Interestingly enough, Machiavelli seems to use the term "tyrant" in precisely the way rejected by Rousseau: *Discourses on Titus Livy*, I, 10 (ed. Crick, pp. 135–138).

[101]Compare Hobbes, *Leviathan*, Part 2, chap. 30: "there be also [some] that maintain, that there are no grounds, nor principles of reason, to sustain those essential rights, which make sovereignty absolute. Wherein they argue as ill, as if the savage people of America, should deny there were any grounds, or principles of reason, so to build a house, as to last as long as the materials, because they never yet saw any so well built. Time and industry, produce every day new knowledge. And as the art of well building is derived from principles of reason, observed by industrious men, that had long studied the nature of materials, and the divers effects of figure, and proportion, long after mankind began, though poorly, to build; so, long time after men have begun to constitute commonwealths, imperfect, and apt to relapse into disorder, there may be principles of reason found out, by industrious meditation, to make their constitution, excepting by external violence, everlasting" (ed. Oakeshott, p. 220).

[102]On this analogy between the "constitution of man" and that "of the State," compare Hobbes, *Leviathan*, Author's Introduction (ed. Oakeshott, p. 5) and *Political Economy* (pp. 211–212). The next paragraph echoes *Geneva Manuscript*, II, ii, paragraph ten.

[103]As prior editors have pointed out, Rousseau's argument reflects his criticism of the Genevan government, which refused to allow the *Conseil Général* to meet with full authority. See *Lettres Écrites de la Montagne*, especially VIII (Pléiade, III, 837–858), IX (pp. 885–887), et passim. Compare *Government of Poland*, chap. VII (ed. Watkins, pp. 191–192, 195), where Rousseau applies this principle to practice.

[104]Compare *Constitutional Project for Corsica* (ed. Watkins, pp. 291–293), where Rousseau does not follow his own advice, with *Government of Poland*, chap. V (ed. Watkins, pp. 181–182), where Rousseau proposes a federal system. The argument of the next paragraph could be supported by the process of rapid urbanization in the "developing" countries. See E. F. Schumacher, *Small is Beautiful* (New York: Harper & Row, 1973), Part III. To emphasize Rousseau's preference for small communities, the word *"ville"* has been consistently translated *"town"* as distinct from *"City"* (*"Cité"*)—which for Rousseau has the special meaning of the classical *polis* or city-state.

[105]On Rousseau's judgment of England, compare *Lettres Écrites de la Montagne*, XIX (Pléiade, III, 877–879). Rousseau's vigorous rejection of the concept of representation distinguishes his political theory from modern constitutional doctrines. Cf. Hobbes's notion of the Sovereign as "representative" of the "body politic": *Leviathan*, Part 1, chap. 16 and Part 2, chap. 18 (ed. Oakeshott, pp. 107, 113). Rousseau was aware that his principles were hard if not impossible to realize under modern conditions, as the rest of this chapter makes clear. Hence it should not be surprising that he proposes for Poland a system of "Deputies" who are "bound by their instructions." The details of this proposal, which is explicitly described as being "deduced" from the "principle" set forth in the *Social Contract*, provide a good example of how Rousseau applied his theory to political practice: see *Government of Poland*, chap. VII (ed. Watkins, pp. 193–195). Compare *Political Economy*, editorial note 27.

[106]Since this note implies that the existing text of Book III was drafted before Rousseau abandoned the projected *Political Institutions*, it could be taken as evidence that the missing half of the *Geneva Manuscript* was detached and used with only minor changes as the final version (compare editorial notes 4 and 68). Although some might be tempted to see the *Federalist Papers* as the fulfillment of Rousseau's project, Hamilton and Madison follow Montesquieu, favoring a commercial republic based on

the separation of powers and indirect, representative legislatures. For a sketch of Rousseau's likely approach to confederations, see Vaughan, I, 95–102 and the texts there cited. It is possible that a manuscript containing Rousseau's conception of confederations was destroyed during the French Revolution (Vaughan, II, 135–136). Rousseau's reticence to publish his ideas on this topic may have been based on fears expressed in his *Jugement sur le Projet de Paix Perpétuelle*. Having shown that the Abbé de Saint Pierre's projected European confederation combined "individual profit" and the "common good" (Pléiade, III, 591), Rousseau concludes: "Let us admire such a beautiful plan, but let us console ourselves not to see it executed, for that could not be done except by means that are violent and dangerous for humanity. One does not see federative leagues established in any other way except by revolutions, and on this principle who would dare say if this European League is to be desired or feared?" (Pléiade, III, 600). On this work, see *Social Contract*, editorial note 119.

[107]The next three chapters return to questions of political "principle" as they relate to the practical problem of establishing and maintaining any legitimate government. On Rousseau's view of the social contract as "the bonds" of society, "obligating all members of the state without exception"—and not a contract between the people and its rulers—see *Second Discourse*, Part 2 (ed. Masters, pp. 168–169).

[108]This phrase—and the "two propositions that can never be omitted" at the regular assemblies (see the end of this chapter, p. 107)—were key passages cited by the Procureur Général of Geneva, J. L. Tronchin, as grounds for condemning the *Social Contract* (Pléiade, III, 1490–1491). Compare editorial note 103. On the importance of the next paragraph, see Introduction, pp. 20–24.

[109]Rousseau uses an old legal term, *le cas odieux*. As Beaulavon pointed out: "It is a case in which the exercise of the claimed right appears to be dangerous; one then invokes the maxim of Roman law, "*odia restringenda, favores ampliandi*—i.e., harmful rights must be limited as much as possible, and on the contrary advantageous rights given all the latitude possible." (Pléiade, III, 1490). On the example of the Roman Decemvirs, cited later in this paragraph, see II, vii, and editorial note 56.

[110]See Grotius, *Droit de la Guerre et de la Paix,* II, v, § 24 (cited Pléiade, III, 1491). On this crucial point, the conventional distinction between modern totalitarianism and constitutional regimes follows Rousseau's principle.

[111]Compare this bucolic image with the description of the early Swiss as "good and just without ever knowing what justice and virtue were" in *Constitutional Project for Corsica* (ed. Watkins, pp. 295–296), the Neufchâtel mountainside depicted in the *Letter to d'Alembert* (ed. Bloom, pp. 60–62), and Rousseau's assertion that the *Social Contract* takes Geneva as "a model of political institutions," *Lettres Écrites de la Montagne*, VI (Pléiade, III, 809). The argument of the remainder of this chapter, with its assertion that the general will "is always constant, unalterable, and pure," follows from the conception set forth in I, vi–II, vi (see especially editorial note 30).

[112]Rousseau's ironical defense of free speech has confused some editors, who read the last clause as a serious statement of principle; such an interpretation is unlikely given the next chapter as well as Book II, chap. iii.

[113]Tacitus, *Histories*, I.85 (ed. Hadas, pp. 471–472).

[114]Unlike the first sentence of I, i, here Rousseau unambiguously uses the present tense (*"tout homme étant né libre . . ."*). Earlier editors have remarked that the principle of consent, spelled out in this paragraph and the following one, follows Pufendorf, Locke, and Burlamaqui (Pléiade, III, 1493). See also Hobbes, *Leviathan*, "A Review and Conclusion" (ed. Oakeshott, pp. 461–463). On residence as tacit consent, compare the last paragraph of III, xviii.

[115]The foregoing passage deserves particular emphasis, since it reinforces the interpretation of the "general will" as the logic implicit in the principle of majority rule. Note, however, that for Rousseau, popular votes should *not* be viewed as an expression of differing interests: compare the distinction between the general will and the will of all, based on the notion "that the agreement of all interests is formed in opposition to the interest of each" (II, iii and Rousseau's first note). Compare editorial notes 28 and 44.

[116]Compare II, iii, and III, xiii–xv, xviii, with IV, iv–vii.

[117]Montesquieu, *Esprit des Lois*, II, ii (ed. Caillois, p. 242). Montesquieu goes on, however, to add that election by lot "is defective by itself"; in the remainder of the chapter, Rousseau seems to disagree in principle, but agree in practice.

[118]Poor members of the Venetian nobility who inhabited the quarter called St. Barnabas (Pléiade, III, 1494). Voltaire criticized this comparison between Venice and Geneva as exaggerated (Ibid.); beyond such questions of historical detail, the passage suggests that not merely Venice, but virtually every republic, is a "mixed regime" in Rousseau's terminology. See III, vii: "Properly speaking, there is no simple government" and editorial note 79. On Venice, compare Machiavelli, *Discourses on Titus Livy*, I, 6 (ed. Crick, pp. 119–121).

[119]Rousseau refers to *Polysynodie*, by the Abbé de Saint Pierre (1718). The two had met just before the Abbé's death (1743), and Rousseau was subsequently asked to edit an abridgment of his works. As a result, in 1761 Rousseau published the *Extract of the Project of Perpetual Peace by Monsieur the Abbé de Saint Pierre* (Pléiade, III, 563–589). Although written at the same time, Rousseau's *Judgment on the Project of Perpetual Peace* (Ibid., pp. 591–600), his edition of *Polysynodie of l'Abbé de St. Pierre* and *Judgment on the Polysynodie* (Ibid., pp. 617–645) were only published posthumously in 1782. The Abbé was a rationalist if not utopian, who imagined a European parliament as the means to universal peace as well as the sweeping reform of the French monarchy to which Rousseau here refers. For the details of Abbé de St. Pierre's proposal, see *Polysynodie*, especially chap. IV–VIII (Pléiade, III, 622–632).

[120]Some editors have not taken this sentence seriously. For example, Vaughan speaks of IV, iv–vii, as "barely relevant to the subject, and quite unworthy of the setting in which they stand" (Vaughan, II, 109). Derathé echoes this feeling, adding that "for Rousseau, it was a matter of filling up this fourth book, even at the price of a digression, in order to be able to insert the chapter on civil religion" (Pléiade, III, 1495). These judgments ignore Rousseau's continued admiration for Rome, the "model of all free peoples." (*Second Discourse*, Dedication [ed. Masters, p. 80]). Moreover, at least one internal reference suggests that these four chapters weren't inserted at the last minute (see *Social Contract*, editorial note 116 as well as *Geneva Manuscript*, editorial note 37). Finally, but most important of all, a comparison of Machiavelli's *Discourses on Titus Livy* and Montesquieu's *Considerations on the Greatness of the Romans* or *Esprit des Lois* shows very clearly the difference between Rousseau's view of Rome and that of his predecessors.

[121]Rousseau's note, like his epigraph from the *Aeneid* (editorial note 3), implies that Rome was founded on violence rather than free consent. Compare *Government of Poland*, chap. ii: "Those who have seen in Numa only a creator of religious rites and ceremonies have sadly misjudged this great man. Numa was the true founder of Rome. If Romulus had done no more than to bring together a pack of brigands who could have been scattered by a single set-back, his imperfect work would not have been able to withstand the ravages of time. It was Numa who made it solid and enduring by uniting these brigands into an indissoluble body . . . " (ed. Watkins, p. 165). Compare *Geneva Manuscript*, I, ii and especially II, iv: "for law comes before justice and not justice

before law." Although the history of Romulus and Numa may be a "fable," it nonetheless reflects the true origin of Rome (see ed. de Jouvenel, p. 331). Compare Montesquieu's dismissal of "Numa's long and peaceful reign" as "ideal for keeping Rome in a state of mediocrity" (*Considerations on the Greatness of the Romans*, chap. 1 [ed. Lowenthal, pp. 23–24]) with Machiavelli, *Discourses on Titus Livy*, I, 11 (ed. Crick, pp. 140–141).

[122]The passages from Varro, *De Re Rustica*, III. i, and Pliny, *Hist. Nat.*, XVIII.iii, are both apparently cited from Sigonius, *De antiquo jure civium romanorum*—a work which, as editors since Dreyfus-Brisac have noted, seems to have been a major source of Rousseau's account of Rome (Pléiade, III, 1494–1495; Vaughan, II, 109). For Montesquieu's account of the Roman institutions described in this chapter, see *Considerations on the Greatness of the Romans*, chap. viii (ed. Lowenthal, pp. 86–87). As remarked in editorial note 104, the word "town" has been used throughout for the French "*ville*", both because Rousseau attaches a special meaning to "*Cité*" (translated "City") and because he refers to an urban agglomeration smaller than contemporary New York, Paris, or Tokyo.

[123]Rousseau's awareness of the bias in favor of wealth in the Roman centuries should be underlined—especially since he adds that they represented "all the majesty of the Roman people" whereas the comitia by tribes, albeit "favorable to popular government," failed to include "the senate and the patricians" (p. 119). Despite his egalitarian principles, Rousseau knew the impossibility of avoiding some degree of social inequality in a complex society. For examples of the process to which Rousseau refers, at least at the end of the Republic, see Lucy Ross Taylor, *Party Politics in the Age of Caesar* (Berkeley, Calif.: University of California Press, 1961).

[124]Cicero, *Laws*, III.xv.33–xvii.39 (ed. Keyes [London: Loeb Classical Library, 1959], pp. 496–505), to which Montesquieu had referred in *Esprit des Lois*, II, ii (ed. Caillois, p. 243). On the secret ballot, which is of course generally practiced in modern democracies, compare editorial note 46. On Rousseau's judgment concerning this change in Roman law, compare Machiavelli, *Discourses on Titus Livy*, III, 24–26 (ed. Crick, pp. 473–477).

[125]In his *Lettres Écrites de la Montagne*, Rousseau rejects a criticism of the tribunes as a cause of the fall of the Roman Republic, adding a reference to this chapter as containing "some good maxims" on such an institution (Pléiade, III, 879–880). As the examples of the Spartan ephors and Venetian Council of Ten indicate, Rousseau clearly has in mind a political function that exists in other regimes; one can wonder how he would have analyzed the United States Supreme Court.

[126]As earlier editors note, in this chapter Rousseau seems to follow Machiavelli, *Discourses on Titus Livy*, I, 33–34 (ed. Crick, pp. 193–198). Compare Montesquieu, *Esprit des Lois*, II, iii.

[127]On the Roman censors, see Machiavelli, *Discourses on Titus Livy*, I, 40 (ed. Crick, p. 230): "For in that the censors became the arbiters of Roman customs, they constituted a very powerful instrument which the Romans used in order to postpone the advent of corruption." Compare Montesquieu's explanation of how the censors "greatly contributed to upholding Rome's government": *Considerations on the Greatness of the Romans*, chap. viii (ed. Lowenthal, pp. 85–86).

[128]The French word translated here as elsewhere as "mores" is *moeurs*; it means both the "morals" and "manners" of a society—that is, "customs" from a moral as well as descriptive point of view. Compare translator's note 3 in *Letter to d'Alembert* (ed. Bloom, pp. 149–150).

[129]In the copy of the *Social Contract* given to d'Ivernois, Rousseau noted: "They were from Chios and not Samos; but given the things in question, I never dared use this

word in the text. Although I think that I am as bold as others, it isn't permissible for anyone to be dirty and crude, in any possible situation. The French have put so much decency in their language that one can no longer tell the truth in it." (Pléiade, III, 1497). Rousseau thus avoided the play on words which would have resulted if he had spoken of "*Chiots*" or "*Chiens*."

[130]For the first version of this chapter, see the final section of the *Geneva Manuscript*: paragraph seven of the draft became paragraphs four and six, with the remainder of the draft starting at paragraph fifteen of the final version (see also editorial note 135). Although the concept of a "civil religion" has understandably been viewed with great suspicion by those who lived through the excesses of Hitler and Stalin, Rousseau's frame of reference should be borne in mind. Compare Montesquieu, *Considerations on the Greatness of the Romans*, chap x (ed. Lowenthal, p. 98): "Aside from the fact that religion is always the best guarantee one can have of the morals of men, it was a special trait of the Romans that they mingled some religious sentiment with their love of country." Similarly, for Machiavelli, "the religion introduced by Numa was among the primary causes of Rome's success. . . . And as the observance of divine worship is the cause of greatness in republics, so the neglect of it is the cause of their ruin." *Discourses on Titus Livy*, I, 11 (ed. Crick, p. 141).

[131]*Judges*, xi.28. Compare the translation of the *Jerusalem Bible* (p. 276): "Do you not possess all that Chemosh your god took from its owners? In the same fashion, whatever Yahweh our God took from its owners, that we possess too."

[132]As Grimsley notes in his edition (p. 222): "Phocaea was one of the large towns of Asia Minor. In 356 B.C. a religious war broke out between the Phocaeans and the Thebans because the Phocaean leaders, who had been accused of cultivating sacred lands, refused to pay the heavy fine demanded of them by the Amphictyons. Sparta and Athens went to help the Phocaeans and Philip of Macedon the Thebans, who were ultimately victorious." Compare Thucydides' account of the role of the "curse of the goddess" and the "curse of Taenarus" in the origin of the Peloponnesian War: *History*, I.118–135 (ed. Finley [New York: Modern Library, 1951], pp. 65–75).

[133]In a manuscript (Neuchâtel 7842), Rousseau noted: "For the last chapter of the Social Contract: *They have broken every one of Caesar's edicts by claiming that there is another emperor, Jesus. Acts, XVII.7.*" (Pléiade, III, 1501). The Biblical translation is from *Jerusalem Bible*, pp. 178–179; Rousseau's French Bible read "*Roy*" (king), not emperor.

[134]"I have seen, writes Grotius, the Treatise *Of the Citizen*. I approve what is there in favor of kings, but I could not approve the foundations on which the author bases his opinions. He thinks that all men are naturally in a state of war, and he establishes some other things that are not in agreement with my principles. He even goes so far as to assert that it is the duty of each private individual to follow the religion approved in his homeland by the public authorities, if not adopting it in his heart, at least in professing it and submitting to it obediently." Rousseau presumably read this letter in Barbeyrac's Translator's Preface to the French edition of Grotius, *Droit de la Guerre et de la Paix* (cited in Pléiade, III, 1502). For Hobbes's own statement, see *De Cive*, chap. vi, paragraph 11 (ed. Gert, pp. 179–180); chap. xv, paragraph 17 (pp. 303–305); chap. xv, paragraphs 7–18 (pp. 313–328); chap. xvii, paragraph 27 (pp. 364–367); chap. xviii, paragraphs 13–14 (pp. 383–386).

[135]At this point, the final version picks up the draft in *Geneva Manuscript,* starting with its second paragraph. The opposition between the "religion of man and that of the citizen" reminds one of the distinction between the "natural man" and the "citizen" in *Émile*, I (Pléiade, IV, 249). For a fuller statement of Rousseau's "natural religion"—here called "true theism" or "natural divine right"—see the "Profession of Faith of the Savoyard Vicar" in *Émile*, IV (Pléiade, IV, 565–635); the Profession of Faith of Julie in *Nouvelle Héloïse,* VI, xi (Pléiade, II, 714–716), as well as V, v (pp. 587–

596); and Masters, *Political Philosophy of Rousseau*, pp. 54–89. On Rousseau's intention to reconcile "the tolerance of the philosopher *(philosophe)* and the charity of the Christian," see *Lettres Écrites de la Montagne*, I (Pléiade, III, 697) and Pléiade, IV, 1600.

[136]"Let him be damned." This formula was used when a citizen was cut off from other citizens and left to the judgment of the gods (ed. Grimsley, p. 226). Rousseau's violent criticism of Catholicism is very much based on the realization that among believers, the power of excommunication—and even the refusal of the sacraments—is the most serious penalty. As Hobbes had put it: "For no man can serve two masters; nor is he less, but rather more a master, whom we believe we are to obey for fear of damnation, than he whom we obey for fear of temporal death." *De Cive*, chap. vi, paragraph 11 (ed. Gert, p. 179). Compare Rousseau's note on the clergy (above, p. 127) with that on marriage, especially in its original form at the end of the *Geneva Manuscript*.

[137]As Derathé points out, this sentence—and the following criticism of Christianity on political grounds—was heavily attacked. By "particular societies" and "social spirit," Rousseau meant political communities: "The great society, human society in general, is founded on humanity, or universal benevolence; I say and I have always said that Christianity is favorable to that society. But the particular societies, political and civil societies, have an entirely different principle. They are purely human establishments from which, as a consequence, the true Christianity detaches us as from all that is only earthly . . . " Letter to Usteri, July 18, 1763 (cited Pléiade, III, 1503). Compare *Geneva Manuscript* I, ii (the long chapter deleted from the final version): in a sense, Rousseau's rejection of a "general society of the human species," based solely on reason, requires in its place a civil religion. Hence IV, viii, of the *Social Contract* is perhaps best understood as Rousseau's replacement of I, ii, of the *Geneva Manuscript*.

[138]Compare Nietzsche's treatment of Judaism, and especially Christianity, as "the slave revolt in morality." *Genealogy of Morals*, I, 10 (ed. Kaufmann [New York: Vintage, 1969], p. 36) et passim.

[139]The passage quoted in this note has not been found in the published version of the Marquis d'Argenson's *Considérations* (Pléiade, III, 1504). On Rousseau's four citations of d'Argenson, see Masters, *Political Philosophy of Rousseau*, pp. 306–309.

[140]Rousseau's endorsement of the death penalty for behavior violating the dogmas of the civil religion indicates a "toughness" in his thought that is often overlooked. Nonetheless, it must be stressed that for Rousseau, only *behavior*—and never opinion or belief—can be punished by society: "I am indignant that everyone's faith is not in the most perfect freedom, and that man dares to inspect the interior of consciences, where he cannot penetrate, as if it depended on us to believe or not believe in matters where there is no proof . . ." Letter to Voltaire, August 18, 1756 (cited Pléiade, III, 1505). Hence Rousseau asserted elsewhere: ". . . . no true believer could be intolerant or a persecutor. If I were the magistrate, and the law provided for the death penalty against atheists, I would begin by having burned as one whoever came to denounce another." *Nouvelle Héloïse*, V, v, note (Pléiade, II, 589).

[141]These dogmas should be compared to the "Profession of Faith" in both *Émile* and *Nouvelle Héloïse* (see editorial note 135 above). Rousseau's attempt to combine religious belief and toleration will strike many modern readers as anachronistic. But it is curious that the political practice of Western democracies—most notably the United States—resembles Rousseau's precept: along with toleration of varied religious beliefs, one finds a general hostility to avowed atheism. Conversely, where atheism has been publicly proclaimed—as in the Soviet Union—there has been a tendency to convert the ruling political ideology into a kind of state religion.

[142]This note, which was softened from the first draft (See the end of the *Geneva*

Manuscript and editorial note 42 thereto), was the source of considerable concern to Rousseau. After the *Social Contract* had been printed, he wrote to his publisher: "I want this note eliminated, whatever the cost, for your advantage as well as for my own." Letter to Rey, March 14, 1762 (cited Pléiade, III, 1507). Rey therefore had to reset the last pages of the book without this note, which was only published in the posthumous edition of 1782.

[143]Henry IV's reasoning is described as follows: "A historian reports that the King had a debate between Doctors of both churches conducted in his presence, and seeing that a [Protestant] Minister agreed that one could be saved in the Catholic Religion, his Majesty spoke as follows to the Minister: *What? Do you agree that one can be saved in the religion of those men over there?* The Minister replied that he did not doubt it, provided that one lived well. The King replied very judiciously: *Prudence indicates, then, that I be of their religion and not yours, because being in theirs I can be saved according to them and according to you, and being of yours I can be saved according to you but not according to them. Now prudence indicates that I follow the most assured* [religion]." Hardouin de Péréfixe, *Histoire du roy Henry le Grand* (ed. 1616, p. 200, cited Pléiade, III, 1506).

[144]On Rousseau's approach to foreign policy, and his decision to delete such considerations when abandoning his projected *Political Institutions*, see editorial notes 4, 106, 119. In the last analysis, Rousseau seems to have been less interested by problems which he called "external and relative" than by those that seemed to him "internal and absolute" (II, ix).

On The Social Contract

OR

ESSAY ABOUT THE
FORM OF THE REPUBLIC[1]

(First Version, commonly called the
Geneva Manuscript)

BOOK I

PRELIMINARY CONCEPTS OF THE SOCIAL BODY

Chapter I: Subject of this Work[2]

So many famous authors have dealt with the maxims of government and the rules of civil right that there is nothing useful to say on this subject that has not already been said. But perhaps there would be greater agreement, perhaps the best relationships of the social body would have been more clearly established if its nature had been better determined at the outset. This is what I have tried to do in this work. It is, therefore, not a question here of the administration of this body, but of its constitution. I make it live, not act. I describe its mechanisms and its parts, and set them in place. I put the machine in running order. Wiser men will regulate its movements.

Chapter II: On the General Society of the Human Race[3]

Let us begin by inquiring why the necessity for political institutions arises.

Man's force is so proportioned to his natural needs and his primitive state that the slightest change in this state and increase in his needs make the assistance of his fellow men necessary; and when his desires finally encompass the whole of nature, the cooperation of the entire human race is barely enough to satisfy them. Thus the same causes that make us wicked also make us slaves, and reduce us to servitude by depraving us. The feeling of our weakness comes less from our nature than from our cupidity. Our needs bring us together in proportion as our passions divide us, and the more we become enemies of our fellow men, the less we can do without them.[4] Such are the first bonds of general society; such are the foundations of that universal goodwill, which seems to be stifled as a feeling once recognized as a necessity, and from which everyone would like to benefit without being obliged to cultivate it. As for our natural identity, its effect here is null because it is as much a subject of quarrel as of union for men, and is as frequently a source of competition and jealousy as of mutual understanding and agreement.

This new order of things gives rise to a multitude of relationships lacking order, regulation and stability, which men alter and change continually—a hundred working to destroy them for one working to establish them. And since the relative existence of a man in the state of nature is dependent on a thousand other continually changing relationships, he can never be sure of being the same for two moments in his life. Peace and happiness are only momentary for him; nothing is permanent except the misery that results from all these vicissitudes. Even if his feelings and ideas could rise to the love of order and the sublime concepts of virtue, it would be impossible for him ever to apply these principles with certainty in a state of things that would not allow him to discern either good or evil, either the decent man or the wicked one.

The kind of general society that mutual needs can engender does not, therefore, offer any effective assistance to man once he has become miserable, or at least it gives new force to him who already has too much, whereas the weak man—lost, stifled, crushed in the multitude—finds no place of refuge, no source of support for his weakness, and finally perishes as a victim of the deceptive union from which he expected happiness.

[Once one is convinced that among the motives causing men to unite by voluntary bonds nothing relates to the union for its own sake; that far from proposing a goal of shared felicity from which each individual would derive his own, one man's happiness is the other's misfortune; if, finally, one sees that rather than all striving toward the general good, men only come together because all are moving away from it; then one must also feel that even if such a state could subsist, it would only be a source of crimes and miseries for men, each of whom would see only his interest, follow only his inclinations, and listen only to his passions.][5]

Thus nature's gentle voice is no longer an infallible guide for us, nor is the independence we have received from her a desirable state. We lost peace and innocence forever before we had appreciated their delights. Unfelt by the stupid men of earliest times, lost to the enlightened men of later times, the happy life of the golden age was always a state foreign to the human race, either because it went unrecognized when humans could have enjoyed it or because it had been lost when humans could have known it.[6]

There is even more. Even had this perfect independence and unregulated freedom remained joined to ancient innocence, it would always have had an essential vice, harmful to the development of our most excellent faculties, namely the lack of that liaison between the parts which constitutes the whole. The earth would be covered with men between whom there was almost no communication. We would have some similarities but none would unite us. Everyone would remain isolated among the others, and would think only of himself. Our understanding would be unable to develop. We would live without feeling anything; we would die without having lived. Our total happiness would consist in not knowing our misery. There would be neither goodness in our hearts nor morality in our actions, and we would never have enjoyed the soul's most delicious feeling, which is love of virtue.

[Certainly the term *human race* suggests only a purely collective idea which assumes no real union among the individuals who constitute it. Let us add to it, if you wish, this supposition, and conceive of the human race as a moral person having—along with a feeling of common existence which gives it individuality and constitutes it as one—a universal motivation which makes each part act for an end that is general and relative to the whole. Let us conceive that this common feeling is humanity, and that natural law is the active principle of the entire machine. Next let us observe what results from the constitution of man in his relations with his fellow men, and completely to the contrary of what we have supposed, we will find that the development of society stifles humanity in men's hearts by awakening personal interest, and that concepts of the natural law, which should rather be called the law of reason, begin to develop only when the prior development of the passions renders all its precepts impotent. It is apparent from this that the so-called social treaty dictated by nature is a true illusion, since the conditions for it are always either unknown or impracticable, and men must necessarily be in ignorance of them or violate them.[7]

If the general society did exist somewhere other than in the systems of philosophers, it would be, as I have said, a moral being with qualities separate and distinct from those of the particular beings constituting it, somewhat like chemical compounds which have properties that do not belong to any of the elements composing them. There would be a universal language which nature would teach all men and which would be their first means of mutual communication. There would be a kind of central nervous system which would connect all the parts. The public good or ill would not be merely the sum of private goods and ills as in a simple aggregation, but would lie in the liaison uniting them. It would be greater than this sum, and public felicity, far from being based on the happiness of private individuals, would itself be the source of this happiness.]

It is false that in the state of independence, reason leads us to cooperate for the common good out of a perception of our own interest. Far from there being an alliance between private interest and the general good, they are mutually exclusive in the natural order of things, and social laws are a yoke that each wants to impose on the other without having to bear himself. "I am aware that I bring horror and confusion to the human species," says the independent man who is stifled by the wise man, "but either I must be unhappy or I must cause others to be so, and no one is dearer to me than myself.[8] I would try in vain," he might add, "to reconcile my interest with that of another man. Everything you tell me about the advantages of the social law would be fine if while I were scrupulously observing it toward others, I were sure that all of them would observe it toward me. But what assurance of this can you give me, and could there be a worse situation for me than to be exposed to all the ills that stronger men would want to cause me without my daring to make up for it against the weak? Either give me guarantees against all unjust undertakings or do not expect me to refrain from them in turn. You try vainly to tell me that in renouncing the duties that natural law imposes on me, I deprive myself at the same time of its rights and that my violence will justify every violence that others would like to use against me. I am all the more willing to agree because I fail to see how my moderation could protect me. Furthermore, it will be my business to get the strong on my side, by sharing with them the spoils from the weak. This would be better than justice for my own advantage and for my security." The proof that this is how the enlightened and independent man would have reasoned is that this is how every sovereign society accountable for its behavior only to itself does reason.

What solid answer can be made to such a speech without bringing religion to the aid of morality and making God's will intervene directly to bind the society of men? But the sublime concepts of a God of the wise, the gentle laws of brotherhood He imposes upon us, the social virtues of pure souls— which are the true cult He desires of us—will always escape the multitude. Gods as senseless as itself will always be made for the multitude, which will sacrifice worthless things in honor of these Gods in order to indulge in a thousand horrible, destructive passions. The whole earth would be covered with blood and the human race would soon perish if philosophy and laws did not hold back the furies of fanaticism and if the voice of men was not louder than that of the Gods.

Indeed, if concepts of the great Being and of natural law were innate in every heart, it was surely superfluous to teach them both explicitly. It was teaching us what we already knew, and the way it was done was far better suited to make us forget. If these concepts were not innate, all those to whom God did not give them are excused from knowing them. Ever since special teaching became necessary, each people has its own ideas which it is taught are the only valid ones, and which lead to carnage and murder more often than to harmony and peace.

Let us, therefore, set aside the sacred precepts of the various religions, whose abuse causes as many crimes as their use can avoid, and give back to the philosopher the examination of a question that the theologian has never dealt with except to the detriment of the human race.[9]

But the philosopher will send me back to the human race itself, which alone ought to decide because the greatest good of all is the only passion it has. He will tell me that the individual should address himself to the general will in order to find out to what extent he should be man, citizen, subject, father, child, and when it is suitable for him to live and to die.[10] "I admit that I see in this the rule that I can consult, but I do not yet see," our independent man will say, "the reason for subjecting myself to this rule. It is not a matter of teaching me what justice is, but of showing me what interest I have in being just." Indeed, no one will deny that the general will in each individual is a pure act of the understanding, which reasons in the silence of the passions about what man can demand of his fellow man and what his fellow man has the right to demand of him. But where is the man who can be so objective about himself; and if concern for his self-preservation is nature's first precept, can he be forced to look in this manner at the species in general in order to impose on himself duties whose connection with his particular constitution is not evident to him? Don't the preceding objections still exist and doesn't it still remain to be seen how his personal interest requires his submission to the general will?

Furthermore, since the art of generalizing ideas in this way is one of the most difficult and belated exercises of human understanding, will the average man ever be capable of deriving his rules of conduct from this manner of reasoning? And when it would be necessary to consult the general will concerning a particular act, wouldn't it often happen that a well-intentioned man would make a mistake about the rule or its application, and follow only his inclination while thinking that he is obeying the law? What will he do, then, to avoid error? Will he listen to the inner voice? But it is said that this voice is formed only by the habit of judging and feeling within society and according to its laws. It cannot serve, therefore, to establish them. And then it would be necessary that there had never arisen in his heart any of those passions that speak louder than conscience, muffle its timid voice, and cause philosophers to assert that this voice is nonexistent.[11] Will he consult the written principles of right, the social actions of all peoples, the tacit conventions even of the enemies of the human race? The initial difficulty still remains, and it is only from the social order established among us that we derive ideas about the one we imagine. We conceive of the general society on the basis of our particular societies; the establishment of small republics makes us think about the large one, and we do not really begin to become men until after we have been citizens. It is apparent from this what should be thought of those supposed cosmopolites who, justifying their love of the homeland by means of their love of the human race, boast of loving everyone in order to have the right to love no one.

What reasoning demonstrates to us in this regard is perfectly confirmed by the facts, and simply by turning back to very ancient times one easily sees that the healthy ideas of natural right and the brotherhood of all men were disseminated rather late and made such slow progress in the world that it was only Christianity that generalized them sufficiently. And even then the ancient acts of violence, not only against declared enemies but also against anyone who was not a subject of the Empire, can still be found authorized in many respects in the laws of Justinian, so that the humanity of the Romans extended no further than their domination.

Indeed, it was long believed, as Grotius remarks, that it was permissible to rob, pillage, and mistreat foreigners, and especially barbarians, until they were reduced to slavery. This led to the questioning of strangers, without offending them, as to whether they were brigands or pirates, because this trade, far from being ignominious, was then considered honorable. The first heroes, like Hercules and Theseus, who made war on brigands, nonetheless engaged in brigandage themselves, and the Greeks often used the term peace treaties for treaties made between peoples who were not at war. The words foreigners and enemies were long synonymous for several ancient peoples, even among the Latins. *Hostis enim,* says Cicero, *apud majores nostros dicebatur, quem nunc peregrinum dicimus.*[12] Hobbes's mistake, therefore, is not that he established the state of war among men who are independent and have become sociable, but that he supposed this state natural to the species and gave it as the cause of the vices of which it is the effect.

But although there is no natural and general society among men, although men become unhappy and wicked in becoming sociable, although the laws of justice and equality mean nothing to those who live both in the freedom of the state of nature and subject to the needs of the social state, far from thinking that there is neither virtue nor happiness for us and that heaven has abandoned us without resources to the depravation of the species, let us attempt to draw from the ill itself the remedy that should cure it. Let us use new associations to correct, if possible, the defect of the general association. Let our violent speaker himself judge its success.[13] Let us show him in perfected art the reparation of the ills that the beginnings of art caused to nature. Let us show him all the misery of the state he believed happy, all the falseness in the reasoning he believed solid. Let him see the value of good actions, the punishment of bad ones, and the sweet harmony of justice and happiness in a better constituted order of things. Let us enlighten his reason with new insights, warm his heart with new feelings; and let him learn to enlarge upon his being and his felicity by sharing them with his fellow men. If my zeal does not blind me in this undertaking, let us not doubt that with a strong soul and an upright mind, this enemy of the human race will at last abjure his hate along with his errors; that reason which led him astray will bring him back to humanity; that he will learn to prefer his properly understood interest to his apparent interest; that he will become good, virtuous, sensitive, and finally—to sum it all up—rather than the ferocious brigand he wished to become, the most solid support of a well-ordered society.

Chapter III: On the Fundamental Compact[14]

Man was/is born free, and nevertheless everywhere he is in chains. One who believes himself the master of others is nonetheless a greater slave than they. How did this change occur? No one knows. What can make it legitimate? It is not impossible to say.[15] If I were to consider only force, as others do, I would say that as long as the people is constrained to obey and does so, it does well; as soon as it can shake off the yoke and does so, it does even better. For in recovering its freedom by means of the same right used to steal it, either the people is well justified in taking it back, or those who took it away were not justified in doing so. But the social order is a sacred right that serves as a basis for all the others. However, this right does not have its source in nature; it is therefore based on a convention. The problem is to know what this convention is and how it could have been formed.

As soon as man's needs exceed his faculties and the objects of his desire expand and multiply, he must either remain eternally unhappy or seek a new form of being from which he can draw the resources he no longer finds in himself. As soon as obstacles to our self-preservation prevail, by their resistance, over the force each individual can use to conquer them, the primitive state can no longer subsist and the human race would perish if art did not come to nature's rescue. Since man cannot engender new forces but merely unite and direct existing ones, he has no other means of self-preservation except to form, by aggregation, a sum of forces that can prevail over the resistance; set them to work by a single motivation; make them act conjointly; and direct them toward a single object. This is the fundamental problem which is solved by the institution of the State.

If, then, these conditions are combined and everything that is not of the essence of the social compact is set aside, one will find that it can be reduced to the following terms: "Each of us puts his will, his goods, his force, and his person in common, under the direction of the general will, and in a body we all receive each member as an inalienable part of the whole."

Instantly, in place of the private person of each contracting party, this act of association produces a moral and collective body, composed of as many members as there are voices in the assembly, and to which the common self gives formal unity, life, and will. This public person, formed thus by the union of all the others, generally assumes the name body politic, which its members call *State* when it is passive, *Sovereign* when active, *Power* when comparing it to similar bodies. As for the members themselves, they take the name *People* collectively, and individually are called *Citizens* as members of the City or participants in the sovereign authority, and *Subjects* as subject to the laws of the State. But these terms, rarely used with complete precision, are often mistaken for one another, and it is enough to know how to distinguish them when the meaning of discourse so requires.

This formula shows that the primitive act of confederation includes a reciprocal engagement between the public and private individuals, and that each individual, contracting with himself so to speak, finds that he is doubly engaged, namely toward private individuals as a member of the sovereign and toward the sovereign as a member of the State. But it must be noted that the maxim of civil right that no one can be held responsible for engagements toward himself cannot be applied here, because there is a great difference between being obligated to oneself, or to a whole of which one is a part. It must further be noted that the public deliberation that can obligate all of the subjects to the sovereign—due to the two different relationships in which each of them is considered—cannot for the opposite reason obligate the sovereign toward itself, and that consequently it is contrary to the nature of the body politic for the sovereign to impose on itself a law that it cannot break. Since the sovereign can only be considered in a single relationship, it is then in the situation of a private individual contracting with himself. It is apparent from this that there is not, nor can there be, any kind of fundamental law that is obligatory for the body of people. This does not mean that this body cannot perfectly well enter an engagement toward another, at least insofar as this is not contrary to its nature, because with reference to the foreigner, it becomes a simple being or individual.

As soon as this multitude is thus united in a body, one could not harm any of its members without attacking the body in some part of its existence, and it is even less possible to harm the body without the members feeling the effects. For in addition to the common life in question, all risk also that part of themselves which is not currently at the disposition of the sovereign and which they enjoy in safety only under public protection.[16] Thus duty and interest equally obligate the two contracting parties to be of mutual assistance, and the same persons should seek to combine in this double relationship all the advantages that are dependent on it. But there are some distinctions to be made insofar as the sovereign, formed solely by the private individuals composing it, never has any interest contrary to theirs, and as a consequence the sovereign power could never need a guarantee toward the private individuals, because it is impossible for the body ever to want to harm its members. The same is not true of the private individuals with reference to the sovereign, for despite the common interest, nothing would answer for their engagements to the sovereign if it did not find ways to be assured of their fidelity. Indeed, each individual can, as a man, have a private will contrary to or differing from the general will he has as a citizen. His absolute and independent existence can bring him to view what he owes the common cause as a free contribution, the loss of which will harm others less than its payment burdens him; and considering the moral person of the State as an imaginary being because it is not a man, he might wish to enjoy the rights of the citizen without wanting to fulfill the duties of a subject, an injustice whose spread would soon cause the ruin of the body politic.

In order for the social contract not to be an ineffectual formula, therefore, the sovereign must have some guarantees, independently of the consent of the private individuals, of their engagements toward the common cause. The oath is ordinarily the first of such guarantees, but since it comes from a totally different order of things and since each man, according to his inner maxims, modifies to his liking the obligation it imposes on him, it is rarely relied on in political institutions; and it is with reason that more real assurances, derived from the thing itself, are preferred. So the fundamental compact tacitly includes this engagement, which alone can give force to all the others: that whoever refuses to obey the general will shall be constrained to do so by the entire body. But it is important here to remember carefully that the particular, distinctive character of this compact is that the people contracts only with itself; that is, the people in a body, as sovereign, with the private individuals composing it, as subjects—a condition that creates all the ingenuity and functioning of the political machine, and alone renders legitimate, reasonable, and without danger engagements that without it would be absurd, tyrannical, and subject to the most enormous abuse.

This passage from the state of nature to the social state produces a remarkable change in man, by substituting justice for instinct in his behavior and giving his actions moral relationships which they did not have before. Only then, when the voice of duty replaces physical impulse, and right replaces appetite, does man, who until that time only considered himself, find that he is forced to act upon other principles and to consult his reason before heeding his inclinations. But although in this state he deprives himself of several advantages given him by nature, he gains such great ones, his faculties are exercised and developed, his ideas broadened, his feelings ennobled, and his whole soul elevated to such a point that if the abuses of this new condition did not often degrade him even beneath the condition he left, he ought ceaselessly to bless the happy moment that tore him away from it forever, and that changed him from a stupid, limited animal into an intelligent being and a man.

Let us reduce the pros and cons to easily compared terms. What man loses by the social contract is his natural freedom and an unlimited right to everything he needs; what he gains is civil freedom and the proprietorship of everything he possesses. In order not to be mistaken in these estimates, one must distinguish carefully between natural freedom, which is limited only by the force of the individual, and civil freedom, which is limited by the general will; and between possession, which is only the effect of force or the right of the first occupant, and property, which can only be based on a legal title.

On Real Estate

Each member of the community gives himself to it at the moment of its formation, just as he currently is—both himself and all his force, which includes the goods he holds. It is not that by this act possession, in changing hands, changes its nature and becomes property in the hands of the sovereign. But as the force of the State is incomparably greater than that of each private individual, public possession is by that very fact stronger and more irrevocable, without being more legitimate, at least in relation to foreigners. For in relation to its members, the State is master of all their goods through a solemn convention, the most sacred right known to man. But with regard to other States, it is so only through the right of the first occupant, which it derives from the private individuals, a right less absurd, less odious than that of conquest and yet which, when well examined, proves scarcely more legitimate.

So it is that the combined and contiguous lands of private individuals become public territory, and the right of sovereignty, extending from the subjects to the ground they occupy, comes to include both property and persons, which places those who possess land in a greater dependency and turns even their force into security for their loyalty. This advantage does not appear to be well known to ancient kings, who seem to have considered themselves leaders of men rather than masters of the country. Thus they only called themselves Kings of the Persians, the Scythians, the Macedonians, whereas ours more cleverly call themselves Kings of France, Spain, England. By thus holding the land, they are quite sure to hold its inhabitants.

What is admirable in this alienation is that far from plundering private individuals of their goods, by accepting them the community thereby only assures them of legitimate disposition, changes usurpation into a true right, and use into property. Then, with their title respected by all the members of the State and maintained with all its force against foreigners, through a transfer that is advantageous to the community and even more so to themselves, they have, so to speak, acquired all they have given—an enigma easily explained by the distinction between the rights of the sovereign and of the proprietor to the same resource.

It can also happen that men start to unite before possessing anything, and that subsequently taking over a piece of land sufficient for all, they use it in common or else divide it among themselves either equally or according to certain proportions established by the sovereign. But however the acquisition is made, the right of each private individual to his own goods is always subordinate to the community's right to all, without which there would be neither solidity in the social bond nor real force in the exercise of sovereignty.

I shall end this chapter with a comment that should serve as the basis of the whole social system. It is that rather than destroying natural equality, the fundamental compact on the contrary substitutes a moral and legitimate equality for whatever physical inequality nature may have placed between men, and that although they may be naturally unequal in force or in genius, they all become equal through convention and by right.

Chapter IV: What Sovereignty Consists of and What Makes it Inalienable[17]

There is, therefore, in the State, a common force that supports it and a general will that directs this force, and the application of the one to the other constitutes sovereignty. It is apparent from this that the sovereign is by its nature only a moral person, that it has only an abstract and collective existence, and that the idea attributed to this word cannot be likened to that of a simple individual. But since this is one of the most important propositions in the whole matter of political right, let us try to make it clearer.

I believe I can establish as an incontestable maxim that the general will alone can guide the forces of the State according to the end for which it was instituted, which is the common good. For if the opposition of private interests made the establishment of civil societies necessary, it is the agreement of these same interests that made it possible. It is what these different interests have in common that forms the social bond, and if there were not some point at which all these interests are in agreement, society could not exist. Now since the will always tends toward the good of the being who wills, since the private will always has as its object private interest and the general will common interest, it follows that this last alone is or ought to be the true motivation of the social body.

I agree that it is possible to question whether a private will could agree in all things with the general will, and consequently, assuming that such a private will existed, whether the entire direction of the public force could without drawback be confided to it. But without anticipating the solutions to this question that I shall give later, everyone should see by this time that a private will substituted for the general will is superfluous when they agree and harmful when they are opposed. One should also see that such a supposition is absurd and impossible by the nature of things, because private interest always tends toward preferences and public interest toward equality.

Furthermore, even if the two wills were found to be momentarily in agreement, one could never be sure that this agreement would last through the following moment and that no opposition would ever arise between them. The order of human things is subject to so many revolutions, and ways of thinking as well as ways of being changed so easily, that it would be foolhardy to affirm that one will want tomorrow what one wants today; and if the general will is less subject to this inconstancy, nothing can protect the private will from it. Thus, even if the social body could say at a given time, "I now want everything that a particular man wants," it could never say in speaking about the same man, "What he will want tomorrow I shall still want." Now the general will that should direct the State is not that of a past time but of the present moment, and the true characteristic of sovereignty is that there is always agreement on time, place, and effect between the direction of the general will and the use of public force, an agreement one can no longer be sure of as soon as another will, whatever it may be, commands this force. It is true that in a well-regulated State, an act of the will of the people can always be inferred to continue in effect as long as the people does not destroy it by a contrary act. But it is always by virtue of current, tacit consent that the prior act continues to be in effect. The conditions necessary in order to presume this consent will be seen in what follows.

Just as the action of the soul on the body with respect to man's constitution is unfathomable in philosophy, so the action of the general will on the public force with respect to the constitution of the State is unfathomable in politics. Here, all legislators have gone astray. In what follows I shall present the best means that have been used for this, and I shall only trust evaluation based on reasoning insofar as this is justified by experience. If willing and doing are the same for every free being, and if the will of such a being measures exactly the amount of his force that he uses to accomplish it, it is evident that in everything that does not go beyond the public power, the State would always faithfully execute everything that the sovereign wills just the way it is willed—provided that the will was as simple an act and the action as immediate an effect of this same will in the civil body as they are in the human body.

But even if the bond of which I speak were as well established as possible, all the difficulties would not disappear. The works of men—always less perfect than those of nature—never go so directly toward their end. In politics as in mechanics one cannot avoid acting more weakly or more slowly, and losing force or time. The general will is rarely the will of all, and the public force is always less than the sum of the private forces, so that in the mechanism of the State there is an equivalent of friction in machines, which one must know how to reduce to the least possible amount and which must at least be calculated and subtracted in advance from the total force, so that the means used will be exactly proportionate to the effect desired. But without going into this difficult research which constitutes the science of the legislator, let us finish determining the idea of the civil State.

Chapter V: False Concepts of the Social Bond[18]

There are a thousand ways to bring men together; there is only one way to unite them. That is why in this work I give only one method for the formation of political societies, although in the multitude of aggregations that now exist under this name, there may not even be two that were formed in the same manner and not one according to the manner I establish. But I seek right and reason, and do not argue over facts. Using these rules, let us try to find out how one should judge other paths to civil association, such as the ones supposed by most of our writers.

1. It is readily conceived that the natural authority of the father of the family over his children extends even beyond their weakness and need, and that as they continue to obey him, they end up doing through habit and gratitude what they did at first through necessity; and the bonds that can unite the family are easy to see. But that when the father dies, one of the brothers usurps from brothers of comparable age, and even from outsiders, the power that the father had over all, is without either reason or foundation. For the natural rights of age, force, paternal tenderness, and the duties of filial gratitude are all lacking in this new order, and the brothers are imbeciles or unnatural to subject their children to the yoke of a man who, according to the natural law, should give every preference to his own. One no longer sees in this situation the ties that unite leader and members. Force acts alone and nature no longer speaks.

Let us stop for a moment on this parallel emphasized by so many authors. First, even if there were as many similarities between the State and the family as they claim, it would not necessarily follow that the rules of conduct appropriate to one of these two societies would be suited to the other. They differ too much in size to be administered in the same way, and there will always be a very great difference between household government, where the father sees everything for himself, and civil government, where the leader sees almost nothing except through the eyes of others. For things to become equal in this respect, the talents, force, and faculties of the father would have to increase in relation to the size of his family, and the soul of a powerful monarch would have to be, compared to that of the ordinary man, what the extent of his empire is to the inheritance of a private individual.

But how could the government of the State be like that of the family, whose principle is so different? Because the father is physically stronger than his children, paternal power is correctly thought to be established by nature for as long as they need his help. In the large family, all of whose members are naturally equal, political authority—purely arbitrary as regards its institution—can only be founded on conventions, and the magistrate can only command the citizen by virtue of the laws. The father's duties are dictated by natural feelings, and in such a way that he can rarely disobey. Leaders have no similar rule and are not really obligated to the people except for what they have promised to do, which the people has the right to require them to carry out. Another even more important difference is that since the children have nothing except what they receive from the father, it is evident that all property rights belong to, or emanate from, him. It is just the opposite in the large family, where the general administration is only established in order to assure private possession, which is antecedent to it. The main object of the entire household's work is to preserve and increase the father's patrimony, so that some day he can divide it among his children without impoverishing them, whereas the prince's wealth, far from adding anything to the welfare of private individuals, almost always costs them their peace and plenty. Finally, the small family is destined to die out and to split up someday into several other similar families, whereas the large one is made to last always in the same state. The former must increase in order to multiply, whereas not only does it suffice for the latter to preserve itself, but it can even be proved that all growth is more harmful than useful to it.

For several reasons derived from the nature of things, the father should command in the family. First, the authority of the father and mother should not be equal; rather there must be a single government, and when opinions are divided, there must be a dominant voice that decides. Second, however slight the incapacitations peculiar to the wife are thought to be, since they are always an inactive period for her, this is sufficient reason to exclude her from primacy, because when the balance is perfectly equal, the smallest thing is enough to tip it. Furthermore, the husband should oversee his wife's conduct, because it is important to him that the children he is forced to recognize do not belong to anyone other than himself. The wife, who has no such thing to fear, does not have the same right over her husband. Third, children should obey their father, at first through necessity, later through gratitude. After having their needs met by him for half their lives, they should devote the other half to attending to his needs. Fourth, as regards domestic servants, they too owe him their services in return for the livelihood he gives them, unless they break the exchange when it no longer suits them. I do not speak of slavery, because it is contrary to nature and nothing can authorize it.

Nothing of this kind exists in political society. Far from the leader's having a natural interest in the happiness of private individuals, it is not unusual for him to seek his own happiness in their misery. Is the crown hereditary? Often a child is in command of men.* Is it elective? Elections present a thousand drawbacks. And in either case all the advantages of paternity are lost. If you have only one leader, you are at the discretion of a master who has no reason to love you. If you have several, you must simultaneously bear their tyranny and their dissensions. In short, abuses are inevitable and their consequences disastrous in all societies, where the public interest and the laws have no natural force and are continuously assailed by the personal interest and passions of leader and members.

Although the functions of the father of a family and of the prince should be directed toward the same goal, the paths they take are so different, their duties and rights are so dissimilar, that one cannot confuse them without

---

*French law on the coming of age of kings proves that very sensible men and long experience have taught peoples that it is a greater misfortune to be governed by regencies than by children.

forming the most erroneous ideas about the principles of society, and without making mistakes that are fatal to the human race. Indeed, while nature's voice is the best advice a father can heed to fulfill his duties, for the magistrate it is a false guide, working continuously to separate him from his people, and bringing him sooner or later to his downfall or to that of the State unless he is restrained by prudence or virtue. The only precaution necessary to the father of a family is to protect himself from depravity, and to prevent his natural inclinations from becoming corrupt, whereas it is these very inclinations which corrupt the magistrate. To do what is right, the former need only consult his heart; the latter becomes a traitor the moment he heeds his. Even his own reason should be suspect to him, and he should follow only the public reason, which is the law. Besides, nature has made a multitude of good fathers of families, but I do not know whether human wisdom has ever made a good king. Look in Plato's *Statesman* at the qualities this royal man should have, and cite someone who has had them.[19] Even if one were to suppose that this man had existed and had worn a crown, does reason allow the rule for human governments to be established on a marvel? It is therefore certain that the social bond of the city neither could nor should have been formed by extension of the family bond or on the same model.

2. That a rich and powerful man, having acquired immense possessions in land, might impose laws on those wishing to establish themselves there; that he might allow them to do so only on condition that they recognize his supreme authority and obey all his wishes: I can also conceive of that. But how can I conceive of a treaty that presupposes antecedent rights as the first basis of right; and in this tyrannical act isn't there a double usurpation, namely of the property of the land and of the freedom of its inhabitants? How can a private individual seize an immense territory and deprive the human race of it except through a punishable usurpation, since this act takes away from the rest of the world's inhabitants the dwelling place and foods that nature gives them in common. Let us grant to need and labor the right of the first occupant. Can't we place some limits on this right? Will setting foot on a piece of common ground be sufficient to claim on the spot to be its exclusive proprietor?* Will having the force to drive away all others be sufficient to deprive them of the right to return? To what extent can the act of taking possession establish property? When Nuñez Balboa, standing on the shore, took possession of the South Sea and all of South America in the name of the crown of Castile, was this enough to dispossess all the inhabitants and exclude all the princes of the world? On that basis such ceremonies multiplied rather ineffectually, for all the Catholic King had to do was to take possession of the entire universe all at once from his study, sub-

---

*In a work entitled, I think, the *Dutch Observer,* I saw a rather amusing principle, which is that all land inhabited only by savages should be considered vacant, and that one may legitimately seize it and drive the inhabitants away without doing them any wrong according to natural right.[20]

sequently eliminating from his empire what had been previously possessed by other princes.

What then are the necessary conditions to authorize the right of the first occupant to any land whatsoever? First, that it not yet be inhabited by anyone. Second, that one occupy only the amount one needs for subsistence. Third, that one take possession not by a vain ceremony but by labor and cultivation, the only sign of property that others ought to respect. The rights of a man prior to the state of society cannot go any further, and everything else, being only violence and usurpation contrary to the right of nature, cannot serve as a foundation for social right.

Now, when I have no more land than is necessary to maintain myself, and enough hands to cultivate it, if I give some away there will be less left than I need. What then can I yield to others without taking away my subsistence, or what agreement could I make with them to give them possession of what does not belong to me? As for the conditions of this agreement, it is very evident that they are illegitimate and null for those who are thereby subjected without qualification to the will of another. For besides the fact that such submission is incompatible with the nature of man, and taking away all his freedom of will is taking away all morality from his actions, it is a vain, absurd, impossible convention to stipulate absolute authority on one side, and on the other unlimited obedience. Isn't it clear that one is in no way engaged toward a person from whom one has the right to demand everything, and doesn't this condition alone, incompatible with any other, entail the nullification of the act? For how could my slave have rights against me, since all he has belongs to me, and his right being mine, my right against myself is a meaningless word?

3. That by the right of war, the victor, instead of killing his captives, reduces them to eternal servitude is doubtless profitable for him; but since he does this to them only by right of war, the state of war does not end between the conquered and himself, because it can end only by means of a free and voluntary convention just as it began. If he does not kill them all, this so-called grace is not one in fact when it must be paid for with the freedom that alone can give life a value. Because these captives are more useful to him alive than dead, he lets them live for the sake of his interest, not theirs. They owe him nothing, therefore, except obedience for as long as they are forced to obey him; but the moment the subjugated people can shake off a yoke imposed by force, and get away from its master—that is, from its enemy—if it can do so it should; and in recovering its legitimate freedom, it only makes use of the right of war which does not end so long as the violence authorized by it persists. But how could the state of war serve as the basis of a treaty of union, whose sole object is justice and peace? Can one conceive of anything more absurd than to say, "We are united in a single body since there is still war between us?" But the falseness of this so-called right to kill captives has become so well recognized that there is no longer any civilized man who

dares to exercise or claim this fantastic, barbaric right, nor even a paid sophist who dares to affirm it.

First, then, I say that since the victor does not have the right to put the vanquished to death as soon as they surrender, he cannot establish their slavery on a nonexistent right. Second, that even if the victor had this right and did not take advantage of it, this could never produce a civil state, but merely a modified state of war.

Let us add that if by the word *war* one means public war, this supposes prior societies whose origin is not explained. If one means private war between man and man, this will yield only a master and slaves, never a leader and citizens. And to create this latter relationship, it is necessary to suppose some social convention that makes a body of the people and unites the members among themselves as well as to the leader.

This, in fact, is the true character of the civil State. A people is a people independently of its leader, and if the prince dies, there are still bonds that maintain them as a national body. You will not find anything like this in the principles of tyranny. As soon as the tyrant ceases to exist, everything comes apart and falls into dust, like an oak into a pile of ashes when the fire that has devoured it dies out.[21]

4. That by the lapse of time a violent usurpation finally becomes a legitimate power, that prescription by itself can change a usurper into a supreme magistrate and a crowd of slaves into a national body is something many learned men have dared to affirm, and lacks no authority except that of reason. Far from a long period of violence being able to transform itself by the force of time into a just government, it is on the contrary undebatable that when a people is foolish enough voluntarily to give its leader arbitrary power, this power could not be transmitted to other generations; and its duration alone is enough to make it illegitimate, because one cannot presume that children yet to be born will approve their fathers' extravagance, nor with any justice make them bear the punishment for a fault they did not commit.

We will be told, I know, that as what does not exist has no status, the child yet to be born has no rights, so that his parents can renounce their rights for themselves and for him without his having ground for complaint. But to destroy such a crude sophism, it suffices to distinguish between rights that a son owes only to his father, such as the property of his goods, and rights he owes only to nature and to his status as a man, such as freedom. There is no doubt that by the law of reason a father can alienate the former, of which he is the sole owner, and deprive his children of them. But the same is not true of the latter, which are direct gifts of nature and of which, therefore, no man can deprive them. Let us suppose that a conqueror, clever and zealous for the happiness of his subjects, persuaded them that with one less arm they would be calmer and happier. Would this suffice to obligate all their children in perpetuity to have an arm cut off to fulfill their fathers' engagements?

With respect to the tacit consent invoked as a legitimation of tyranny, it is easy to see that it cannot be presumed even from the longest silence, because in addition to the fear that prevents individuals from protesting against a man who has the public force at his disposal, the people, which can manifest its will only in a body, lacks the power to assemble and declare it. On the contrary, the silence of citizens is enough to reject an unrecognized leader. They must speak, and speak in full freedom, in order to give him authority. Besides, all that is said on this subject by jurists and others who are paid to do so does not prove that the people does not have the right to take back its usurped freedom, but only that it is dangerous to try. It is also something that must never be done when one knows greater evils than having lost one's freedom.

This whole dispute about the social compact seems to me to come down to one very simple question. What can have engaged men to join together voluntarily into a social body if not their common utility? The common utility is therefore the foundation of civil society. Given this, how are legitimate States to be distinguished from forced, unauthorized groupings, if not by considering the object or end of each? If the form of the society tends toward the common good, it follows the spirit of its institution; if it envisages only the interest of the leaders, it is illegitimate by right of reason and humanity. Because even though the public interest might sometimes be consistent with tyranny, this passing consistency could not suffice to authorize a government not based on the principle of the public interest. When Grotius denies that all power is established in favor of the governed, he is only too right with respect to facts, but it is the matter of right with which we are concerned. His only proof is strange; he derives it from the power of a master over his slave, as if one fact could authorize another, and slavery itself were less wicked than tyranny. It is precisely the right of slavery that had to be proved. It is not a matter of what is, but of what is suitable and just; nor of the power one is forced to obey, but of that which one is obligated to recognize.

Chapter VI: On the Respective Rights of the Sovereign and the Citizen[22]

If the common interest is the object of the association, it is clear that the general will should be the rule of the social body's actions. This is the fundamental principle I have tried to establish. Now let us see what power this will should have over private individuals, and how it becomes manifest to everyone.

As the State or City constitutes a moral person whose life consists in the cooperation and union of its members, the first and most important of its concerns is that of its own preservation. This concern requires a universal, compulsory force to move and arrange each part in the manner best suited to the whole. Thus, just as nature gives each man absolute power over his members, the social compact gives the body politic absolute power over its members; and it is the exercise of this same power, directed by the general will, which as I have said bears the name sovereignty.

But since we have to consider, in addition to the public person, the private persons who compose it and whose life and existence are naturally independent of it, this matter requires some discussion.

Everything consists in making a clear distinction between the sovereign's rights over the citizens and those it should respect in them, and between the duties they have to fulfill as subjects and the natural right to which they are entitled as men. It is certain that each person alienates through the social compact only that part of his natural faculties, goods, and freedom whose possession matters to the society.

Thus a citizen owes the State all the services he can render it, and the sovereign, for its part, cannot burden the subjects with any chain that is useless to the community. For under the law of reason nothing is done without a cause, any more than under the law of nature. But one must not confuse what is appropriate with what is necessary, simple duty with narrow right, and what can be required of us with what we should do voluntarily.[23]

The engagements that bind us to the social body are obligatory only because they are mutual, and their nature is such that one cannot work for someone else without at the same time working for oneself. Why is the general will always right, and why do all constantly want the happiness of each, if not because there is no one who does not secretly apply this word *each* to himself, and does not think of himself as he votes for all? Which proves that equality of right, and the concept of justice that flows from it, are derived from each man's preference for himself, and consequently from the nature of man; that the general will, to be truly such, should be general in its object as well as in its essence; that it should come from all to return to all, and that it loses its natural rectitude as soon as it is applied to an individual, determinate subject. Because then, judging what is not ourselves, we have no true principle of equity to guide us.

Indeed, as soon as it is a matter of fact or a particular right concerning a point that has not been regulated by a prior, general convention, the affair is in dispute. It is a lawsuit where the interested private individuals constitute one party and the public the other, but in which I see neither what law must be followed nor what judge should decide. In this case it would be ridiculous to want to turn to an express decision of the general will, which can only be the conclusion of one of the parties and which, for the other party, is consequently only a private will, subject on this occasion to injustice or error. Thus, just as a private will cannot represent the general will, the general will in turn cannot, without changing its nature, become a private will; it cannot pass judgment by name on either a man or a fact. When the people of Athens, for example, appointed or dismissed its leaders, awarded a recompense to one or imposed a fine on another, and by means of a multitude of particular decrees performed indistinguishably all the acts of government, the people then no longer had a general will properly speaking. It no longer acted as sovereign, but as magistrate.

It should be understood from this that what generalizes the public will is not the number of voters, but the common interest that unites them, because in this institution everyone necessarily subjects himself to the conditions he imposes on others, an admirable agreement between interest and justice which confers on common deliberations a quality of equity that vanishes in the discussion of private matters, for want of a common interest that unites and identifies the will of the judge with that of the party.

However one traces the principle, one always reaches the same conclusion, namely that the social compact establishes an equality of right between citizens such that they all engage themselves under the same conditions and should all benefit from the same advantages. Thus, by the very nature of the compact, every act of sovereignty, which is to say every authentic act of the general will, obligates or favors all citizens equally, so that the sovereign knows only the nation as a body and makes no distinctions between any of those who compose it. What really is an act of sovereignty then? It is not an order given by a superior to an inferior, nor a command given by a master to a slave, but a convention between the body of the State and each of its members. A convention that is legitimate, because it has the social contract as a basis; equitable, because it is voluntary and general; useful, because it can have no other object than the good of all; and solid, because it has the public force and the supreme power as guarantees. As long as subjects are subordinated only to such conventions, they do not obey anyone, but solely their own will; and to ask how far the respective rights of the sovereign and of private individuals extend is to ask how far the latter can engage themselves to one another, each to all and all to each.

It follows from this that the sovereign power, albeit entirely absolute, entirely sacred, and entirely inviolable, does not and cannot exceed the limits of the general conventions, and that every man can fully dispose of the part of his goods and freedom that has been left to him by these conventions. So that the sovereign never has the right to burden one private individual more than another, because then the matter becomes individual, and its power is no longer competent.

Once these distinctions are acknowledged, it is so false that the social contract involves any true renunciation on the part of private individuals that their situation, by the effect of this contract, is actually preferable to what it was beforehand; and instead of a simple alienation, they have only exchanged to their advantage an uncertain, precarious mode of existence for another that is better and safer; natural independence for civil freedom, the power to harm others for their personal safety, and their force, which others could overcome, for a right that the social union renders invincible. Their life itself, which they have dedicated to the State, is constantly protected by it; and when they risk or lose it for the State's defense, what are they then doing that they did not do more often and with greater danger in the state of nature when, waging inevitable fights, they defend at the risk of life that which preserves it for them? It is true that everyone has to fight, if need be, for the homeland, but also no one ever has to fight for himself. Don't we still gain by risking, for something that gives us security, a part of what we would have to risk for ourselves as soon as our security is taken away?

Chapter VII: Necessity for Positive Laws[24]

It seems to me that these are the most accurate ideas one can have about the fundamental compact that is the basis of every true body politic; ideas that it was all the more important to develop because, for want of having conceived them clearly, all those who have dealt with this subject have always founded civil government on arbitrary principles which do not flow from the nature of this compact. In what follows, it will be seen how easily the whole political system is deduced from the principles I have just established, and how natural and enlightened its consequences are. But let us finish laying down the foundations of our construction.

Since the social union has a determinate object, its fulfillment must be sought as soon as the union is formed. In order for each person to want to do what he ought to do according to the engagement of the social contract, each must know what it is that he ought to want. What he ought to want is the common good; what he ought to avoid is the public ill. But since the State has only an ideal and conventional existence, its members have no natural, common sensitivity by means of which they are promptly alerted to receive a pleasant impression from what is useful to it and a painful impression as soon as it is harmed. Far from anticipating the ills that attack it, they are rarely in time to effect a remedy when they begin to feel them. Yet these ills must be foreseen long in advance to be avoided or cured. How then could private individuals safeguard the community from ills they can neither see nor feel until they have struck? Besides, how is it possible to be assured that men who are constantly reminded of their primitive condition by nature will never neglect this other, artificial condition whose advantage they can only sense through consequences that are often far removed? Let us assume that they are always subject to the general will. How can this will manifest itself on all occasions? Will it always be evident? Will the illusions of private interest never obscure it? Will the people always remain assembled to declare it, or will they rely for this on private individuals who are ever ready to substitute their own interest? Finally, how will they all act together, how will they organize their affairs, what means of agreement will they have, and how will they divide the common tasks among themselves?

These difficulties, which must have appeared insurmountable, were removed by the most sublime of all human institutions, or rather by a celestial inspiration that taught people to imitate here on earth the immutable decrees of the divinity. By what inconceivable art could the means have been found to subjugate men in order to make them free; to use the goods, the labor, even the life of its members in the service of the State, without forcing and without consulting them; to bind their will by their own consent; to make their agreement predominate over their refusal; and to force them to punish themselves when they do what they did not want? How can it be that all obey while none commands, that they serve and have no master, and are all the freer, in fact, because under what appears as subjugation, no one loses any of his freedom except what would harm the freedom of another. These marvels are the work of the law. It is to law alone that men owe justice and freedom. It is this healthy instrument of the will of all that reestablishes, as a right, the natural equality among men. It is this celestial voice that tells each citizen the precepts of public reason, and teaches him to behave according to the maxims of his own judgment and not to be constantly in contradiction with himself. Laws are the sole motivation of the body politic, which is active and sensitive only through them. Without laws, the newly formed State is only a body without a soul; it exists but cannot act. For it is not enough for everyone to be subject to the general will; to follow it, one must know it. From this arises the necessity for legislation.

Laws are properly speaking only the conditions of the civil association. The people that is subject to the laws ought therefore to be their author, because only those who are forming an association have the right to declare the conditions under which they are willing to be associated. But how will they declare these conditions? Will it be in common accord and by sudden inspiration? Does the body politic have an organ to enunciate its will? Who will give it the necessary foresight to formulate acts and publish them in advance, or how will it pronounce them in time of need? How is it to be expected that a blind multitude, which often does not know what it wants because it rarely knows what is good for it, can formulate and carry out by itself such a difficult undertaking as a system of legislation, which is the most sublime effort of human wisdom and foresight? By itself, the people always wants the good, but by itself it does not always see it. The general will is always right; it is never a question of correcting it. But it is necessary to know how to consult it appropriately. It must be presented with objects as they are, or sometimes as they should appear to be; shown the good path it wants to follow; safeguarded against the seduction of private wills; shown how to assimilate considerations of time and place; taught to weigh the illusion of present, tangible advantages against the danger of remote, hidden ills. Private individuals see the good they reject; the public wants the good it does not see. All are equally in need of guides. The former must be obligated to make their wills conform to their reason; the latter must be taught to know what it wants. Then public enlightenment will result in the virtue of private individuals; and this union of understanding and will in the social body, from the complete cooperation of the parts and the greatest force of the whole. From this arises the necessity for a legislator.

BOOK II

ESTABLISHMENT OF THE LAWS

Chapter I: End of Legislation[25]

Through the social compact, we have given the body politic existence and life; the issue now is to give it movement and will through legislation. For the original act which forms and unites this body does not thereby determine anything about what it should do to preserve itself. This is the noble objective to which the science of legislation is devoted. But what is this science? Where should one look for a genius who knows it, and what virtues are necessary for the individual who dares to practice it? This research is imposing and difficult; it is even discouraging for anyone who hopes to see the emergence of a well-instituted State.

Chapter II: On the Legislator[26]

Indeed, the discovery of the best rules of society that are suited to nations would require a superior intelligence, who knew all of men's needs but felt none of them; who had no relationship to our nature, yet saw all the relationships suited to it; whose happiness was independent of us, yet who was nevertheless willing to attend to ours. In short, a God would be needed to give the human race good laws; and just as herdsmen are of a species superior to the livestock they tend, so the shepherds of men, who are their leaders, ought to be of a more excellent species than the people.

This reasoning, used by Plato with respect to right in defining the civil or royal man he seeks in the *Statesman,* Caligula used in fact, according to Philo, to prove that the masters of the world were of a nature superior to the rest of mankind. But if it is true that a great prince is a rare man, what about a great legislator? For the former only has to follow the model that the latter should propose. The latter is the mechanic who invents the machine; the former is only the workman who puts it together or starts it running. At the birth of societies says Montesquieu, the leaders of republics create the institutions; thereafter it is the institutions that form the leaders of republics.

One who thinks he is capable of forming a people should feel that he can, so to speak, change human nature. He must transform each individual, who by himself is a perfect and solitary whole, into a part of a larger whole from which this individual receives, in a sense, his life and his being. He must in a sense mutilate man's constitution in order to strengthen it; substitute a partial and moral existence for the physical and independent existence we have all received from nature. He must, in short, take away all man's own, innate forces in order to give him forces that are foreign to him and that he cannot make use of without the help of others. Now the more these natural forces are dead and destroyed, and the acquired ones great and lasting, the more the institution as well is solid and perfect. So that if each citizen can do nothing except with all the others, and if the force acquired by the whole is equal or superior to the sum of the natural forces of all the individuals, it may be said that legislation has reached its highest possible point of perfection.

The legislator is an extraordinary man in the State in all ways. If he should be so by his talents, he is no less so by his function. It is not magistracy; it is not sovereignty. This function, which constitutes the republic, does not enter into its constitution. In a way, it is a particular and almost divine activity that has nothing in common with human dominion. For if one who has authority over men should not have authority over laws, one who has authority over laws should also not have authority over men. Otherwise his laws, being made to serve his passions, would often only perpetuate his injustices, and he could never avoid having private views alter the sanctity of his work. Thus the variations of written law prove the private motives that dictated the decisions: an immense, formless, contradictory compilation; the work of an imbecilic emperor, a fallen woman, and a corrupt magistrate who published a law to authorize each violent act he wanted to commit.[27]

When Lycurgus wanted to give his homeland laws, he began by abdicating sovereignty. It was the custom of most Greek cities to entrust the drafting of their laws to foreigners. During its finest period, Rome revived in its midst all the crimes of tyranny, and nearly perished as a result of combining legislative authority and sovereign power in the same hands.

Not that it was ever imagined that the will of one man could become law without the consent of the people. But how can this consent be refused to someone who is known to be the master and in whom are combined the public confidence and force. Reasonable people have difficulty making themselves heard; weak people dare not speak; and the forced silence of subjects has so often passed for tacit approval that since the Roman Emperors, who under the name tribunes arrogated to themselves all the rights of the people, men have dared to place the will of the prince above the law, even though the law is the only source of his authority.[28] But we are dealing with rights and not abuses.

He who drafts the laws, therefore, does not or should not have any legislative power. And the people itself cannot divest themselves of this supreme right, because according to the fundamental compact only the general will obligates private individuals, and one can never be assured that a private will is in conformity with the general will without submitting it to the free vote of the people.

If it is said that once an entire people has subjected itself voluntarily, solemnly, and without constraint to one man, all the objects of this man's will should, by virtue of this subjection, be considered as so many acts of the general will, one states a sophism which I have already refuted. I shall add that the voluntary and supposed subjection of the people is always conditional; that it is not given for the prince's benefit but for its own; that if each private individual promises to obey without reservation, it is for the good of all; that in this situation the prince also makes engagements on which those of the people depend, and that even under the most absolute despotism, he cannot break his oath without at the same moment relieving his subjects from theirs.

Even if a people were stupid enough to stipulate nothing in exchange for its obedience except the right to command it, this right would still be conditional in nature. To clarify this truth, it must be carefully noted that those who claim that a gratuitous promise rigorously obligates the one who makes it, nonetheless distinguish with care between promises that are purely gratuitous and those that contain some tacit, but obvious, conditions. In the latter case, they all agree that the validity of promises depends on the execution of the implied condition; for example, when a man engages himself in the service of another, he obviously assumes that this other man will give him food. Similarly, a people that chooses one or several leaders for itself and promises to obey them, obviously assumes that its freedom, which is thereby alienated, will only be used to the people's own advantage; for without this the people would be insane and its engagements null. With regard to the same alienation extorted by force, I have already shown that it is null, and that one is obligated to obey force only as long as one is constrained to do so.

It is, therefore, always necessary to know whether the conditions are fulfilled and consequently whether the will of the prince is really the general will, a question of which the people is the sole judge. Thus the laws are like pure gold, which cannot be denatured by any possible operation and which the first test promptly returns to its natural form. Moreover, it is contrary to the nature of will, which has no dominion over itself, to engage itself for the future. One can obligate oneself to do, but not to will; and there is a great difference between executing what one has promised, because one has promised it, and continuing to will it, even when one has not previously promised to do so. Today's law should not be an act of yesterday's general will, but of today's, and we have engaged ourselves to do not what everyone has willed, but what everyone now wills, on the understanding that the sovereign, whose resolutions as sovereign concern only itself, is always free to change them. It follows from this that when the law speaks in the name of the people, it is in the name of the people at present and not that of former times. Even existing laws only have lasting authority insofar as the people, being free to revoke them, nonetheless does not do so, which proves current consent. Nor can it be doubted that in the assumed case, the public will of the legitimate prince obligates private individuals for as long as the nation, being able to assemble and oppose it without any obstacle, gives no sign of disavowal.

These clarifications show that since the general will is the continuing bond of the body politic, the legislator is never allowed, whatever his previous authorization might be, to act otherwise than by directing this same will by persuasion, nor to prescribe anything to private individuals that has not first received the sanction of general consent, for fear of destroying from the outset the very essence of the thing one wants to form, and of breaking the social tie in trying to strengthen the society.

Therefore, I see two things together in the work of legislation that seem mutually exclusive: an undertaking beyond all human force and, to execute it, an authority that amounts to nothing.

Another difficulty deserves attention. Wise men often made the mistake of using their own language rather than that of the common people; thus the people never understood them. There are a thousand kinds of ideas that have only one language and are impossible to translate for the people. Overly general views and overly remote objects are equally beyond its grasp. For example, each individual, seeing no other aspect of government than his private happiness, has difficulty perceiving the advantages he should obtain from the continual deprivations imposed by good laws. In order for an emerging people to feel the noble maxims of justice and the fundamental rules of statecraft, the effect would have to become the cause; the social spirit, which should be the result of the institution, would have to preside over the founding of the institution itself, and men would have to be prior to laws what they should become by means of laws. Since the legislator is unable to use either force or reasoning, he must necessarily have recourse to another order of authority, which can win over without violence and persuade without convincing.

This is what has always forced the fathers of nations to have recourse to celestial intervention and to attribute their own wisdom to the Gods; so that the peoples, subjected to the laws of the State as to those of nature, and recognizing the same power in the formation of the physical body as in that of the moral body, might obey with freedom and bear with docility the yoke of public felicity. It is this sublime reason, which rises above the grasp of common men, whose decisions the legislator places in the mouths of the immortals, in order to subjugate by means of divine authority those who cannot be moved by human prudence. But it is not every man who can make the Gods speak or be believed when he declares himself their interpreter. The grandeur of the things said in their name has to be sustained by superhuman eloquence and vigor. The fire of enthusiasm should be combined with profundity of wisdom and constancy of virtue. In short, the legislator's great soul is the true miracle that should prove his mission. Any man can engrave stone tablets, buy an oracle, pretend to have a secret relationship with some divinity, train a bird to talk in his ear, or find some other crude way to impress the people. One who knows only that much might even assemble, by chance, a crowd of madmen, but he will never found an empire, and his extravagant work will soon die along with him. For if false tricks can form a fleeting bond, wisdom alone can make it durable. The Jewish law, which is still in existence, and the law of the son of Ishmael, which has ruled half the world for eleven centuries, still bear witness today to the great men who formulated them; and whereas proud philosophy or blind partisan spirit regards them merely as lucky imposters, the true political theorist admires in their institutions that great and powerful genius which presides over lasting establishments.

One must not conclude from all this, as Warburton does, that politics and religion can have a common object, but rather that one sometimes serves as an instrument of the other. [Everyone is quite aware of the usefulness of political union for making certain opinions permanent and maintaining them as a body of doctrine and as a sect. And as for the contribution of religion to the civil establishment, one also sees that it is no less useful to be able to give the moral tie an internal force that reaches into the soul and is always independent of goods, of misfortunes, of life itself, and of all human events.

I don't believe that this chapter contradicts what I said before concerning the limited usefulness of the oath in the contract of society, for there is a great difference between remaining faithful to a State solely because one has sworn to do so, or because one considers its institution to be divine and indestructible.]

Chapter III: On the People To Be Founded[29]

Although I am dealing here with right and not with expediency, I cannot refrain from taking a passing glance at those matters of expediency which are indispensable to every good institution.

Just as a skillful architect, before putting up a building, observes and tests the ground to see whether it can bear the weight, so the wise founder does not start by drafting laws at random, but first examines whether the people for whom he intends them is suited to bear them. For this reason, Plato refused to give laws to the Arcadians and Cyrenians, knowing that both were rich and could not tolerate equality. For this reason there were good laws and wicked men in Crete, because Minos had disciplined only a people full of vices. A thousand nations that have long flourished on earth could never have tolerated good laws, and even those that could were only so disposed for a very short time during their entire existence. Peoples, like men, are easy to handle only in their youth. They become incorrigible as they grow older. Once customs are established and prejudices have taken root, it is a dangerous and foolhardy undertaking to want to touch them. People cannot even tolerate talk of making them happy, like those stupid and cowardly patients who tremble at the sight of a doctor. There are few nations debased by tyranny that care at all about freedom, and those that would still want it are no longer in condition to endure it.

To be sure, just as men's minds are unhinged and their memories of the past erased by certain illnesses, so there sometimes occur, during the lifetime of States, violent periods when revolutions have the same effect on peoples as do certain crises on individuals; when horror of the past is equivalent to amnesia, and when the State, set afire by civil wars, is reborn so to speak from its ashes and resumes the vigor of youth by escaping from death's clutches. Sparta in the time of Lycurgus and Rome after the Tarquins were like this; and among us so were Switzerland and Holland after the expulsion of the tyrants.

But these events are rare; they are exceptions that can always be explained by the particular constitution of the exceptional State. In general, peoples that are worn out by a long enslavement and the resulting vices lose both the love of country and the sentiment of happiness. They console themselves for their misfortune by imagining it is impossible to be better off. They live together without any real union, like men grouped on the same piece of land but separated by deep ravines. Their misery is not in the least obvious to them because ambition blinds them and no one looks at the position he is in, but rather at the one to which he aspires.

A people in this state is no longer fit for a healthy institution, because its will is no less corrupt than its constitution. It has nothing more to lose; it cannot gain anything more. Dazed by enslavement, it scorns the good things it does not know. Disturbances can destroy it, but revolutions cannot reestablish it, and as soon as its chains are broken, it falls apart and no longer exists. Thus, henceforth it must have a master, and never a liberator.

A people that is not yet corrupt can have vices in its size that are not in its substance. Let me explain.

Just as nature has set limits to the stature of a well formed man, outside of which there are only giants or dwarfs, so with regard to the best constitution of a State there are limits to the dimensions it should have, in order that it be neither too large to be well governed, nor too small to be self-sustaining. It is hard to imagine anything more foolish than the maxims of those conquering nations that believed they always increased their power by extending their territory beyond all measure. It is beginning to be obvious that every body politic has a maximum force which it cannot exceed, and of which it often falls short by growing larger. But perhaps it is not yet sufficiently obvious that the more the social bond stretches, the looser it becomes, and that in general a small State is always proportionately stronger than a large one.

Only a glance at history is needed to be convinced of this maxim by experience, and a thousand reasons can prove it. First, administration becomes more difficult over long distances, as a weight becomes heavier at the end of a large lever. It also becomes more burdensome as the number of levels multiplies, because each city has its own administration paid for by the people; each district has one, again paid for by the people; next, each province; then, the large-scale governments—the satrapies and viceroyalties—that cost more the higher up one goes. Finally, there is the supreme administration which crushes everything. There barely remain resources for emergencies, and when it is necessary to have recourse to them, the State is always on the brink of ruin. The government has less vigor and speed to enforce the laws, forestall harassment, correct abuses, and repress seditious undertakings that may occur in distant places. The people has less affection for leaders it never sees, for the homeland which is like the whole world in its eyes, and for its fellow citizens most of whom are foreigners to it. The same laws cannot be suited to such a variety of nations, which have different mores, live in contrasting climates, and cannot tolerate the same form of government. Different laws only produce discord and confusion among peoples who, living under the same leaders and in constant communication, continually move to each other's areas and, being subjected to other customs, are never sure whether their patrimony is really theirs. Talents are buried, virtues unknown, vice unpunished in this multitude of men who do not know one another and who are gathered together in one place by the location of the administration. Leaders overburdened with work see nothing by themselves. Finally, all the public attention is absorbed by the steps that must be taken to maintain everywhere the general authority, which so many distant officials always want to avoid or abuse. Nothing is left for the people's happiness, and there is barely anything left for its defense if necessary. And thus a State that is too big for its constitution always perishes, crushed by its own weight.

On the other hand, the State ought to procure a sufficient basis to be solid and withstand the upheavals it is sure to go through and the efforts it will be forced to sustain, for all peoples have a kind of centrifugal force by which they constantly act upon each other and tend to grow at the expense of their neighbors. Thus the weak risk being rapidly swallowed up, and one cannot hope to preserve oneself except by establishing a sort of equilibrium with all the others which approximately equalizes the pressure.

It is apparent from this that there are reasons to expand and reasons to shrink; and it is not the least of the political theorist's talents to find among these reasons the proportion most advantageous to the preservation of the

State. In general it can be said that the former, being purely external and relative, should always be subordinated to the latter, which are interior and absolute. For a strong, healthy constitution is the first thing that must be sought, and one should rely more on the vigor born of a good government than on the resources furnished by a large territory.

Besides, there have been States so constituted that the necessity for conquests was in their constitution itself, and that were forced to grow endlessly to maintain themselves. Perhaps they took great pride in this happy necessity, though it showed them, along with the limit of their size, the inevitable moment of their downfall.

In order for the State to be well governed, its size—or, to be more precise, its extent—would have to be measured by the faculties of those who govern it; and given the impossibility that great geniuses will succeed one another endlessly in the government, calculations should be based on average competence.[30] This explains why nations that have grown under illustrious leaders necessarily decline in the hands of the imbeciles who never fail to succeed them, and why if the State is the least bit large, the prince is almost always too small. When, on the contrary, it happens that the State is too small for its leader, which is very rare, it is still badly governed, because the leader, always pursuing his grand views and ambitious plans, forgets the people's interests and by misusing his excessive talents, makes it no less unhappy than does a stupid leader who is limited by his lack of talents. The drawback of the administration of a monarchy, even one that is well regulated, is most strongly felt when it is hereditary and the leader is not chosen by the people but determined by birth. The kingdom would, so to speak, have to expand or shrink with each reign depending on the competence of the prince. In contrast, since the talents of a senate are more stable, the State can have invariable boundaries without causing the administration to suffer thereby.

Moreover, a fundamental rule for every well-constituted and legitimately governed society would be that all the members could be easily assembled every time this would be necessary, for it will be seen later that assemblies by deputation can neither represent the body nor receive from it sufficient powers to make laws in its name as sovereign.[31] From this it follows that the State ought to be limited to one town at the most; and that if there are several, the capital will always be sovereign in fact and the others subjects— a kind of constitution in which tyranny and abuse are inevitable.

It must be noted that a body politic can be measured in two ways, namely by the extent of its territory or by the number of its people. There is a necessary ratio between these two numbers if the State is to be given its true size. For it is the men who make up the State and the land that feeds the men. This ratio consists in there being enough land for the maintenance of its inhabitants and as many inhabitants as can be fed by the land. The maximum force of a given number of people is to be found in this proportion, for if there is too much land, its defense is burdensome, its cultivation inadequate, and its output superfluous; if there is not enough land, the State finds itself dependent on its neighbors for the supplement.

The implications of this important topic would take us too far afield if we were to stop here to consider them. For example, it is certain that one could not calculate arithmetically a fixed ratio between the amount of land and the number of men that are mutually sufficient, as much because of differences in qualities of the terrain, its degrees of fertility, the nature of its products, and the influence of climate, as because of differences noted in the temperaments of the men who inhabit them, some of whom consume little in a fertile country, others a great deal on more sterile soil. Moreover, attention must be paid to the greater or lesser fecundity of women, to whatever the country offers that is more or less favorable to population, to the numbers that the legislator can hope to attract there by means of what he establishes. Hence, the legislator's judgment should not always be based on what he sees, but on what he foresees; nor should he give as much consideration to the present state of the population as to the state it should naturally attain. Finally, there are a thousand occasions when the peculiarities of a place require or permit the inclusion of more or less land than appears necessary. Thus one expands considerably in mountainous country where natural products, namely woods and pastures, require less human labor; where experience shows that women are more fecund than on the plains; and where a large amount of sloping land provides only a small horizontal area, which is all that can be counted on for vegetation. On the contrary, it is possible to shrink by the sea, even on nearly barren rocks and sand, because fishing can substitute substantially for products of the land; because men should be gathered more closely together to repulse privateers and pirates; and because it is, in addition, easier to rid the country of surplus inhabitants by means of commerce and colonies.

To these conditions must be added one that cannot substitute for any other, but without which all the rest are useless: the enjoyment of prosperity and profound peace. For the time when a State is organized, like that when a battalion is formed, is the instant when the body is weakest, least capable of resisting, and easiest to destroy. There would be better resistance during absolute disorder than during a moment of ferment, when everyone is concerned about his status rather than the danger. Should a war, famine, or sedition occur in this time of crisis, the State is inevitably overthrown. To be sure, many governments are established during such storms, but then it is these very governments that destroy the State. Usurpers always bring about or choose these times of trouble, taking advantage of public panic to pass destructive laws that the people would never adopt when calm. It can be said that the moment of the founding is one of the surest ways to distinguish the work of a legislator from that of a tyrant.

At the risk of repetition, let us recapitulate what the legislator should consider before undertaking the founding of a people, for these considerations are important if time and authority are not to be used in vain.[32] First, he should not try to change the institution of a people that is already subject to laws, let alone try to restore an institution that has been abolished or to revive worn out mechanisms. For the force of laws is like the flavor of salt. Thus it is possible to create vigor in a people who never had any, but not to restore it in a people who has lost it. I consider this maxim fundamental. Agis tried to revive the discipline of Lycurgus in Sparta; the Maccabees wanted to restore Moses' theocracy in Jerusalem; Brutus wanted to restore Rome's ancient freedom; Rienzi tried to do the same thing later. All were heroes, even the last one for a brief time in his life. All died in the course of their undertaking.

Every large nation is incapable of discipline. A State that is too small lacks stability. But average size sometimes does no more than to combine these two defects.

It is necessary, furthermore, to take the surrounding area into consideration. What enabled the small Greek States to survive was the fact that they were themselves surrounded by other small States, and that all together they were as good as a very big one when they united through common interest. It is an unfortunate position to be between two powerful neighbors who are jealous of each other. It is hard to avoid getting involved in their quarrels and being crushed along with the weaker of the two. Any State that is an enclave within another should be counted as nothing. Any State too big for its inhabitants or overpopulated for its territory is hardly worth more, unless this imbalance is accidental and there is a natural force that returns things to their correct proportion.

Finally, the circumstances must be taken into consideration, for example because one should not talk about rules to starving people, nor about reason to fanatics; and war, which silences existing laws, can hardly allow for their establishment. But famine, frenzy, and war do not last forever. There is scarcely any man or people who will not listen to reason at some better period and some moment of his life. That is the instant that must be seized.

What people, then, is suited for legislation? One that has never yet borne the yoke of laws, that has neither customs nor superstitions that are entrenched, yet is already bound by some union of origin or interest. One that does not risk being crushed by a sudden invasion and can, without becoming involved in its neighbors' quarrels, resist each alone or use the help of one to drive away another. One whose members can all be known to each other, and where it is not necessary to impose on any man a greater burden than a man can bear. One that does not depend on other peoples and on whom no other people depends.* One that is neither rich nor poor and is self-

*If one of two neighboring peoples could not do without the other, the situation would be very hard for the former, but very dangerous for the latter. In such a case, any wise nation will very quickly try to relieve the other of its dependency.

sufficient. In short, one that combines the stability of an ancient people with the docility of a young people. What makes the work of legislation difficult is not so much what must be established as what must be destroyed. And what makes success so rare is the impossibility of finding the simplicity of nature together with the needs of society. All these conditions are hard to find together, I admit; hence one sees few well-constituted States.

Chapter IV: On the Nature of Laws and the Principle of Civil Justice[33]

Whatever is good and in accordance with order is so by the nature of things, independently of all human convention.

All justice comes from God; He alone is its source. But if we knew how to receive it from on high, we would need neither government nor laws. There is without doubt a universal justice for man emanating from reason alone and founded on the simple right of humanity; but to be acknowledged, this justice must be reciprocal. Considering things from a human point of view, the laws of justice are ineffectual between men for want of a natural sanction; they only profit wicked people and burden the just man should the latter observe them toward all men while no one observes them toward him. Therefore, there must be conventions and laws to combine rights with duties and to bring justice back to its object. In the state of nature where everything is common, I owe nothing to those to whom I have promised nothing; I recognize nothing as belonging to someone else except what is useless to me.

But it is important to explain here what I mean by the word law. Because as long as one is satisfied to attach vague, metaphysical ideas to this word, one could know what a law of nature is, yet continue to be ignorant of what a law is in the State.

We have said that the law is a public, solemn act of the general will, and since everyone has subjected himself to this will through the fundamental compact, it is from this compact alone that all law derives its force. But let us try to give a more precise idea of this word *law* taken in the proper, restricted sense relevant to this work.

The substance and form of laws constitute their nature. The form consists of the authority that enacts laws; the substance consists of the thing enacted. The latter, which is the only part considered in this chapter, seems to have been badly understood by those who have discussed laws.

As the thing enacted is necessarily related to the common good, it follows that the object of the law should be general, as is the will dictating it; and it is this double universality which creates the true character of the law. Indeed, when a particular object has different relationships to different individuals, each one having its own will concerning this object, there is no general will that is perfectly unified concerning this individual object.

What do these words *Universality* and *Generality*—which are the same here—signify? The genus considered as an abstraction, or what is suited to the whole in question; and the whole is such only with respect to its parts. That is why the general will of a whole people is not general for an individual foreigner, because that private individual is not a member of this people. Now the moment a people considers a particular object, even if it is one of its own members, a relation between the whole and its part is formed which makes of them two separate entities, one of which is the part and the other of which is the whole minus that part. But the whole minus a part is not the whole, and for as long as this relationship lasts, there is no whole, but rather two unequal parts.

On the contrary, when the entire people enacts something concerning the entire people, it considers only itself, and if a relationship is formed then, it is between the whole object viewed in one way and the whole object viewed in another, without any division of the whole. Then the object of the enactment is general like the will that enacts, and it is this act that I call a law.

When I say that the object of the laws is always general, I mean that the law considers the subjects as a body and actions by their genera or species, never one man in particular or one unique individual action. Thus the law can very well enact that there will be privileges, but it cannot confer them on anyone by name. It can create several classes of citizens, and even designate the qualities determining who has a right to each of these classes, but it cannot specify the particular people to be admitted to them. It can establish a royal government and hereditary succession, but it cannot elect a king or name a royal family. In short, any function that relates to an individual object does not belong to the legislative power [and that is one of the reasons why the law cannot be retroactive, because it would be an enactment concerning a particular fact rather than enacting generally on a species of actions that have not yet been done by anybody and that, therefore, have nothing individual about them until after the publication of the law and by the will of those who perform them].

Given this idea, one easily sees that it is no longer necessary to ask who should make laws, since they are acts of the general will, nor whether the prince is above the laws, since he is a member of the State; nor whether the law can be unjust, since no one is unjust toward himself; nor how one is free yet subject to the laws, since they merely record our wills.

Furthermore, one sees that since the law combines the universality of the will and the object, what any man, whoever he may be, orders on his own authority is not a law. Whatever is ordered even by the sovereign concerning a particular object is not a law either, but rather a decree, nor is it an act of sovereignty but of magistracy, as I shall explain later.

The greatest advantage of this concept is that it shows us clearly the true foundations of justice and natural right.[34] Indeed, the first law, the only truly fundamental law that flows directly from the social compact, is that each man prefer the greatest good of all in all things.

Now the specification of the actions that contribute to this greatest good, by means of a number of particular laws, is what constitutes right in the narrow, positive sense. Everything that is seen to contribute to this greatest good, but that laws do not specify, constitutes acts of civility,* of goodwill; and the habit that disposes us to practice these acts even to our own disadvantage is what is called force or virtue.

Extend this maxim to the general society of which the State gives us an idea. Protected by the society of which we are members or by the one in which we live, the natural repugnance to do evil is no longer counterbalanced in us by the fear of being wronged, and we are simultaneously moved by nature, by habit, and by reason to treat other men approximately as we do our fellow citizens. From this disposition, transformed into actions, arise the rules of rational natural right, different from natural right properly so called, for the latter is based only on a true but very vague sentiment that is often stifled by love of ourselves.

This is how the first concepts of the just and unjust are formed in us, for law comes before justice and not justice before law; and if law cannot be unjust, it is not because justice is its basis, which might not always be true, but because it is contrary to nature for one to want to harm himself, which is true without exception.

It is a beautiful and sublime precept to do unto others as we would have done unto ourselves, but isn't it evident that far from providing a basis for justice, this precept is itself in need of a basis? For where is the clear, solid reason for me, just as I am, to behave according to the will I would have if I were someone else? Furthermore, it is clear that this precept is subject to a thousand exceptions for which only sophistic explanations have been given. Wouldn't a judge who condemns a criminal want to be absolved if he were a criminal himself? Where is the man who would not want never to be refused anything? Does it follow that we must grant everything that is asked of us? What is the basis of that other axiom, *cuique suum*, which serves as the basis of all right of property, if not the right of property itself?[36] And if I do not say, along with Hobbes, everything is mine, why wouldn't I at least recognize as mine in the state of nature all that is useful to me and that I can get hold of?

The true principles of the just and unjust must, therefore, be sought in the fundamental and universal law of the greatest good of all, and not in the private relations between one man and another; and there is no particular rule of justice that cannot be easily deduced from that first law. Hence *cuique suum*, because private property and civil freedom are the bases of the community. Hence *love thy neighbor as thyself*, because the private self extended to the whole is the strongest bond of the general society, and because the State has the highest degree of force and life it can have when all

---

*I do not need to caution, I think, that this word must not be understood in the French manner.[35]

our private passions are combined in it. In short, there are a thousand cases when it is an act of justice to harm one's neighbor, whereas every just action necessarily has as its rule the greatest common utility; this is without exception.

Chapter V: Classification of Laws[37]

Various relations have to be considered in order to organize the whole or give the commonwealth the best possible form. First, the action of the entire body acting upon itself—that is, the relationship of the whole to the whole, or of the sovereign to the State; and this relationship is composed of the relationship of intermediary forces, as we shall see later. The laws that regulate this relationship are named political laws and are also called fundamental laws, not without a degree of reason if these laws are wise. For if there is only one correct way to organize each State, the people that has found it should never change anything in it, but if the established order is bad, why should one accept, as fundamental, laws that prevent it from being good? Besides, in any event the people always has the power to change its laws, even the best; for if it pleases a man to harm himself, who has the right to prevent him from doing so?

The second relation is that of the members to each other or to the entire body. And this relationship should be as small as possible with respect to the former and as large as possible with respect to the latter, so that each citizen is in a position of perfect independence from all the others and of excessive dependence upon the City. This is always achieved by the same means, because only the force of the State creates the freedom of its members. It is from this second relationship that civil laws arise.

The laws that regulate the exercise and form of sovereign authority with respect to private individuals were called laws of majesty in Rome, such as the one that forbade appealing popular judgments to the senate and the one that made the person of the tribunes sacred and inviolable.

As for the particular laws regulating the respective duties and rights of the citizens, they are called civil laws with respect to domestic relations and the property of goods, and police with regard to good public order and the safety of people and things.

It is possible to consider a third type of relation between man and the law, namely that of disobedience and penalty. And this gives rise to the establishment of criminal laws, which are basically not so much a particular type of law as a sanction for all the others.

To these three types of laws is added a fourth, the most important of all; which is not engraved on marble or bronze, but in the hearts of the citizens; which is the true constitution of the State; which gains fresh force each day; which, when other laws age or die out, revives or replaces them, preserves a people in the spirit of its institution, and imperceptibly substitutes the force of habit for that of authority. I am speaking of mores and customs—a part of the laws unknown to our political theorists, but on which the success of all the others depends; a part to which the great legislator attends in secret, while appearing to limit himself to the particular regulations that are merely the sides of the arch of which mores, slower to arise, form at last the unshakable keystone.

Among these various types of laws, I limit myself in this work to the discussion of political laws.

Chapter VI: On Various Systems of Legislation[38]

If one seeks to define precisely what constitutes that greatest good of all which ought to be the basis of every system of legislation, one will find that it comes down to these two principal objects: *freedom* and *equality*. Freedom, because all private dependence is that much force subtracted from the body of the State; equality, because freedom cannot last without it.

I have already said what civil freedom is. With regard to equality, this word must not be understood to mean that degrees of power and wealth should be exactly the same, but rather with regard to power, it should be incapable of all violence and never exerted except by virtue of status and the laws; and with regard to wealth, no citizen should be so opulent that he can buy another, and none so poor that he is constrained to sell himself. This presumes moderation in goods and influence on the part of the upper classes and moderation in avarice and covetousness on the part of the lower classes.

This equality is said to be a speculative fantasy that cannot exist in practice. What? Because an effect is inevitable, does it follow that it must not at least be regulated? It is because the force of things always tends to destroy equality that the force of legislation should always tend to maintain it.

But these general objects of all good institutions should be modified in each country according to the relationships that arise as much from the local situation as from the character of the inhabitants; and it is on the basis of these relationships that each people must be assigned a particular system of legislation that is the best, not perhaps in itself, but for the State for which it is intended. For example, is the soil unprofitable and barren, or the country too small for its inhabitants? Turn to industry and the arts, the products of which can be exchanged for the foodstuffs you lack. On the contrary, do you inhabit rich plains and fertile hillsides? Do you lack inhabitants on good terrain? Apply all your efforts to agriculture, and chase out the arts for fear that they may complete the country's depopulation by concentrating its small number of inhabitants in a few locations—for it is known that, all things being equal, the population expands less in towns than in the countryside. Do you inhabit extensive, convenient shores? Cover the seas with ships, cultivate commerce and navigation. Is your coast merely a place where the sea meets almost inaccessible rocks? Remain barbarians and fish eaters; you will live more peacefully, better perhaps, and surely more happily. In short, apart from the maxims common to all, each people contains within itself some cause that organizes it in a particular manner and renders its legislation appropriate for it alone. Thus the Hebrews long ago and the Arabs recently have had religion as their principal object; the Athenians, letters; Carthage and Tyre, commerce; Rhodes, navigation; Sparta, war; and Rome, virtue. The author of *The Spirit of Laws* has given a large number of examples of the art by which the legislator directs the institution toward each of these objects.

The constitution of a State is made truly solid and enduring when matters of expediency are so well observed that natural relationships and the laws always agree on the same points and the latter only secure, accompany, and rectify, so to speak, the former. But if the legislator makes a mistake about his objective and adopts a different principle from the one arising from the nature of things—whether one tends toward servitude and the other toward freedom, one toward wealth and the other toward population growth, or one toward peace and the other toward conquest—the laws will imperceptibly weaken, the constitution will be altered, and the State will not cease being agitated until it is either destroyed or changed, and invincible nature has regained its dominion.

BOOK III

ON POLITICAL LAWS, OR
ON THE INSTITUTION OF GOVERNMENT[39]

Before discussing the various forms of government, it will be well to determine the precise meaning that must be given to this word in a legitimate society.

Chapter I: What the Government of a State Is

I warn readers that this chapter requires close attention and that I do not know the art of being clear for those who are not willing to be attentive.

Every free action has two causes that combine to produce it. One is moral, namely the will that determines the act; the other is physical, namely the power that executes it. When I walk toward an object, I must first want to go there and in the second place my feet must take me there. A paralyzed man who wants to run or an agile man who does not want to do so will both remain where they are. The body politic has the same motivating causes; force and will are distinguishable within it in the same sense, the latter under the name legislative power and the former under the name executive power.* Nothing is or should be done there without their cooperation.

We have seen that the legislative power belongs to the people and can belong only to it. It is easy to see similarly, that the executive power cannot belong to the people.

[On Civil Religion][41]

As soon as men live in society, they must have a religion that keeps them there. A people has never subsisted nor ever will subsist without religion, and if it were not given one, it would make one itself or would soon be destroyed. In every State that can require its members to sacrifice their lives, anyone who does not believe in the afterlife is necessarily a coward or a madman. But we know only too well the extent to which the hope of an af-

---

*I say executive and legislative, not executor's and legislator's, because I treat these two words as adjectives. In general, I do not attach great importance to all these grammatical trifles, but I believe that in didactic works one should frequently pay less attention to usage than to analogy, when the latter makes the meaning more exact.[40]

terlife can bring a fanatic to scorn this life. Take away this fanatic's visions and give him the same faith as the reward for virtue, and you will turn him into a true citizen.

Considered in relation to society, religion can be divided into two types, namely the religion of man and that of the citizen. The former, without temples, altars, or rituals, limited to the purely spiritual cult of the supreme God and to the eternal duties of morality, is the pure and simple religion of the Gospel, or true theism. The latter, confined so to speak to a single country, gives it its own tutelary Gods; its ceremonies, its rituals, its external cult are prescribed by the laws. Outside of the single nation that observes it, everything else is considered infidel, foreign, barbarous; it only extends the duties and rights of man as far as its Gods and its laws. Such were the religions of all ancient peoples, without any exception.

There is a third, more bizarre type of religion that gives men two leaders, two laws, and two homelands, subjects them to contradictory duties, and prevents them from ever being simultaneously pious men and citizens. The religion of the Lamas is like this, as is that of the Japanese and Roman Catholicism. It can be called the religion of the priest.

Considered from a political point of view, each of these three types of religions has its faults. The third is so manifestly bad that it is a waste of time to amuse oneself by proving it.

The second is good in that it combines the divine cult and love of the laws, and by making the homeland the object of the citizens' prayers, it teaches them that to serve the State is to serve God. It is a kind of theocracy in which the State ought to have no priests other than its magistrates. Then, to die for one's country is to be martyred, to disobey the laws is to be impious and sacrilegious, and to subject a criminal to public execration is to deliver him to the celestial anger of the Gods: *sacer estod.*

But this religion is bad in that, being based on error and falsehood, it deceives men, makes them credulous and superstitious, and drowns the true cult of divinity in empty ceremonial. It is bad, too, whenever it becomes exclusive and tyrannical and makes a people bloodthirsty and intolerant to the point where it lives only for murder and massacre, and believes it performs a holy act by killing whoever does not accept its Gods and its laws. It is not permissible to strengthen the bond of a particular society at the expense of the rest of the human race.

If under paganism, when each State had its cult and its tutelary Gods, there were no wars of religion, it was for the very reason that each State, having its own particular cult as well as its government, did not distinguish between its Gods and its laws. War, by being purely civil, was everything it could possibly be. The departments of the Gods were, so to speak, fixed by the boundaries of nations. The God of one people had no rights over another people. The Gods of the pagans were not jealous Gods. They divided dominion over the world peacefully among themselves, and watched its division by mortals without concern. The obligation to embrace a religion came only from that of being subject to the laws that prescribed it. Therefore, since there was no other way to convert a people except to subjugate it, it would have been ridiculous to say "worship my Gods or I will attack you." As the obligation to change cult was tied to victory, it was necessary to start by winning before talking about it. In short, far from men fighting for the Gods, it was—as in Homer—the Gods who fought for the men. Before capturing a place, the Romans called upon its Gods to abandon it; and when they let the people of Tarantum keep their angry Gods, it was because at that point the Romans considered them as subject to their own and forced to pay them homage. They let the vanquished keep their Gods as they let them keep their laws. A gold crown for the Capitoline Jupiter was often the only tribute they demanded.

Now if pagan superstition, despite this mutual tolerance and in the midst of culture and a thousand virtues, engendered so many cruelties, I do not see how it is possible to separate those very cruelties from that very zeal, and reconcile the rights of a national religion with those of humanity. It is better, then, to bind the citizens to the State by weaker and gentler ties, and to have neither heroes nor fanatics.

There remains the religion of man, or Christianity—not that of today, but that of the Gospel. Through this saintly, sublime, true religion, men—children of the same God—all acknowledge one another as brothers, and the society that unites them is all the closer because it is not dissolved even by death. However, this same religion, having no particular relation to the constitution of the State, leaves political and civil laws with only the force that natural right gives them, without adding any other force to them; and because of this, one of the greatest supports of society remains without effect in the State.

We are told that a people of true Christians would form the most perfect society that can be imagined. The most perfect in a purely moral sense, perhaps; certainly not the strongest or the most lasting. The people would be subject to the laws, the leaders would be fair, the soldiers would scorn death, I agree. But all that is not enough.

Christianity is a totally spiritual religion which detaches men from worldly things. The Christian's homeland is not of this world. He does his duty, it is true, but he does it with profound indifference for the outcome of the efforts he makes. It matters little to him whether things go well or badly here on earth. If the State is flourishing, he modestly enjoys the public felicity; if the State declines, he blesses the hand of God that weighs heavily on his people. In order for the society to be peaceful and for harmony to last, all citizens without exception would have to be equally good Christians. But if unfortunately there were an ambitious man or a hypocrite—a Catiline, for example, or a Cromwell—he would very certainly get the better of his pious compatriots. As soon as he has learned the secret of how to deceive them through some ruse and seize a part of the public authority for himself, at once he is powerful. It is God's will to obey him; he is the rod with which He punishes His children. It would be against conscience to chase out the usurper, for it would be necessary to shed blood, use violence, and disturb the public tranquillity. All of that is in no way consistent with the gentleness of a Christian. And after all, what does it matter whether one is free or in chains in this vale of tears. The essential thing is to go to heaven, and resignation is but an additional means of doing so. A slave can be saved just as well as a free man.

What if a foreign war breaks out? The citizens march to combat, none of them thinks of fleeing; they do their duty, but they have little passion for victory. They know how to die rather than to win. What does it matter if they are victors or vanquished? Providence knows better than they what is good for them. Imagine how an impetuous, active, passionate enemy can take advantage of their stoicism. Confront them with those generous and proud peoples consumed by a burning love of glory and homeland. Suppose that your Christian republic is face to face with Sparta or Rome. The Christians will be beaten, crushed, destroyed before they have had time to look around, or they will owe their salvation only to the scorn their enemies will conceive for them. The oath taken by the soldiers of Fabius was a fine one, it seems to me. They did not swear to win or to die; they swore to return as victors, and they did so. Christians would never dare take an oath like that, for they would believe they were tempting God.

But I am mistaken when I speak of a Christian republic; these two words are mutually exclusive. Christianity preaches nothing but servitude and dependence. The spirit of Christianity is so favorable to tyranny that tyranny always profits from it. True Christians are made to be slaves. They know it and are scarcely moved thereby; this brief life is of too little worth to them.

Christian troops are excellent, I shall be told. I deny this. Let someone show me some. For myself, I don't know of any Christian troops. The crusades will be cited. Without arguing over the valor of the crusaders, I shall be content to remark that very far from being Christians, they were soldiers of the priest. They were citizens of the church fighting for their spiritual country. Properly understood, this amounts to paganism; since the Gospel is not a civil religion, any war of religion is impossible among Christians.

Under the pagan Emperors, Christian soldiers were brave; I can well believe it. There was a kind of war of honor between them and the pagan troops. As soon as the Emperors were Christian, this emulation ceased and their troops did nothing more that was worthwhile.

Let us return to right and determine its principles. The right that the social compact gives the sovereign over the subjects does not exceed, as I have said, the limits of public utility. The subjects, therefore, do not have to account for their opinions to the sovereign, except insofar as these opinions matter to the community. Now it matters greatly to the State that each citizen have a religion, but the dogmas of that religion matter to it only insofar as they relate to morality. All others are outside of its competence, and everyone can have whatever opinions he pleases beyond that, without the sovereign having to know what they are.

There are positive dogmas, that the citizen should accept as advantageous to the society, and negative dogmas, that he should reject as harmful.

These various dogmas constitute a purely civil profession of faith that it is for the law to prescribe, not exactly as religious dogmas, but as sentiments of sociability without which it is impossible to be a good citizen or a faithful subject. The law cannot obligate anyone to believe them, but it can banish from the State anyone who does not believe them. The law can banish him not for being impious, but for being unsociable; for being incapable of sincerely loving the laws, justice, the homeland, and of giving his life, if need be, for his duties.

Every citizen should have to pronounce this profession of faith before the magistrate, and give express recognition to all the dogmas. If someone does not acknowledge them, he should be cut off from the City, but he should be allowed to take all his goods away with him in peace. If someone who has acknowledged these dogmas behaves as though he does not believe them, he should be punished with death. He has committed the greatest of crimes: he lied before the laws.

The dogmas of the civil religion will be simple, few in number, stated with precision, and without explanation or commentary: the existence of a beneficent, powerful, intelligent, foresighted and providential divinity; the afterlife; the happiness of the just and the punishment of the wicked; the sanctity of the social contract and the laws. These are the positive dogmas. As for the negative ones, I limit them to a single one: intolerance.

Those who make a distinction between civil and ecclesiastical intolerance are mistaken. One leads necessarily to the other; these two intolerances are inseparable. It is impossible to live in peace with people whom one believes are damned. To love them would be to hate God who punishes them. They must necessarily be either converted or persecuted. A necessary and indispensable article in the civil profession of faith is therefore as follows: I do not believe that any person is guilty before God for not thinking as I do about His cult.

I shall go further. It is impossible for intolerant men joined by the same dogmas ever to live in peace among themselves. As soon as they have the right to inspect one another's faith, they all become enemies, alternatively persecuted and persecutors, one against all and all against one. The intolerant person is Hobbes's man; intolerance is war with humanity. The society of the intolerant is like that of demons: they only agree in order to torment each other. The horrors of the inquisition never prevailed except in countries where everyone was intolerant. In these countries, it is purely a matter of chance that the victims are not the executioners.

You must think as I do in order to be saved. This is the horrible dogma that desolates the world. You will never do anything for public peace if you do not remove this infernal dogma from the City. Whoever does not find it execrable can be neither Christian, citizen, nor man; he is a monster who must be sacrificed for the sake of the tranquillity of the human race.

Once this profession of faith is established, it should be solemnly renewed each year, and this solemnity should be accompanied by an august and simple cult of which the magistrates alone are the ministers, and which revives love of the homeland in all hearts. That is all the sovereign is permitted to prescribe concerning religion. Beyond this, one should allow the introduction of all opinions that are not contrary to the civil profession of faith and all cults that are compatible with the public cult. And neither religious disputes nor holy wars should be feared. No one will think of refining the dogmas when there is so little interest in discussing them. No apostle or missionary will have the right to come and criticize the errors of a religion that serves as the basis for all the religions in the world and that condemns none of them. And if someone comes to preach his horrible intolerance, he will be punished as seditious and rebellious against the laws, unless he prefers to go and relate his martyrdom in his own country. It was very difficult for ancient peoples to understand those troublemaking, seditious men called missionaries. Thus the advantages of the religion of man and the religion of the citizen will be combined. The State will have its cult and will not be the enemy of anyone else's. With divine and human laws being always united on the same object, the most pious theists will also be the most zealous citizens, and the defense of the holy laws will be the glory of the God of men.

Now that there is no longer and can never again be an exclusive national religion, one should tolerate all those religions that tolerate others, provided that their dogmas are in no way contrary to the duties of the citizen. But whoever says there is no salvation outside of the Church should be chased out of the State, unless the State is the Church. This intolerant dogma should be accepted only in a theocratic government; in any other it is absurd and pernicious.

[The Marriage of Protestants][42]

It is clear that the civil registration of marriage ought to entail all the civil consequences, such as the status and name of children, the inheritance of goods, etc. The consequences of the sacrament ought to be purely spiritual. But this is not so at all. Everything has been so confounded that the status of citizens and the inheritance of goods depend solely on priests. It is absolutely up to the clergy whether not a single legitimate child is born in the whole kingdom of France, whether no citizen has a right to his father's goods, and whether thirty years from now all of France will be populated solely by bastards. As long as the functions of priests have civil consequences, the priests will be the true magistrates. The assemblies of the clergy of France are, in my opinion, the real government of the nation.

Do you want a certified, yet almost unbelievable example of this? You need only consider how the Protestants in the kingdom are treated.

I see no reason why the clergy of France could not extend to all citizens, whenever it wishes to do so, the rights it currently exercises toward French Protestants. Once experience proved how greatly the revocation of the Edict of Nantes weakened the monarchy, there was a desire to retain in the kingdom, along with the remainder of the persecuted sect, the only remaining source of subjects. Ever since then, these unfortunates, reduced to the most horrible situation in which any people has found itself since the world began, can neither stay nor flee. They are allowed to be neither foreigners, nor citizens, nor men. The very rights of nature are taken from them. Marriage is forbidden; and divested all at once of homeland, family, and goods, they are reduced to the status of beasts. Consider how this unheard-of treatment follows from a sequence of badly conceived principles. The laws of the kingdom have prescribed the solemn forms that legitimate marriages should take, and this is very well conceived. But the administration of these forms has been attributed by laws to the clergy, and combined with the so-called sacrament. The clergy for its part refuses to administer the sacrament to anyone who is not a child of the Church, and one cannot criticize this refusal as unjust. The Protestant, therefore, cannot marry according to the forms prescribed by the laws without renouncing his religion, and the magistrate recognizes as legitimate marriages only those which satisfy the forms prescribed by the laws. Thus the Protestant people is simultaneously tolerated and outlawed. There is simultaneously the wish for them to live and to die. In vain does the unfortunate man marry and in his misery respect the purity of the bond he has established. He sees himself condemned by the magistrates, his family divested of his goods, his wife treated as a concubine and his children as bastards. All of it, as you see, juridically and in consequence of the laws. This situation is unique, and I hasten to put down my pen for fear of yielding to the natural cry which rises and laments to its author.

Experience teaches that of all the Christian sects, Protestantism, as the wisest and gentlest, is also the most peaceful and social. It is the only one in which the laws can maintain their dominion and the leaders their authority.

FRAGMENTS

[The following fragments are found in the *Geneva Manuscript*, on the back of various pages. Fragment 5 appears in the eleventh paragraph of *Social Contract*, I, iv.]

1. That sovereignty is indivisible.

2. Moral signs are uncertain, difficult to calculate. Safety, tranquillity, freedom itself.

3. Several peoples, in the midst of wars and internal dissensions,

nonetheless multiply rapidly. In other governments, on the contrary, peace itself is devouring and consumes the citizens.

4. In a free state, men, often gathered among themselves, live very little with women. The laws of Sparta, rather than guaranteeing property, destroyed it. Where the laws were the mores, the mores became the laws.

5. But it is clear that this supposed right to kill the conquered in no way comes from the state of war. War is not a relation between men, but between powers, in which the private individuals are enemies only by accident, less as citizens than as soldiers. The foreigner who robs, pillages, and detains subjects without declaring war on the prince is not an enemy but a brigand; and even in the midst of war a just prince seizes everything in an enemy country that belongs to the public, but respects the person and goods of private individuals. He respects the rights on which his own power is based. The end of war is the destruction of the enemy State. One has the right to kill its defenders as long as they are armed, but as soon as they lay down their arms and surrender, they cease to be enemies, or rather instruments of the enemy, and one no longer has a right to their lives. One can kill the State without killing a single one of its members. War confers no right that is not necessary to its end.

[the following fragment appears in the Vaughan edition, but not in the Pléiade.]

The Pope is the true king of kings in the Roman Church. The entire division of peoples into States and governments is only apparent and illusory. At bottom, there is only one State in the Roman Church. The true magistrates are the bishops, the clergy is the sovereign, the citizens are the priests; laymen are nothing at all. It should . . .

EDITOR'S NOTES

[1]Rousseau hesitated between *Du Contract Social* and *De la Société Civile* as the title, and tried three other subtitles: *Essai sur la constitution de l'État, Essai sur la formation du corps politique,* and *Essai sur la formation de l'État,* before finally making up his mind (Pléiade, III, 1410). On the term "social contract" and the Platonic version of the original subtitle, see Introduction, pages 13–15 and 18–20.

[2]This chapter was deleted from the final version, perhaps because it is almost apologetic in tone; compare the Introduction to Book I in the final version. The clear distinction between the "nature" of the "social body" and its "relationship" is, however, worth stressing; by "relationships," Rousseau means the "matters of expediency" described in *Geneva Manuscript,* II, iii and II, vi or *Social Contract,* II, xi. The distinction thus parallels the difference between "the idea of the civil state" and the "science of the legislator" (*Geneva Manuscript* I, iv); in the final draft of the *Social Contract,* a similar distinction is made between "principles of right" and "maxims of politics" (III, xviii) or between "right" and "political considerations" (IV, viii). On the implications of these passages, see Introduction, pp. 20–24.

³Although deleted from the final version, this chapter is of great importance. It contains Rousseau's rejection of the concept of a "general will of the human species," which Diderot had proposed in the article *Natural Right* (*Encyclopédie*, Volume V). See Introduction pp. 15–18; Vaughan, I, 440–444; Pléiade, III, 1410–1411. Since Diderot's definition of the "general will" anticipates Kant's "categorical imperative" to a striking extent, the logic of Rousseau's criticism could also be applied to Kantian ethics. Without minimizing the impact of Rousseau's thought on Kant—and the affinities between their ideas—attempts to read Kantian ethics back into Rousseau's political teaching must consider this evidence carefully. Compare Ernst Cassirer, *Rousseau, Kant and Goethe* (New York: Harper Torchbooks, 1963), and Andrew Levine, *The Politics of Autonomy: A Kantian Reading of Rousseau's Social Contract* (Amherst, Mass.: University of Massachusetts Press, 1976).

⁴On Rousseau's argument that the emergence of social "bonds" was preceded by an evolution away from man's "natural needs" and "primitive state," see *Second Discourse*, Part 1 (ed. Masters, especially pp. 126–128) and Part 2 (especially pp. 151–152) as well as *Essay on the Origin of Language*, chap. 2 (ed. Moran and Gode, p. 12) and chap. 9 (p. 32). What the next paragraph calls a "state of nature" among humans who have developed reason, passions, and speech should thus be compared to the "state of war" in *Second Discourse*, Part 2 (ed. Masters, pp. 157–160).

⁵Paragraphs in brackets are crossed out in the *Geneva Manuscript* itself. Note that this passage explains Rousseau's attempt—stated at the outset of the final version—"to reconcile . . . what right permits with what interest prescribes" (*Social Contract*, I, Introduction). In other words, Rousseau will assume that humans are both selfish and capable of rationally defining their self-interest.

⁶So much for Rousseau's supposed praise for the "noble savage"—a phrase which, to my knowledge, he never used. Compare *Second Discourse*, Part 2 (ed. Masters, pp. 150–151) and *Essay on the Origin of Languages*, chap. 9 (ed. Moran and Gode, p. 33): while "savage society" was the "happiest and most durable epoch" of human evolution, the "golden age" of the past was also "barbaric."

⁷Rousseau here restates his attack on the natural law tradition, according to which human society and moral duty are derived from a natural law discovered by "right reason." See *Second Discourse*, Preface (ed. Masters, pp. 94–96) and Part 1 (p. 133). For examples of this natural law tradition, see Aristotle, *Nicomachean Ethics*, V.vii. 1134b–1135a (ed. Ostwald, pp. 131–133); Cicero, *De Re Publica*, III.xxii.33 (ed. Keyes, p. 211); St. Thomas Aquinas, *Summa Theologica*, I–II, Q. 93–94 (in *The Political Ideas of St. Thomas Aquinas*, ed. Bigongiari, pp. 34, 47–50), as well as the works of Grotius, Pufendorf, Barbeyrac, and Burlamaqui cited in Masters, *Political Philosophy of Rousseau*, p. 78, note 88.

⁸This sentence, which Rousseau attributes to "the independent man," is a direct quotation from Diderot's *Natural Right*, where it introduces a speech by what is called a "violent reasoner" who will be "stifled" by Diderot (Vaughan, I, 430–431). In answer to Rousseau's *Second Discourse*, Diderot argues that "man is not only an animal, but an animal who reasons" (Ibid.) Hence the combination of selfishness and rationality— which for Rousseau characterizes man in the "state of war" immediately preceding the social contract (*Second Discourse*, Part 2 [ed. Masters, pp. 155–158])—for Diderot describes a "ferocious beast" who is either "crazy" or "morally wicked" (*Natural Right*,§ iv [Vaughan, I, 431]). To represent Rousseau's position before attacking it, Diderot had therefore imagined the following speech being given by a rational egoist in a state of nature: " '*I am aware that I bring horror and confusion to the human species, but either I must be unhappy or I must cause others to be so, and no one is dearer to me than myself. Don't blame me for this terrible inclination; it isn't freely chosen. It is*

the voice of nature, which is never clearer to me than when it speaks in my favor. But is it only in my heart that it is heard with such violence? O men, it is to you that I appeal. Which of you, on the point of dying, would not buy his own life at the expense of the largest part of the human race, if he was sure to do so with impunity and in secret? But,' he will continue, 'I am equitable and sincere. If my happiness requires that I do away with all those existences which intrude on me, it is also necessary that an individual, whoever he is, can do away with my [existence] if it intrudes on his. Reason demands it and I accept. I am not so unjust that I require of another a sacrifice that I do not want to make for him.' " *Natural Right*, § iii (Vaughan, I, 430), italics added to indicate the passage quoted by Rousseau. Diderot's imaginary speaker seems to equate natural right with an unlimited right of self-preservation, as Hobbes did when describing the "natural condition of mankind" as a "time of war, where every man is enemy to every man." Thomas Hobbes, *Leviathan*, Part 1, chap. 13 (ed. Oakeshott, p. 82). It is, therefore, with surprise that we note that Diderot intends the speech to represent Rousseau—and that Rousseau accepts the attribution, treating Diderot as a "wise man." But whereas Diderot had described the speaker as a "violent reasoner," Rousseau quotes the position as that of an "independent man" who seeks "guarantees" against the "unjust undertakings" of others. The disagreement between Rousseau and Diderot, while at first philosophical, led to a bitter personal break; see Masters, *Political Philosophy of Rousseau*, p. 97.

[9]The strongly anticlerical tone of these three paragraphs is retained in the final version: see *Social Contract*, II, vi, second paragraph; II, vii, last three paragraphs; and IV, viii. But when Rousseau dismisses the "theologian" on the grounds that religion tends to produce fanaticism, his phrase has a double meaning: to give the question of natural right "back to the philosopher *(philosophe)*" could mean either to return it to philosophers in general—or to a member of the group known as the *philosophes*, namely Diderot. Compare Introduction, p. 26. On Rousseau's religious teaching, see also *Social Contract*, II, vii; III, viii; and editorial note 135.

[10]Again, Rousseau quotes Diderot, who had written: "But if we take from the individual the right to decide the nature of the just and unjust, where will we bring this great question? Where? Before the human species, *which alone ought to decide, because the good of all is the only passion it has.* Individual wills are suspect, they could be good or wicked; but the general will is always good; it has never been mistaken, and it never will be. . . . *The individual should address himself to the general will in order to find out to what extent he should be man, citizen, subject, father, child, and when it is suitable for him to live and to die.*" *Natural Right*, §vi–vii (Vaughan, I, 431–432), italics added to indicate Rousseau's quotation. Note that Rousseau inserts the superlative "greatest" before "good of all." Although *la volonté générale* ("general will") had been used by Fontenelle and Malebranche, it is not unlikely that this passage by Diderot inspired Rousseau's use of the term. See Vaughan, I, 424–427, and ed. de Jouvenel, pp. 105–112. For other antecedents of the notion of a "single" or "general will," however, see Samuel Pufendorf, *Le Droit de la Nature et des Gens*, VII, ii, § 5 and 13 (ed. 1706; II, 203, 213); Hobbes, *Leviathan*, Part 2, chap. 17 (ed. Oakeshott, p. 112); Montesquieu, *Esprit des Lois*, I, iii and XI, vi (ed. Caillois, pp. 237, 398); as well as Rousseau, *Second Discourse*, Part 2 (ed. Masters, p. 169).

[11]Rousseau here alludes to his notions of "natural pity" and the "conscience" as the "voice of nature": *First Discourse*, Part 2 (ed. Masters, p. 64); *Second Discourse*, Preface (pp. 95–96) and Part 1 (pp. 130–133); *Émile*, IV (Pléiade, IV, 522–523, 547–548) and "Profession of Faith" (Pléiade, IV, 594–606). Rousseau's statement that the *philosophes* "assert that this voice is nonexistent" is confirmed by the absence of any reference to the "conscience" in *Natural Right*. As if addressing Rousseau directly, Diderot had written: "But you will say to me: Where is this general will found? Where

can I consult it? *In the written principles of right of all civilized nations, in the social actions of savage and barbarian peoples, in the tacit conventions that the enemies of the human race make* amongst themselves; and even in indignation and resentment, the two passions that nature seems to have even given to animals to make up for the absence of social laws and public vengeance." *Natural Right,* § viii (Vaughan, I, 432), italics added to indicate the indirect quotation in Rousseau's next sentence. Both Diderot and Rousseau speak of social practice as a possible source of natural law, but where Rousseau speaks of pity and the conscience, Diderot emphasizes "indignation and resentment"—that is, natural passions that serve as punishments rather than bonds or obligations to others. Compare Masters, *Political Philosophy of Rousseau,* chap. ii.

12"Among our ancestors they called 'enemies' those we today call 'foreigners.' " Cicero, *De Officiis,* I.xii. All of the paragraph up to this quotation is a paraphrase of Grotius, *Droit de la Guerre et de la Paix,* II, xv, § 5 (see Pléiade, III, 1414–1415).

13By "violent speaker" Rousseau presumably designates the rational egoist or Hobbesian he previously called "the independent man," but whom Diderot calls "a violent reasoner" (compare editorial note 8 above)—unless of course the "violent speaker" is Diderot himself.

14The first paragraph of this chapter was revised to become Book I, chap. i, of the final version. The second, third, and fourth paragraphs became Book I, chap. vi; the next three paragraphs—"This formula shows . . . enormous abuse"—became Book I, chap. vii; paragraphs eight and nine—"This passage from the state of nature . . . legal title" became the first two paragraphs of Book I, chap. viii; and the section "On Real Estate" became the chapter with that title (I, ix). On Rousseau's revision of Book I, see editorial note 18 below.

15Compare the final version of this passage, which became the first paragraph of Book I, chapter i: when Rousseau converted these sentences into his explosive introduction, he *personalized* the answers to the two questions. Since his original draft of chapter i in Book I was also personalized, it would seem that Rousseau intentionally begins the *Social Contract* by writing in the first person singular. (Compare Introduction, pp. 27–33.) The negative answer to the question: "How did this change [from freedom to chains] occur?" is sometimes taken as a repudiation of the *Second Discourse*; this is clearly unnecessary, since Rousseau explicitly says that his account of the "events" *between* man's "primitive condition" of freedom and "the bonds of servitude" could "have happened in several ways" and hence that he gives only the "conjectures" that are the "most probable." *Second Discourse,* Part 1 (ed. Masters, pp. 140–141).

16Although this sentence was deleted from the final version, it stresses an important point: each individual in society retains—as a *social* right—the use of all land, goods, and personal faculties that are not being devoted to communal activity. Compare *État de Guerre,* quoted in editorial note 26 to the *Social Contract.* As Rousseau indicates, however, it is "only under public protection" that private property can be enjoyed "in safety." Cf. Hobbes, *Leviathan,* Part 1, chap. 13 (ed. Oakeshott, pp. 82–82); Locke, *Second Treatise,* chap. xi, para. 137–140 (ed. Laslett, pp. 377–380).

17This chapter was revised to become Book II, chap. i. For a possible reason for the deletion of the first paragraph, see *Social Contract,* editorial note 36. On the importance of the last paragraph, see Introduction, pp. 18–20.

18This chapter, with its rejection of alternative principles, was divided and only partially used in the final version. The first two paragraphs were deleted; a long discussion of paternal authority (paragraphs three to seven) appears in *Political Economy:* (pp. 209–211); most of the next two paragraphs are in *Social Contract,* I, ix;

part of the next paragraph in Book I, chapter iv, of the final version, and the remainder essentially rewritten in the first chapters of the definitive text. These details are primarily significant as an indication of Rousseau's reorganization of the work. Whereas the *Geneva Manuscript* begins by rejecting Diderot's notion of a "general will of the human species" (I, ii), poses Rousseau's own principles (I, iii–iv), and only then rejects alternative positions in general (I, v), the *Social Contract* rejects all contrary explanations of the origin of the social bond (I, i–v) before presenting Rousseau's theory of the general will (I, vi–ix)—and ignores Diderot completely. It would be hard to deny that the final organization is more logical than the first draft. On the first paragraph, compare *Social Contract*, editorial notes 3 and 30. Because part of this chapter appears in *Political Economy*, which was published in 1755, some commentators have argued that the *Geneva Manuscript* was written before that date, and that Rousseau's use of a passage required a rewriting of the final version of the *Social Contract* (Pléiade, III, 1417–1418). Compare editorial note 20 below.

[19]See especially *Statesman*, 293a. On the difference between paternal and political authority, compare Aristotle, *Politics*, I.i.1252a (ed. Barker, p. 1).

[20]Rousseau refers to a pro-French propaganda tract generally attributed to Jacob N. Moreau: *L'Observateur Hollandois, ou Lettres de M. Van ** à M. H ** de la Haye, sur l'état présent des affaires de l'Europe*, 8 vols. (La Haye, 1755–1759), II, 41–48. Since the passage is in a letter dated January 2, 1756, the *Geneva Manuscript* as it stands must be subsequent to that date. The substance of this note reflects Rousseau's strong opposition to colonial empires. Moreau, writing to defend French land claims which contributed to the Seven Years' War (1756–1763), had asserted that "we can, in the present dispute, consider as vacant lands all those that are only inhabited by savages" (pp. 44–45). It is not surprising that the author of the *Second Discourse* was outraged by such an attitude toward the native inhabitants of North America. Compare Locke, *Second Treatise*, chap. v, especially para. 41–43 (ed. Laslett, pp. 314–316). Rousseau's omission of this note in the final version (I, ix) might well be due to the fact that it openly criticizes the French claims in a war that was being fought when the *Social Contract* was published. Compare Masters, *Political Philosophy of Rousseau*, pp. 280–282. Rousseau's anticolonialism, while prudently stated, can be traced elsewhere: "Who will we judge as more courageous, the odious Cortez subjugating Mexico by means of gunpowder, deceit, and treachery? Or the unfortunate Guatimozin, stretched out on hot coals by decent Europeans in order to get his treasures, and reprimanding one of his officers, who groaned a bit under the same treatment, by proudly saying: 'And me, am I lying on roses?' " *Dernière Réponse* (Pléiade, III, 91).

[21]Compare *Social Contract*, I, v, first paragraph, and editorial note 28.

[22]This chapter became Book II, chap. iv, of the final version. The deletion of the first paragraph was probably necessary because the last paragraphs of the preceding chapter of the *Geneva Manuscript* had also been cut. But this change did obscure the link between Rousseau's "general will" and the traditional concepts of the "common good" or "common interest."

[23]This sentence, like most of Rousseau's explicit references to the distinction between "strict right" and what is "appropriate" or "convenient," was deleted in the final version. See Introduction, pp. 18–24.

[24]Only the last paragraph of this chapter found its way into the final version of the *Social Contract*, serving as the conclusion of Book II, chap. vi. Most of the third paragraph, however, is used in *Political Economy* (p. 214). On the possible reason for Rousseau's deletion of the paragraph which speaks of the State as having "only an ideal and conventional existence," see *Social Contract*, editorial note 36.

[25]The first two sentences of this chapter became the opening of *Social Contract*, II, vi; the remainder, along with other explicit references to the "science of legislation" in the first draft, was deleted. Compare Masters, *Political Philosophy of Rousseau*, pp. 305–313.

[26]With the deletion of a long section (paragraphs eight to eleven), this chapter was used as Book II, chap. vii, of the final version. The deleted material refers to the nature of laws, rather than the legislator per se, and thus might well have struck Rousseau as redundant. In addition to the revisions described in the next two notes, Rousseau crossed out the last paragraph and a half in the *Geneva Manuscript* itself.

[27]This sentence, referring to the codification of Roman law by Justinian, was deleted in the final version. Compare the fragment "Des Lois" (Vaughan, I, 331).

[28]Rousseau here refers to two formulas of Roman law dating from the Empire: *Quod principi placuit legis habet vigorem*—"Whatever the prince wants has the power of law" (*Digest*, I.iv.1) and *Princeps legibus solutus*—"The prince is not bound by the laws" (*Digest*, I.iii.31). In the final version, Rousseau deleted this reference, instead citing the practice of Roman Decemvirs: *Social Contract*, II, vii and editorial note 56.

[29]This chapter was divided into three, becoming *Social Contract*, II, viii–x. On the distinction between "right" and "expedience," which was deleted from the final version, see Introduction, pp. 18–24. Rousseau also deleted several other passages in revising the text.

[30]This paragraph was placed in Book III, chap. vi, of the final version. Rousseau's argument could be taken as a rejection of Plato's conception of philosophic rulers. Compare *Republic*, IX, 591c–592b.

[31]Although this paragraph as written was deleted from the final version, see *Social Contract*, III, xii–xiii.

[32]This paragraph and the three following ones were deleted from the definitive text, doubtless because Rousseau himself found them "repetitious."

[33]Paragraphs one to three and seven to eleven of this chapter were used in *Social Contract*, II, vi. The remainder—including Rousseau's interesting discussion of natural law at the end—was deleted.

[34]The rest of this chapter of the *Geneva Manuscript* was not used in the final version, perhaps because the discussion is so closely related to the rejection of Diderot's "general society" (*Geneva MS*, I, ii), which was also cut. It is, nonetheless, a very interesting statement, again emphasizing Rousseau's *historical* interpretation of the foundation of ethical principles. Whereas the tradition speaks of "natural law," therefore, Rousseau speaks of "the rules of rational natural right, different from natural right properly so called." Another conceivable reason for deleting this discussion, however, might have been the dangerous implications if an unscrupulous politician read such statements as: "the law comes before justice," and "there are a thousand cases when it is an act of justice to harm one's neighbor." Compare *Social Contract*, editorial notes 3, 17, 36, and 52.

[35]In using the French work *civilité*, Rousseau obviously wants to refer to the ancient *Cité* (Greek *polis*) rather than modern "politeness." Compare *Social Contract*, editorial notes 32 and 104.

[36]*cuique suum* = "to each his own." For Rousseau, the historical origin of human concepts of justice makes it impossible to base either civil rights or ethics directly on the presumed "natural rights" of individuals. As a result, Rousseau bases private property, civil freedom, and the moral duties of civilized individuals on a rational

discovery of "the greatest good of all" rather than on "the private relations between one man and another" (next paragraph). While explicitly an attack on Hobbes, it is interesting to wonder if knowledge of this passage would have influenced Kant.

[37]This chapter was used, with the deletion of paragraphs three and four, as Book II, chap. xii, of the final version. The reference to what the Romans called "laws of majesty" in paragraph three makes it likely, however, that from the first Rousseau included an extensive study of Rome in the *Social Contract*. Compare Pléiade, III, 1495 and *Social Contract*, editorial note 120.

[38]This chapter became *Social Contract*, II, xi. The third paragraph was written at the bottom of a page, without an indication of its location in the text; it has been inserted at the point where it was used in the final version (Vaughan, I, 497).

[39]Only a short fragment of the beginning of Book III is found in the *Geneva Manuscript*, which breaks off at this point. For a detailed description of the manuscript itself, as well as hypotheses on its exact date, see Vaughan, I, 434–435 and Pléiade, III, lxxxii–xc.

[40]This note was suppressed in the final version. Montesquieu had contrasted "*la puissance législative*" and "*la puissance exécutrice*" (*Esprit des Lois*, XI, vi), as Derathé points out in his note to the *Geneva Manuscript* (Pléiade, III, 1426–1427). Rousseau thus sought to correct a grammatical anomaly by proposing more consistent terminology. In the final version however, he uses the form here rejected: "*La puissance exécutive ne peut appartenir à la généralité, comme Législatrice ou Souveraine.*"—"executive power cannot belong to the general public in its legislator's or sovereign capacity." *Social Contract*, III, i.

[41]Unlike the manuscript up to the beginning of Book III, which is "written in Rousseau's fairest hand," the chapter "On Civil Religion"—which became *Social Contract*, IV, viii—is "scribbled, in a hand often almost indecipherable" on the back of pages 46–51. Hence, whereas the rest of the *Geneva Manuscript* is apparently written out carefully as if for the printer, this material is clearly Rousseau's own first draft. Based on inferences from Rousseau's correspondence with his publisher Rey, it is probable that the chapter "On Civil Religion" was written in 1761 (Vaughan, I, 434–435; Pléiade, III, lxxxii–lxxxiii; *Confessions*, X ([Pléiade, I, 560]). In any event, there are numerous differences between this preliminary sketch and the definitive text of *Social Contract*, IV, viii.

[42]This note reflects Rousseau's outrage at the condition of his fellow Protestants under the laws of France. An edict of May 14, 1724, forbade Protestants to have their marriages blessed and children baptized by Catholic clergy and prohibited them from leaving the country to get married or from sending their children abroad. These provisions thus extended the official intolerance toward Protestants—which had become royal policy since the revocation of the Edict of Nantes; as a result, it was technically impossible for a French Protestant to have legitimate children and hence to transmit property to his offspring (see Pléiade, III, 1430). This draft was apparently intended to influence the trial of four Protestants in Toulouse; after the accused were executed in February 1762, Rousseau wrote his publisher: "I have deleted the last note, which has become useless now that the fate of our unfortunates has been decided, and concerning which you would perhaps have been given more difficulty [by the censors] than for all the rest of the book. For this note, I have substituted another one which is just as good, and is better directed to the root of the evil." (Letter to Rey, March 11, 1762, cited Pléiade, III, 1506). The replacement, now found in IV, viii, was in turn deleted from the first edition by an anxious Rousseau, afraid of religious persecution. See *Social Contract*, editorial note 142.

Discourse On
Political Economy[1]

ECONOMY or OECONOMY, (*Moral and Political*.) This word comes
from οἶκος, *house,* and νόμος, law, and originally signified only the wise and
legitimate government of the household for the common good of the whole
family. The meaning of the term was subsequently extended to the government of the large family which is the State. In order to distinguish these two
meanings, in the latter case it is called *general,* or *political, economy,* and in
the former *domestic,* or *private, economy.* This article is concerned only with
the first of these. Regarding *domestic economy,* see *FATHER OF THE
FAMILY.*[2]

Even if there were as much similarity between the State and the family
as several authors claim, it would not necessarily follow that the rules of
conduct appropriate to one of these two societies were suited to the other.[3]
They differ too much in size to be administered in the same way, and there
will always be a very great difference between domestic government, where
the father can see everything for himself, and civil government, where the
leader sees almost nothing except through the eyes of others. For things to
become equal in this respect, the talents, force, and faculties of the father
would have to increase in proportion to the size of his family, and the soul of a
powerful monarch would have to be, compared to that of an ordinary man,
what the extent of his empire is to the inheritance of a private individual.

But how could the government of the State be like that of the family,
whose basis is so different? Because the father is physically stronger than his
children, paternal power is correctly thought to be established by nature for
as long as they need his help. In the large family, all of whose members are
naturally equal, political authority—purely arbitrary as regards its institution—can only be founded on conventions, and the magistrate can only com-

mand the citizen by virtue of the laws.[4] The father's duties are dictated by natural feelings, and in such a way that he can rarely disobey. Leaders have no similar rule and are not really obligated to the people except for what they have promised to do, which the people has the right to require them to carry out. Another even more important difference is that since the children have nothing except what they receive from the father, it is evident that all property rights belong to, or emanate from, him. It is just the opposite in the large family, where the general administration is only established in order to assure private property, which is antecedent to it. The main object of the entire household's work is to preserve and increase the father's patrimony, so that someday he can divide it among his children without impoverishing them; whereas the wealth of the public treasury is only a means, often very badly understood, to maintain private individuals in a state of peace and plenty. In short, the small family is destined to die out and split up someday into several other similar families, whereas the large one is made to last always in the same state. The former must increase in order to multiply, whereas not only does it suffice for the latter to preserve itself, but it can easily be proved that all growth is more harmful than useful to it.

For several reasons derived from the nature of things, the father should command in the family.[5] First, the authority of the father and mother should not be equal; rather, there must be a single government, and when opinions are divided, there must be a dominant voice that decides. Second, however slight the incapacitations peculiar to the wife are thought to be, since they are always an inactive period for her, this is sufficient reason to exclude her from primacy, because when the balance is perfectly equal, a straw is enough to tip it. Furthermore, the husband should oversee his wife's conduct, because it is important to him that the children he is forced to recognize do not belong to anyone other than himself. The wife, who has no such thing to fear, does not have the same right over her husband. Third, children should obey their father, at first through necessity, later through gratitude. After having their needs met by him for half their lives, they should devote the other half to attending to his needs. Fourth, as regards domestic servants, they too owe him their services in return for the livelihood he gives them, unless they break the exchange when it no longer suits them. I do not speak for slavery, because it is contrary to nature and no right can authorize it.

Nothing of this kind exists in political society. Far from the leader's having a natural interest in the happiness of private individuals, it is not unusual for him to seek his own happiness in their misery. Is the magistracy hereditary? Often a child is in command of men. Is it elective? Elections present a thousand drawbacks. And in either case all the advantages of paternity are lost. If you have only one leader, you are at the discretion of a master who has no reason to love you. If you have several, you must simultaneously bear their tyranny and their dissensions. In short, abuses are inevitable and their consequences disastrous in all societies, where the public interest and the laws have no natural force and are continuously assailed by the personal interest and passions of both leader and members.

Although the functions of the father of a family and of the prince should be directed toward the same goal, the paths they take are so different, their duties and rights are so dissimilar, that one cannot confuse them without forming false ideas about the fundamental laws of society, and without making mistakes that are fatal to the human race. Indeed, while nature's voice is the best advice a father can heed to fulfill his duties, for the magistrate it is a false guide, working continuously to separate him from his people, and bringing him sooner or later to his downfall or to that of the State unless he is restrained by the most sublime virtue. The only precaution necessary to the father of a family is to protect himself from depravity, and to prevent his natural inclinations from becoming corrupt, whereas it is these very inclinations which corrupt the magistrate. To do what is right, the former need only consult his heart; the latter becomes a traitor the moment he heeds his. Even his own reason should be suspect to him, and he should follow no other rule than the public reason, which is the law. Besides, nature has made a multitude of good fathers of families, but it is doubtful that since the beginning of the world, human wisdom has ever made ten men capable of governing their fellow men.

It follows from everything I have just set forth, that *public economy* is correctly distinguished from *private economy,* and that since the State has nothing in common with the family except the obligation of their leaders to make each of them happy, the same rules of conduct could not be suited to both.[6] I thought these few lines would suffice to reject the odious system that Sir Filmer tried to establish in a work entitled *Patriarcha,* which two famous men have already overly honored by writing books to refute it. Besides, this error is very old, since Aristotle himself saw fit to combat it with reasons that can be found in the first book of his *Politics.*[7]

I urge my readers also to distinguish carefully *public economy,* about which I am to speak, and which I shall call *government,* from the supreme authority, which I call *sovereignty*—a distinction that consists in the one having the legislative right and in certain cases obligating the body of the nation itself, while the other has only the executor's power and can only obligate private individuals. *See POLITICS and SOVEREIGNTY.*[8]

Allow me to use for a moment a common comparison, imprecise in many ways, but suited to making myself better understood.

The body politic, taken individually, can be considered to be like a body that is organized, living, and similar to that of a man. The sovereign power represents the head; the laws and customs are the brain, source of the nerves and seat of the understanding, will, and senses, of which the judges and magistrates are the organs; commerce, industry, and agriculture are the mouth and stomach that prepare the common subsistence; public finances are the blood that a wise economy, performing the functions of the heart, sends out to distribute nourishment and life throughout the body; the citizens are the body and members that make the machine move, live, and work, and that cannot be harmed in any part without promptly sending a painful response to the brain if the animal is in a state of health.

The life of both is the *self* common to the whole, the reciprocal sensitivity and internal correlation of all the parts. What happens if this communication ceases, if formal unity disappears and contiguous parts are related to one another only by their proximity? The man is dead or the State is dissolved.

The body politic is thus also a moral being that has a will; and this general will, which always tends toward the preservation and welfare of the whole and of each part, and which is the source of the laws, is—for all the members of the State in relation to themselves and to it—the rule of what is just and unjust. This truth, let me say in passing, shows how incorrectly many writers have treated as theft the cunning prescribed to Spartan children for obtaining their frugal meal, as if everything that is required by law could fail to be legitimate. *See RIGHT*, for the source of this great and luminous principle, which that article develops.[9]

It is important to note that this rule of justice, infallible in relation to all citizens, can be defective with foreigners. And the reason for this is evident. Then the will of the State, although general in relation to its members, is so no longer in relation to other States and their members, but becomes for them a private and individual will that has its rule of justice in the law of nature, which fits in equally well with the principles established. For then the large town of the world becomes the body politic, of which the law of nature is always the general will and the various States and peoples are merely individual members.

These same distinctions, applied to each political society and its members, give rise to the most universal and infallible rules by which to judge a good or bad government, and in general the morality of all human actions.

All political societies are composed of other, smaller societies of different types, each of which has its interests and maxims. But these societies that everyone perceives, because they have an external, authorized form, are not the only ones that really exist in the State. All the private individuals united by a common interest constitute as many others, permanent or temporary, whose force is no less real for being less apparent, and whose various relationships, well observed, are the true knowledge of mores. It is all these tacit or formal associations which modify in so many ways the appearance of the public will by the influence of their own. The will of these particular societies always has two relations: for the members of the association, it is a general will; for the large society, it is a private will, which is very often found to be upright in the first respect and vicious in the latter. A given man can be a pious priest, or a brave soldier, or a zealous lawyer, and a bad citizen. A given deliberation can be advantageous to the small community and pernicious to the large one. It is true that since particular societies are always subordinate to those that contain them, one ought to obey the latter in preference to the former; the citizen's duties take precedence over the senator's, and the man's over the citizen's. But unfortunately personal interest is always found in inverse ratio to duty, and it increases in proportion as the association becomes narrower and the engagement less sacred—invincible proof that the most general will is also always the most just, and that the voice of the people is in fact the voice of God.[10]

Even so, it does not follow that public deliberations are always equitable. They may not be so concerning foreign affairs; I have stated the reason for this. Thus it is not impossible for a well-governed republic to wage an unjust war. Nor is it impossible for the council of a democracy to pass bad decrees and condemn innocent men. But that will never happen unless the people is seduced by private interests that some wily men have been able to substitute for its own. Then the public deliberation will be one thing and the general will a completely different thing. Do not raise Athens as an objection, then, because Athens was not in fact a democracy, but a highly tyrannical aristocracy, governed by learned men and orators.[11] Examine carefully what happens in any deliberation, and you will see that the general will is always in favor of the common good. But very often a secret split occurs, a tacit confederation, which causes the natural disposition of the assembly to be bypassed for the sake of private views. Then the social body really divides into other bodies whose members adopt a general will that is good and just with respect to these new bodies, unjust and bad with respect to the whole from which each of them has broken away.

This shows how easy it is, using these principles, to explain the apparent contradictions seen in the conduct of many men who are full of scruple and honor in certain respects, deceitful and knavish in others; trampling underfoot the most sacred duties, yet faithful unto death to engagements that are often illegitimate. Thus the most corrupt men always render some sort of homage to the public faith. Thus (as noted in the *article RIGHT*) even brigands who are the enemies of virtue in the large society worship its semblance in their hideouts.[12]

In establishing the general will as the first principle of public *economy* and the fundamental rule of government, I did not believe it was necessary to examine seriously whether the magistrates belong to the people or the people to the magistrates, and whether in public affairs it is the good of the State or that of the leaders that should be consulted. This question was long ago resolved in one way by practice and in another by reason; and in general it would be sheer madness to hope that those who are in fact masters will prefer another interest to their own. It would be appropriate, therefore, to divide public *economy* further into popular and tyrannical. The former is that of all States in which the people and the leaders have the same interest and the same will. The other necessarily exists everywhere that the government and the people have different interests and consequently opposing wills. The maxims of the latter are inscribed all through the archives of history and in Machiavelli's satires.[13] The others are found only in the writings of philosophers who dare to demand the rights of humanity.

I. The first and most important maxim of legitimate or popular government—that is, one that has the good of the people as its object—is therefore, as I have said, to follow the general will in all matters. But in order to follow it, it must be known, and above all well distinguished from the private will, starting with one's own, a distinction that is always extremely difficult to make and on which only the most sublime virtue can shed sufficient light. Since it is necessary to be free in order to will, another difficulty, which is hardly lesser, is to assure both public freedom and the government's authority. Seek the motives that have brought men, united by their mutual needs in the large society, to unite more closely by means of civil societies. You will find none other than that of assuring the goods, life, and freedom of each member by the protection of all. But how can men be forced to defend the freedom of one among them without infringing on that of the others? And how can the public needs be met without altering the private property of those who are forced to contribute to it? Whatever sophisms may be used to disguise all this, it is certain that if someone can constrain my will, I am no longer free, and that I am no longer master of my goods if another can meddle with them. This difficulty,[14] which must have seemed insurmountable, was removed along with the first by the most sublime of all human institutions, or rather by a celestial inspiration that taught man to imitate here on earth the immutable decrees of the divinity. By what inconceivable art could the means have been found to subjugate men in order to make them free; to use the goods, the labor, even the life of all its members in the service of the State without forcing and without consulting them; to bind their will with their own consent; to make their agreement predominate over their refusal; and to force them to punish themselves when they do what they did not want? How can it be that they obey and no one commands, that they serve and have no master, and are all the freer, in fact, because under what appears as subjugation, no one loses any of his freedom except what would harm the freedom of another. These marvels are the work of the law. It is to law alone that men owe justice and freedom. It is this healthy instrument of the will of all that reestablishes, as a right, the natural equality among men. It is this celestial voice that tells each citizen the precepts of public reason, and teaches him to act according to the maxims of his own judgment and not to be in contradiction with himself. It is also through the law alone that leaders must speak when they command; for as soon as a man claims to subject another to his private will independently of the laws, he immediately leaves the civil state, and in relation to the other man places himself in the pure state of nature, where obedience is never prescribed except by necessity.

The most pressing interest of the leader, as well as his most indispensable duty, is therefore to attend to the observation of the laws of which he is the minister and on which all his authority is based. If he must make others observe them, there is even greater reason for him to observe them himself, as the one who enjoys all their benefits. For his example is so powerful that even if the people would tolerate his emancipation from the yoke of the law, he ought to refrain from taking advantage of such a dangerous prerogative, which others would soon attempt to usurp in turn, and often to his detriment. At bottom, since all of society's engagements are reciprocal in nature, it is not possible to be above the law without renouncing its advantages, and no one owes anything to any person who claims he owes nothing to anyone. For the same reason, no exemption from the law will ever be accorded for any reason whatever in a well-regulated government. Even the citizens who most deserve something from the homeland should be rewarded with honors and never with privileges. For the republic is on the brink of ruin as soon as someone can think it is a fine thing not to obey the laws. But if ever the nobility or the military or some other order within the State were to adopt such a maxim, all would be irretrievably lost.

The power of laws depends even more on their own wisdom than on the severity of their ministers, and the public will derives its greatest influence from the reason that dictated it. It is because of this that Plato considers it a very important precaution always to place at the head of edicts a well-reasoned preamble which shows their justice and utility.[15] Indeed, the first of the laws is to respect the laws. Severity of punishments is merely a vain expedient thought up by small minds in order to substitute terror for the respect they can't obtain. It has always been noted that the countries where corporal punishments are most terrible are also those where they are most frequent; so that the cruelty of penalties is hardly anything except a sign of the multitude of lawbreakers, and when everything is punished with equal severity, the guilty are forced to commit crimes to escape punishment for their mistakes.

But although the government is not the master of the law, it is no small thing to be its guarantor and to dispose of a thousand ways of making it beloved. The talent of reigning consists of nothing else. When one has force in hand, there is no art to making everyone tremble, and not even very much to winning men's affection; for experience has long taught the people to be very grateful to its leaders for all the evil they do not do to it, and to worship its leaders when not hated by them. An imbecile who is obeyed can, like anyone else, punish crimes. The true statesman knows how to prevent them. He extends his respectable dominion over wills even more than over actions. If he could create a situation in which everyone did what is right, he himself would have nothing further to do, and the masterpiece of his works would be to be able to remain idle. It is certain, at least, that the greatest talent of leaders is to disguise their power to make it less odious, and to manage the State so peacefully that it seems to have no need for managers.

Therefore, I conclude that just as the legislator's first duty is to make the laws conform to the general will, the first rule of public *economy* is for the administration to be in conformity with the laws. This will even be sufficient for the State not to be badly governed, if the legislator has attended as he should to all that is required by the location, climate, soil, mores, surroundings, and all the particular relationships of the people he was to institute.[16] Not that there do not still remain an infinite number of administrative and economic details left to the wisdom of the government. But it always has two infallible rules for acting correctly on those occasions. One is the spirit of the law, which should help in deciding cases that the law could not foresee. The other is the general will, source and supplement of all the laws, and which should always be consulted when they are lacking. How, I will be asked, can the general will be known in cases where it has not expressed itself? Must the whole nation be assembled at each unforeseen event? Such an assembly is all the less necessary because it is not sure its decision would be the expression of the general will; because this means is impractical for a large people; and because it is rarely necessary when the government is well intentioned.[17] For the leaders know very well that the general will is always for the side most favorable to the public interest—that is, for the most equitable; so that it is only necessary to be just and one is assured of following the general will. Often, when it is too openly offended, it manifests itself despite the terrible restraint of the public authority. I look as near at hand as I can for examples to follow in such a case. In China, the prince follows an unwavering maxim of blaming his officers in all disputes that arise between them and the people. Is bread expensive in one province? The intendant is put in prison. Is there rioting in another? The governor is demoted, and each mandarin answers with his life for all the trouble that occurs in his department. Not that the affair is not later examined in a regular trial. But long experience has made it possible to anticipate the verdict. There is rarely any injustice to remedy in this; and the emperor, convinced that public clamor never arises without cause, always discerns among the seditious cries that he punishes, some just grievances that he rectifies.

It is no small thing to have brought order and peace to all the parts of the republic; it is no small thing that the State is tranquil and the law respected. But if one does nothing more, all this will be more apparent than real, and the government will have difficulty making itself obeyed if it limits itself to obedience. If it is good to know how to use men as they are, it is better still to make them what one needs them to be. The most absolute authority is that which penetrates to the inner man and is exerted no less on his will than on his actions. It is certain that people are in the long run what the government makes them. Warriors, citizens, men when it so pleases; mob and rabble when it wishes. And every prince who scorns his subjects dishonors himself by showing that he did not know how to make them worthy. Train men, therefore, if you want to command men. If you want the laws to be obeyed, make them beloved, so that for men to do what they should, they need only think they ought to do it. That was the great art of the governments of antiquity, in those remote times when philosophers gave laws to peoples, and only used their authority to make them wise and happy. From this came the many sumptuary laws, the many regulations concerning mores, the many public maxims accepted or rejected with the greatest care. Even tyrants did not forget this important part of administration, and they gave as much careful attention to corrupting the mores of their slaves as did the magistrates to correcting the mores of their fellow citizens. But our modern governments, which think they have done all there is to do when they have collected money, don't even imagine that it is either necessary or possible to go that far.

II. The second essential rule of public *economy* is no less important than the first. Do you want the general will to be fulfilled? Make sure that all private wills are related to it; and since virtue is only this conformity of the private will to the general, to say the same thing briefly, make virtue reign.[18]

If political theorists were less blinded by their ambition, they would see how impossible it is for any establishment whatever to function in the spirit of its institution if it is not directed in accordance with the law of duty. They would realize that the greatest wellspring of public authority lies in the hearts of the citizens, and that for the maintenance of the government, nothing can replace good mores. Not only is it worthy men alone who know how to administer laws, but basically it is only honorable men who know how to obey them. Anyone who manages to defy remorse will not long delay in defying corporal punishment, which is a less rigorous and less continuous chastisement and one from which there is at least the hope of escaping. And whatever precautions are taken, those who are only waiting for impunity to do evil, will hardly lack means of eluding the law or escaping a penalty. Then, since all the private interests combine against the general interest which is no longer that of anyone, public vices have more force to weaken the laws than the laws have to repress vices. And the corruption of the people and leaders finally extends to the government, however wise it may be. The worst of all abuses is to obey the laws in appearance only to break them in fact with safety. Soon the best laws become the most pernicious. It would be a hundred times better if they did not exist; it would be one resource that would still exist when no others remain. In such a situation, it is useless to add edicts upon edicts, regulations upon regulations. All that merely serves to introduce other abuses without correcting those that already exist. The more you multiply laws, the more contemptible you make them; and all the overseers you institute are merely new lawbreakers destined to share with the old ones or do their plundering separately. Soon the price of virtue becomes that of brigandage. The vilest men are the best accredited. The greater they are, the more contemptible they are. Their infamy manifests itself in their dignities, and they are dishonored by their honors. If they buy the votes of leaders or the protection of women, it is so they themselves can sell justice, duty, and the State. And the people, who does not see that its own vices are the primary cause of its misfortunes, mutters and cries in despair, "All my ills come only from those whom I pay to protect me."

Then, in place of the voice of duty that no longer speaks in men's hearts, leaders are forced to substitute the cry of terror or the lure of an apparent interest by which they deceive their creatures. Then there must be recourse to all the small, despicable tricks they call *maxims of State* and *cabinet secrets*. All the vigor that remains in the government is used by its members to ruin and replace each other, while business matters remain neglected or are taken up only as personal interest demands and according to its direction. Finally, the whole skill of these great politicians is so to hypnotize those whose help they need that each person believes he is working for his own interest while working for *theirs*. I say theirs if indeed it is in fact the true interest of leaders to annihilate the people in order to subject it, and to ruin their own goods in order to secure possession of them.

But when citizens love their duty, and when the trustees of public authority sincerely apply themselves to encouraging this love through their example and by their efforts, all difficulties vanish and administration becomes so easy that it can do without that shady art whose baseness produces its secrecy. Those ambitious minds, so dangerous and so admired, all those great ministers whose glory is combined with the people's misfortunes, are no longer missed. Good public mores replace the genius of leaders. And the longer virtue reigns, the less necessary are talents. Ambition itself is better served by duty than by usurpation. The people, convinced that its leaders work only for its happiness, spares them by its deference from working to strengthen their power; and history shows us in a thousand places that the authority the people accords to those it loves and by whom it is beloved, is a hundred times more absolute than all the tyranny of usurpers. This does not mean that the government ought to fear using its power, but rather that it should only use it in a legitimate manner. History provides a thousand examples of ambitious or pusillanimous leaders, who have been lost through softness or pride, but none of someone who fared badly because he was only equitable. But negligence should not be confused with moderation, nor gentleness with weakness. To be just, it is necessary to be severe. Tolerating wickedness that one has the right and the power to repress is being wicked oneself.[19]

It is not enough to say to citizens, be good. They must be taught to be so, and example itself, which is the first lesson in this regard, is not the only means that must be used. Patriotism is the most effective, for as I have already said, every man is virtuous when his private will conforms on all matters with the general will, and we willingly want what is wanted by the people we love.

It seems that the sentiment of humanity evaporates and weakens as it is extended over the whole world, and that we can't be moved by calamities in Tartary or Japan as we are by those of a European people. Interest and commiseration must in some way be confined and compressed to be activated. Now since this inclination in us can only be useful to those with whom we have to live, it is good that the feeling of humanity, concentrated among fellow citizens, gains fresh force through the habit of seeing one another and through the common interest that unites them. It is certain that the greatest miracles of virtue have been produced by patriotism. By combining the force of egoism with all the beauty of virtue, this sweet and ardent sentiment gains an energy which, without disfiguring it, makes it the most heroic of all the passions. It produced the many immortal actions whose splendor dazzles our weak eyes, and the many great men whose antique virtues have been thought to be fables ever since patriotism has been turned to derision. We should not be surprised by this. The ecstasies of tender hearts appear as so many chimeras to anyone who has not experienced them. And love of the homeland, a hundred times more ardent and delightful than that of a mistress, likewise cannot be imagined except by being felt. But it is easy to notice, in all hearts that are inflamed by it and in all the actions it inspires, that fiery and sublime ardor which even the purest virtue lacks when separated from this love. Let us dare to compare Socrates himself to Cato. One was more a philosopher, the other more a citizen. Athens was already lost, and Socrates had no homeland other than the whole world. Cato always carried his homeland in the bottom of his heart; he lived for it alone and could not outlive it. Socrates' virtue is that of the wisest of men. But compared to Caesar and Pompey, Cato seems like a God among mortals. One teaches a few private individuals, combats the Sophists, and dies for the truth; the other defends the State, freedom, and the laws against the conquerors of the world, and finally takes leave of the earth when he no longer sees any homeland to serve.[20] A worthy student of Socrates would be the most virtuous of his contemporaries; a worthy emulator of Cato would be the greatest. The former's own virtue would constitute his happiness; the latter would seek his happiness in that of all others. We would be taught by one, but ruled by the other, and that alone would determine our preference. For a people of wise men has never been formed, but it is not impossible to make a people happy.

Do we want peoples to be virtuous? Let us then start by making them love their homeland. But how are they to love it if the homeland is nothing more for them than for foreigners, and accords them only what it cannot refuse to anyone? The problem would be still worse if they did not even enjoy civil safety there, and if their goods, life, or freedom were at the discretion of powerful men, without its being either possible or permitted for them to dare invoke the laws. Then, subjected to the duties of the civil state without even enjoying the rights of the state of nature and without being able to use their force to defend themselves, they would consequently be in the worst possible condition for free men, and the word *homeland* could have only an odious or ridiculous meaning for them. It is not credible that an arm can be harmed or cut off without pain being transmitted to the head. And it is no more credible that the general will would allow any member of the State, whoever he might be, to injure or destroy another, than it is that the fingers of a reasoning man would put out his own eyes. Private safety is so closely connected to the public confederation that were it not for the consideration owed to human weakness, this convention would be dissolved by right if a single citizen perished who could have been saved; if a single one were wrongly held in prison; and if a single suit were lost due to evident injustice. For when the fundamental conventions are violated, one can no longer see what right or what interest could maintain the people in the social union, unless it is restrained by force alone, in which case the civil state is dissolved.

Indeed, isn't the body of the nation under an engagement to provide for the preservation of the humblest of its members with as much care as for all the others? And is the safety of a citizen any less the common cause than that of the whole State? If someone tells us it is good that a single man should perish for all, I shall admire this adage from the lips of a worthy and virtuous patriot who consecrates himself willingly and out of duty to die for the safety of his country. But if this means that the government is allowed to sacrifice an innocent man for the safety of the multitude, I hold this maxim to be one of the most execrable that tyranny ever invented, the most false that might be proposed, the most dangerous that might be accepted, and the most directly opposed to the fundamental laws of society.[21] Rather than that one ought to perish for all, all have engaged their goods and their lives for the defense of each one among them, in order that private weakness always be protected by public force, and each member by the whole State. After conjecturing the subtraction of one individual after another from the people, urge the partisans of this maxim to explain more clearly what they mean by *the body of the State,* and you will see that they finally reduce it to a small number of men who are not the people, but the officers of the people, and who, having obligated themselves by a personal oath to perish for its safety, claim to prove thereby that it is the people who ought to perish for theirs.

Do you want to find examples of the protection that the State owes to its members, and of the respect it owes to their persons? These must be sought only in the most illustrious and courageous nations on earth, and there are scarcely any except free peoples who know the worth of a man. It is known how great the perplexity of the entire republic was in Sparta when a matter of punishing a guilty citizen arose. In Macedonia, the life of a man was held to be so important that even in all his greatness, Alexander—that powerful monarch—would not have dared to put a criminal Macedonian to death in cold blood unless the accused had appeared to defend himself before his fellow citizens and had been condemned by them. But the Romans stood out over all the peoples of the earth for the deference of the government toward private individuals and for its scrupulous attention to the inviolable rights of all members of the State. Nothing was as sacred as the life of the simple citizens. No less than the assembly of the entire people was necessary to condemn one of them. Neither the senate itself nor the consuls in all their majesty had the right to do this; and among the world's most powerful people, the crime and punishment of a citizen was a public desolation. It also appeared so brutal to shed blood for any crime whatever, that by the law *Porcia,* the death penalty was commuted to exile for those who would want to outlive the loss of such a sweet homeland. In Rome and in the armies, everything betokened that love of the citizens for one another and that respect for the name Roman which aroused courage and animated the virtue of anyone who had the honor to bear it. The hat of a citizen freed from slavery or the civic crown of one who had saved another's life were the things viewed with the greatest pleasure at victory celebrations. And it is notable that of the crowns used in war to honor noble actions, only the civic crown and that of the victors were made of grass and leaves; all the others were merely gold. Thus was Rome virtuous, and became the mistress of the world. Ambitious leaders! A shepherd governs his dogs and his flocks, yet he is the humblest of men. If it is noble to command, it is when those who obey us can do us honor. Therefore, respect your fellow citizens, and you will make yourselves respectable. Respect freedom, and your power will be increased daily. Never exceed your rights, and soon they will be limitless.

Let the homeland, then, be the common mother of the citizens; let the advantages they enjoy in their country endear it to them; let the government leave a large enough share of the public administration to them so that they feel at home; and let the laws be in their sight only guarantees of the common freedom. These rights, noble as they are, belong to all men. But without appearing to attack them directly, the bad will of leaders easily reduces their effect to zero. Law that is abused serves the powerful simultaneously as an offensive weapon and as a shield against the weak, and the pretext of the public good is always the most dangerous scourge of the people. What is most necessary and perhaps most difficult in the government is rigorous integrity in providing justice for all, and especially protecting the poor against the tyranny of the rich. The greatest harm is already done when there are poor men to protect and rich ones to restrain. It is only on moderate wealth that the full force of the laws is exerted. Laws are equally powerless against the treasures of the rich and against the indigence of the poor; the first eludes them, the second escapes them; one breaks the net and the other slips through.

It is, therefore, one of the government's most important tasks to prevent extreme inequality of wealth, not by taking treasures away from those who possess them, but by removing the means of accumulating them from everyone; nor by building poorhouses, but by protecting citizens from becoming poor. People unequally distributed over the territory and crowded into one place while others become depopulated; arts of pleasure and pure invention favored at the expense of useful and difficult trades; agriculture sacrificed to commerce; the tax-farmer made necessary by bad administration of the State revenues; venality, finally, pushed to such excess that reputation is measured in coin and the virtues themselves are sold for money: these are the most obvious causes of opulence and indigence, of the substitution of private interest for the public interest, of the mutual hate of citizens, of their indifference to the common cause, of the corruption of the people, and of the weakening of all the mechanisms of the government. Such are, consequently, the evils that are hard to cure once they make themselves felt, but which a wise administration should prevent in order to maintain, along with good mores, respect for the laws, patriotism, and a vigorous general will.

But all these precautions will be insufficient without going still further. I end this part of the public *economy* where I ought to have started it. The homeland cannot subsist without freedom, nor freedom without virtue, nor virtue without citizens. You will have all these if you train citizens; without doing so, you will have only wicked slaves, beginning with the leaders of the State. Now training citizens is not accomplished in a day, and to have them as men they must be taught as children. Someone may tell me that anyone who has men to govern should not seek, outside of their nature, a perfection of which they are not capable; that he should not want to destroy their passions, and that the execution of such a project would not be any more desirable than it is possible. I will agree the more strongly with all this because a man who had no passions would certainly be a very bad citizen. But it must also be agreed that although men cannot be taught to love nothing, it is not impossible to teach them to love one thing rather than another, and what is truly beautiful rather than what is deformed. If, for example, they are trained early enough never to consider their persons except as related to the body of the State, and not to perceive their own existence, so to speak, except as part of the State's, they will eventually come to identify themselves in some way with this larger whole; to feel themselves to be members of the homeland; to love it with that delicate sentiment that any isolated man feels only for himself; to elevate their soul perpetually toward this great object; and thereby to transform into a sublime virtue this dangerous disposition from which all our vices arise. Not only does philosophy demonstrate the possibility of these new directions, but history provides a thousand stunning examples. If they are so rare among us, it is because no one cares whether there are any citizens, and still less does anyone think of doing something early enough to form them. It is too late to change our natural inclinations when they have become entrenched, and habit has been combined with egoism. It is too late to draw us out of our ourselves once the *human self* concentrated in our hearts has acquired that contemptible activity that aborbs all virtue and constitutes the life of petty souls. How could patriotism develop in the midst of so many other passions stifling it? and what is left for fellow citizens of a heart already divided among greed, a mistress, and vanity?

It is from the first moment of life that one must learn to deserve to live; and since one shares the rights of citizens at birth, the instant of our birth should be the beginning of the performance of our duties. If there are laws for maturity, there should be some for childhood that teach obedience to others. And as each man's reason is not allowed to be the unique arbiter of his duties, it is even less appropriate to abandon the education of children to the enlightenment and prejudices of their fathers in that it matters even more to the State than to fathers. For according to the natural course of events, the father's death often deprives him of the final fruits of this education, but the homeland sooner or later feels its effects; the State remains, and the family is dissolved. And if the public authority, by assuming the fathers' place and taking charge of this important function, acquires their rights by fulfilling their duties, the fathers have all the less cause for complaint because in this regard they are actually only changing name, and will have in common, under the name citizens, the same authority over their children that they exercised separately under the name *fathers,* and will be no less well obeyed when they speak in the name of the law than they were when they spoke in the name of nature. Public education, under rules prescribed by the government and magistrates established by the sovereign, is therefore one of the fundamental maxims of popular or legitimate government. If children are raised in common in the midst of equality, if they are imbued with the laws of the State and the maxims of the general will, if they are taught to respect them above all things, if they are surrounded by examples and objects that constantly remind them of the tender mother who nourishes them, her love for them, the inestimable benefits they receive from her, and what they owe in return, there can be no doubt that they will learn from this to love one another as brothers, never to want anything except what the society wants, to substitute the actions of men and citizens for the sterile, empty babble of sophists, and one day to become the defenders and fathers of the homeland whose children they will have been for so long.

I shall not discuss the magistrates destined to preside over this education, which is certainly the State's most important business. It is apparent that if such marks of public confidence were lightly accorded, if this sublime function were not—for those who had worthily fulfilled all the others—the reward for their labors, the honorable and sweet repose of their old age, and the height of all honors, the whole undertaking would be useless, and the education unsuccessful. For everywhere that the lesson is not supported by authority and the precept by example, teaching is fruitless, and virtue itself loses its credit in the mouth of one who does not practice it. But when illustrious warriors, bent by the weight of their laurels, preach courage; when up-right magistrates, grown gray in dignity and at the tribunals, teach justice; all of them will train their virtuous successors, and will transmit from age to age to the generations that follow the experience and talents of leaders, the courage and virtue of citizens, and the emulation common to all of living and dying for the homeland.

I know of only three peoples who in former times practiced public education: namely the Cretans, the Lacedemonians, and the ancient Persians. Among all three it was the greatest success, and produced marvels among the latter two. When the world became divided into nations too large to be well governed, this method was no longer practicable; and other reasons that the reader can easily see have also prevented its being tried by any modern people. It is a very remarkable thing that the Romans could do without it. But Rome was for five hundred years a continual miracle that the world cannot hope to see again. The Romans' virtue, engendered by a horror of tyranny and the crimes of tyrants and by innate patriotism, turned all their homes into as many schools for citizens; and the unlimited power of fathers over their children placed so much severity in the private domain that the father—more feared than magistrates—was the censor of mores and avenger of the laws in his domestic tribunal.[22]

In this way, an attentive and well-intentioned government, ceaselessly careful to maintain or revive patriotism among the people, prevents from afar the evils that sooner or later result from the indifference of citizens concerning the fate of the republic, and confines within narrow limits that personal interest which so isolates private individuals that the State is weakened by their power and cannot hope to gain anything from their goodwill. Wherever the people loves its country, respects the laws, and lives simply, little else remains to do to make it happy. And in public administration, where fortune plays less of a role than in the fate of private individuals, wisdom is so close to happiness that these two objects are indistinguishable.

III.   It is not enough to have citizens and protect them; it is also necessary to think about their subsistence. And providing for the public needs is an evident consequence of the general will and third essential duty of the government. This duty is not, it should be apparent, to fill the granaries of private individuals and dispense them from working, but rather to maintain abundance within their reach so that to acquire it, work is always necessary and never useless. It also extends to all the operations concerning the maintenance of the public treasury and the expenses of the public administration. Thus, after discussing the general *economy* in relation to the government of persons, it remains for us to consider it in relation to administration of goods.

This part offers no fewer difficulties to resolve or contradictions to overcome than the preceding one. It is certain that the right of property is the most sacred of all the rights of citizens, and more important in certain respects than freedom itself, either because it is more closely connected with the preservation of life, or because, since goods are easier to usurp and more difficult to protect than one's person, greater respect should be accorded to what can more easily be stolen, or finally because property is the true basis of civil society and the true guarantee of the citizens' engagements. For if goods were not held accountable for persons, nothing would be so easy as to elude one's duties and scoff at the laws. On the other hand, it is no less certain that the maintenance of the State and the government requires costs and expenses. And since anyone who grants the end cannot refuse the means, it follows that the members of the society should contribute some of their goods to its upkeep. Moreover it is difficult to assure the property of private individuals on the one hand without attacking it on the other, and it isn't possible for all the regulations concerning inheritance, wills, and contracts not to constrain the citizens in certain respects regarding the disposition of their own goods, and consequently regarding their right of property.

But besides what I have already said about the harmony that prevails between the authority of the law and the freedom of the citizens, there is, in relation to the disposition of goods, one important remark to be made that overcomes many difficulties. It is, as Pufendorf has shown, that by the nature of the right of property, it does not extend beyond the life of the proprietor, and that the instant a man is dead, his goods no longer belong to him.[23] Thus prescribing to him the conditions under which he can dispose of them, although in appearance an impairment of his right, is in fact an extension of it.

In general, although the institution of the laws that regulate the power of private individuals in disposing of their own goods belongs to the sovereign alone, the spirit of these laws, which the government should follow in applying them, is that from father to son and kin to kin, the family's goods should leave the family and be alienated as little as possible. There is an obvious reason for this in favor of children, for whom the right of property would be quite useless if their father left them nothing, and who, moreover, having often contributed by their labor to the acquisition of the father's goods, are in their own name associated with his right. But another reason, more remote yet not less important, is that nothing is more pernicious for mores and for the republic than continual changes of status and fortune among the citizens—changes that are the proof and the source of a thousand disorders, that upset and confuse everything, and due to which, since those who have been raised for one thing find themselves destined for another, neither those who rise nor those who fall can adopt the maxims or enlightenment suited to their new status, much less fulfill its duties. I turn now to the topic of public finances.

If the people governed itself and there were nothing intermediary between the administration of the State and the citizens, they would only have to pay their shares as the occasion arose in proportion to the public needs and the capacities of private individuals. And since no one would ever lose sight of the collection or use of State revenues, neither fraud nor abuse could slip into their handling. The State would never be encumbered by debts, nor the people overwhelmed by taxes; or at least the assurance of its proper use would console the people for the hardship of the taxation. But things cannot be thus, and however limited a State's territory may be, its civil society is always too numerous to be able to be governed by all its members. The public revenues must necessarily pass through the hands of the leaders who, besides the interest of the State, all have their private interest, which is not the last to be heeded. On the other hand, the people, perceiving the greediness of leaders and their extravagant expenses rather than the public needs, protests at being divested of necessities to provide superfluities for others. And once these maneuvers have embittered it to a certain degree, the most upright administration could not succeed in reestablishing confidence. Then if contributions are voluntary, they are unproductive; if they are forced, they are illegitimate; and the difficulty of a just and wise *economy* lies in the cruel alternative of letting the State perish or attacking the sacred right of property which is its mainstay.

The first thing that the founder of a republic ought to do after the establishment of the laws is to find capital sufficient for the upkeep of the magistrates and other officers, and for all public expenses. This capital is called *ærarium*, or the *public treasury,* if it is in money; the *public domain* if it is in land; and the latter is much preferable to the former for obvious reasons. Anyone who has given this matter enough thought can hardly have any other opinion than that of Bodin, who views public domain as the most honest and safe of all means of providing for the State's needs.[24] And it is notable that Romulus's first care in the division of land was to designate a third of it for this purpose. I admit that it is not impossible for the proceeds of a badly administered public domain to be reduced to nothing; but it is not of the essence of public domain to be badly administered.

Prior to any use of it, this capital ought to be assigned or accepted by the assembly of the people or Estates of the country, which should then determine its use. After this solemn ceremony which renders this capital inalienable, it changes its nature, so to speak, and its revenues become so sacred that diverting the smallest thing to the detriment of its purpose is not only the most infamous of all thefts, but a crime of high treason. It is a great dishonor for Rome that the integrity of the quaestor Cato was openly discussed, and that an Emperor rewarding a singer's talent with a few coins had to add that the money came from his family's goods and not from the State's. But if there are few men like Galba, where will we find Catos? And once vice is no longer a dishonor, what leaders will be scrupulous enough to abstain from touching the public revenues left to their discretion, and not soon deceive themselves by pretending to confuse their vain and scandalous dissipations with the glory of the State, and the means of extending their authority with those of increasing its power? It is above all in this delicate part of administration that virtue is the only effective instrument and that the magistrate's integrity is the only check capable of restraining his greed. The books and all the records of administrators serve less to reveal their infidelities than to cover them up; and prudence is never as quick to imagine new precautions as is knavery to elude them. Therefore forget registers and papers, and place the finances in faithful hands; it is the only way to have them faithfully administered.

Once the public capital is established, the leaders of the State are by right its administrators; for this administration is a part of the government, always essential, although not always equally so. Its influence increases in proportion as that of other mechanisms diminishes, and it can be said that a government has reached the final degree of corruption when the only thing left of its vitality is money. Now since all governments tend continually to weaken, this reason alone shows why no State can subsist if its revenues do not increase constantly.

The first awareness of the necessity for this increase is also the first sign of internal disorder in the State. And the wise administrator, as he thinks of finding money to meet the present need, doesn't neglect to seek the ultimate cause of this new need, just as a sailor seeing water flood his ship doesn't forget, as he gets the pump into action, to find and plug the leak as well.

From this rule flows the most important maxim of the administration of finances, which is to work much more carefully to prevent needs than to increase revenues. However diligent one is, help that comes only after the harm is done, and more slowly, always leaves the State in distress. While the remedy for one difficulty is being worked out, another is already being experienced, and the resources themselves produce new difficulties. So that in the end the nation is overwhelmed with debts, the people is downtrodden, the government loses all its vigor and it no longer does much of anything with a great deal of money. I believe it was this great maxim, when well established, that gave rise to the marvels of the governments of antiquity, which did more with parsimony than ours with all their treasures. And it is from this, perhaps, that the common meaning of the word *economy* is derived, referring more to the wise handling of what one has than to the means of acquiring what one does not have.

Independently of the public domain which yields to the State in proportion to the probity of those who administer it, if one had sufficient knowledge of the whole force of the general administration, especially when it is limited to legitimate means, one would be amazed at the resources leaders have for anticipating all public needs without touching the goods of private individuals. As they are the masters of all the State's commerce, nothing is easier for them than to direct it in a manner that provides for everything, often without appearing to have any hand in it. The distribution of foodstuffs, money, and merchandise in just proportions according to time and place is the true secret of finances, and the source of their abundance, provided that those who administer them know how to project their views far enough in advance and on occasion accept an apparent and proximate loss in order actually to obtain immense profits at a future time. When a government pays subsidies, rather than to be paid, for the exportation of wheat in years of plenty and for its importation in years of scarcity, one needs to have such facts before one's eyes to think them true; and they would be treated as pure fiction if they had occurred long ago. Suppose that to prevent scarcity in bad years, the establishment of public storehouses was proposed. In many countries wouldn't the upkeep of such a useful establishment serve as the pretext for new taxes? In Geneva, such granaries—established and maintained by a wise administration—provide a public resource in bad years and the principal revenue of the State at all times. *Alit et Ditat*[25] is the noble and just inscription one reads on the facade of the building. In order to present here the economic system of a good government, I have often looked toward the system of that republic, happy thus to find in my homeland the example of wisdom and happiness I would like to see prevail in all countries.

If one examines how the needs of a State grow, this will often be found to happen in about the same way as it does for private individuals, less by true necessity than by an expansion of frivolous desires, and often expenses are increased solely to provide a pretext for increasing income. Thus the State would sometimes profit from not being rich, and such apparent wealth is basically a greater burden than poverty itself would be. There may be the hope, it is true, of holding peoples in stricter dependence by giving them with one hand what has been taken away from them with the other; and this was the policy Joseph used with the Egyptians. But this vain sophism is all the more fatal to the State in that the money does not return to the same hands from which it came, and that maxims of this sort only enrich idlers with spoils taken from useful men.

The taste for conquests is one of the most obvious and dangerous causes of this increase in needs. This taste, often engendered by another type of ambition than the one it seems to represent, is not always what it appears to be; and its true motive is not so much the apparent desire for the growth of the nation as the hidden desire to increase the internal authority of the leaders, with the help of an increased number of troops and by means of the diversion that the war's objectives create in the minds of the citizens.

What is at least very certain is that nothing is as downtrodden or miserable as conquering peoples, and even their successes only increase their miseries. Even if history did not teach us so, reason would be enough to show us that the larger the State, the heavier and more burdensome, in proportion, will become its expenses. For all the provinces must furnish their quota of the expenses of the general administration, and beyond that each province must spend the same amount for its own particular administration as if it were independent. Add the fact that all fortunes are made in one place and consumed in another, which soon breaks the equilibrium between what is produced and what is consumed, and impoverishes a great deal of countryside in order to enrich a single town.

Another source of the increase of public needs is related to the preceding one. A time may come when the citizens, no longer considering themselves interested in the common cause, would cease to be the defenders of the homeland, and when magistrates would prefer to command mercenaries rather than free men, if only in order to use the former at the expedient time and place to subjugate the latter all the better. Such was the state of Rome at the end of the Republic and under the Emperors. For all the victories of the first Romans, like those of Alexander, had been won by brave citizens who knew how to shed blood for the homeland if necessary, but who never sold it.[26] Marius was the first, in the war of Jugurtha, who dishonored the legions by introducing freedmen, vagabonds, and other mercenaries. Having become enemies of the peoples for whose happiness they were responsible, tyrants established standing armies, in appearance to repress foreigners and in fact to oppress the inhabitants. In order to raise these armies, it was necessary to take farmers away from the land, so that the lack of farmers lowered the quantity of foodstuffs and the cost of maintaining them introduced taxes that increased food prices. This first disorder caused the people to protest. To repress them it was necessary to multiply the troops, and consequently indigence. And the more despair increased, the more necessary it was to increase it further to prevent its effects. On the other hand, these mercenaries, whose worth could be judged by the price at which they sold themselves, were proud of their debasement, scorned the laws by which they were protected and their brothers whose bread they ate, and thought it more honorable to be Caesar's satellites than Rome's defenders. Committed to blind obedience, their job was to hold a dagger over their fellow citizens, ready to murder all at the first signal. It would not be difficult to show that this was one of the main causes of the ruin of the Roman Empire.

The invention of artillery and fortifications has, in our times, forced the sovereigns of Europe to reestablish the use of standing armies to defend their fortresses. But although the motives are more legitimate, it is to be feared that the effect will be equally pernicious. It is no less necessary to depopulate the countryside to raise armies and set up garrisons. To maintain them, it is no less necessary to oppress the peoples. And in recent times, these dangerous establishments have been growing so rapidly in all our countries that one can foresee only the future depopulation of Europe and, sooner or later, the ruin of the peoples who inhabit it.

However this may be, it should be apparent that such institutions necessarily upset the true economic system, which derives the principal revenue of the State from the public domain, and leave only the unfortunate resource of subsidies and taxes, which remain for me to discuss.

It is necessary to remember, at this point, that the basis of the social compact is property, and its first condition that each person continue in the peaceful enjoyment of what belongs to him. It is true that by the same treaty, each person obligates himself, at least tacitly, to pay his share of the public needs. But since this engagement cannot undermine the fundamental law and supposes that the taxpayers acknowledge the evidence of need, it is apparent that in order to be legitimate, this payment ought to be made willingly. Not through a private will, as if it were necessary to have each citizen's consent and he only ought to provide what he pleases—which would be directly contrary to the spirit of the confederation—but through a general will, by majority vote, and based on proportional rates that leave no room for an arbitrary assessment of taxes.

This truth—that taxes cannot be legitimately established except by the consent of the people or its representatives—has been generally acknowledged by all the philosophers and legal theorists who have acquired any reputation in matters of political right, including Bodin himself.[27] While a few have established maxims that appear contrary, it is easy to see the private motives that inspired them to do so, they attach so many conditions and restrictions that it all comes down to exactly the same thing. For whether the people can refuse or the sovereign should not require is indifferent in terms of right. And if it is only a question of force, it is completely useless to examine what is or is not legitimate.

The contributions levied from the people are of two kinds: some on property, which are collected on the basis of things, and others personal, which are paid by the head. Both are given the names *taxes* or *subsidies.* When the people sets the total amount it gives, it is called a *subsidy;* when it gives all the proceeds of a form of taxation, it is called a *tax.* In the book *The Spirit of the Laws,* one finds that assessment by head is more in keeping with servitude, and property taxation more suited to freedom.[28] That would be incontestable if all shares by head were equal. For nothing would be as disproportionate as such taxation, and the spirit of freedom consists above all in the precise respecting of proportions. But if taxation by head is exactly proportionate to the means of private individuals, as the French *capitation* could be, and thus has simultaneously both a property and a personal basis, it is the most equitable and consequently the most suited to free men. At first these proportions appear very easy to observe, because being relative to each person's status in the world, the indications are always public. But besides the fact that greed, reputation, and fraud know how to leave no overt traces, it is rare that all the elements that should be included in these calculations are taken into account. First, one should consider the relationship of quantities, according to which—all other things being equal—someone who has ten times more goods than another should pay ten times more. Second, the relationship of use, that is the distinction between the necessary and the superfluous. Someone who has only the bare necessities should pay nothing at all; taxation on someone who has superfluities can, if need be, approach the totality of what exceeds his necessities. To this he will reply that considering his rank, what would be superfluous for an inferior man is necessary for him. But this is a lie. For a nobleman has two legs just like a cowherd, and has only one stomach as he does. Moreover, this so-called necessity is so far from necessary to his rank that if he had the sense to renounce it for a praiseworthy cause, he would be all the more respected. The people would bow before a minister who would go to the council on foot because he had sold his carriages when the State was in urgent need. Finally, the law does not require magnificence of anyone, and decorum never provides a reason to go against right.

A third relationship that is never taken into account, but that should always come first, is that of the utility each person derives from the social confederation, which strongly protects the immense possessions of the rich and barely lets a poor wretch enjoy the hut he built with his own hands. Aren't all the advantages of society for the powerful and the rich? Aren't all the lucrative jobs filled by them alone? Aren't all the pardons and all the exemptions reserved for them? And isn't public authority entirely in their favor? When an esteemed man steals from his creditors or cheats in other ways, isn't he always sure of impunity? The beatings he gives, the violent actions he commits, even the murders and assassinations he is guilty of, aren't these affairs passed over in silence and forgotten after six months? If this same man is robbed, the forces of law and order go into action immediately, and woe to the innocents whom he suspects. Does he have to travel through dangerous places? He is escorted through the countryside. Does the axle of his carriage break? Everyone rushes to his aid. Is it noisy near his door? He says a word and all is silent. Does the crowd annoy him? He gives a sign and everything becomes orderly. Is a cart driver in his way? His men are ready to beat him. And fifty honest pedestrians going about their business will be trampled before an idle good-for-nothing's coach is slowed down. All these attentions don't cost him a penny; they are the rich man's right, and not the price of riches. How different is the picture of the poor man! The more humanity owes him, the more society refuses him. All doors are closed to him, even when he has the right to make them open. And if he sometimes obtains justice, it is with greater difficulty than another would obtain pardon. If there are corvées to do, troops to be raised, he is given preference. In addition to his own burden, he always bears the one from which his richer neighbor has the influence to be exempted. At the slightest accident that happens to him, everyone abandons him. If his poor cart tips over, far from being helped by anyone, I consider him lucky if he avoids the passing insults of the flippant servants of some young duke. In short, all free assistance flees him when needed, precisely because he has nothing with which to pay for it. And I consider him a lost man if he has the misfortune to have an honest soul, an attractive daughter, and a powerful neighbor.

Another point, no less important to note, is that the losses of poor men are far less reparable than those of the rich, and that the difficulty of acquiring always increases in proportion to need. Nothing produces nothing; it is as true in business as in physics. Money breeds money, and the first gold *pistole* is sometimes harder to earn than the second million. But it goes even further. All that the poor man pays is forever lost to him, and remains in, or returns to, the hands of the rich. And since the proceeds of taxes go sooner or later only to those men who take part in the government or who are close to it, they have—even in paying their share—an evident interest in increasing taxes.

Let us summarize in a few words the social compact of the two estates. *You need me, for I am rich and you are poor, so let us come to an agreement between ourselves. I shall permit you to have the honor of serving me on condition that you give me what little you have for the trouble I shall take to command you.*

If all these things are carefully combined, it will be found that in order to impose taxation in an equitable and truly proportional way, assessment should not be made solely in proportion to the goods of taxpayers, but in a proportion composed of the difference between their condition and the superfluity of their goods—a very important and very difficult calculation made daily by multitudes of honest clerks who know arithmetic, but which a Plato or a Montesquieu would only have dared to undertake with trembling and after imploring heaven for enlightenment and integrity.

Another drawback of personal taxation is that it is felt as too heavy a burden and is levied too harshly, which doesn't prevent it from being subject to many unpaid debts, because it is easier to hide one's head than one's possessions from the tax rolls and from prosecution.

Of all other kinds of assessment, the land tax or taille on real estate has always been thought most advantageous in countries where more consideration is given to the amount of proceeds and the certainty of payment than to the least annoyance for the people. Some have even dared to say that the peasant must be burdened to rouse him from his laziness, and that he would do nothing if he had nothing to pay. But experience among all the people of the world belies this ridiculous maxim. It is in Holland and England, where the farmer pays very little, and above all in China, where he pays nothing, that land is best cultivated. On the contrary, everywhere that the farmer is assessed in proportion to the yield of his field, he lets it lie fallow or reaps only exactly what he needs to live. This is because for anyone who loses the fruit of his labor, it is a gain to do nothing; and placing a fine on work is a strange way to abolish laziness.

Taxation on land or on wheat, especially when it is excessive, results in two disadvantages so terrible that they eventually will depopulate or ruin all countries in which it is established.

The first comes from the lack of circulation of currency, for commerce and industry attract all the money from the countryside to the capitals, and since the tax destroys any proportion that might still exist between the farmer's needs and the price of his wheat, money always comes in and never returns. The richer the town, the more miserable the country. The proceeds from the taille pass from the hands of the prince or tax-farmer into those of artists and merchants; and the grower, who never receives any but the smallest part, is finally exhausted by always paying equally and always receiving less. How could a man live if he had only veins and no arteries, or if his arteries only carried his blood to within several inches of his heart? Chardin says that in Persia the king's duties on foodstuffs are also paid in foodstuffs. This usage, which Herodotus indicates was practiced long ago in that same country until the time of Darius, can prevent the evil of which I have just spoken.[29] But unless in Persia the intendants, directors, clerks, and storehouse guardians are a different kind of people than everywhere else, I find it hard to believe that the least bit of all these products ever reaches the king, that the wheat doesn't rot in all the granaries, and that fire doesn't consume most of the storehouses.

The second disadvantage comes from an apparent advantage, which allows problems to grow worse before they are noticed. This is that wheat is a food whose value is not raised by taxes in the countries that produce it, so that despite its absolute necessity, the quantity is diminished without an increase in price. As a result, many people die of hunger although wheat continues to be cheap, and the farmer alone bears the burden of the tax, which he has been unable to pass on in the selling price. It must be carefully noted that the same reasoning should not be applied to the taille on real estate as to duties on all merchandise whose price is thereby increased and which are therefore paid not so much by the merchants as by the buyers. For these duties, however large they may be, are nevertheless voluntary, and are only paid by the merchant in proportion to the merchandise he buys. And since he buys only in proportion to his sales, he dictates the law to private individuals. But the farmer who, whether he sells or not, is constrained to pay a set price for the land he cultivates, is not the master to wait until the market value of his produce attains the price he wants; and even if he weren't to sell it to support himself, he would be forced to sell it to pay the taille, so that sometimes it is the enormity of the assessment that maintains the produce at a very low price.

Notice, further, that the resources of commerce and industry, far from making the taille more bearable by an abundance of money, only render it more burdensome. I shall not dwell on a very obvious point, namely that although a greater or lesser quantity of money in a State can give it more or less credit externally, it in no way alters the real wealth of the citizens, and does not make them any more or less well off. But I shall make two important remarks. One, that unless the State has surplus foodstuffs and the abundance of money comes from the foreign sale of these, the commercial towns are the only places to enjoy this abundance, and the peasant only becomes relatively poorer. The other, that since the price of all things rises as money multiplies, taxes too must rise proportionately, so that the farmer finds himself more burdened without having more resources.

It should be apparent that the taille on lands is actually a tax on their product. While everyone agrees that nothing is so dangerous as a tax on wheat paid by the buyer, how can it be ignored that the evil is a hundred times worse when this tax is paid by the grower himself? Isn't this attacking the source of the State's subsistence? Isn't it working as directly as possible to depopulate the country, and consequently to ruin it in the long run? For there is no worse scarcity for a nation than that of men.

Only the true statesman is able to raise his sights above the financial objective in setting the tax base, to transform burdensome obligations into useful regulations of public policy, and to make the people wonder whether such establishments have not had as their end the good of the nation rather than the proceeds of taxation.

Duties on the importation of foreign merchandise which the inhabitants are eager to have but which the country does not need; on the exportation of domestic merchandise of which the country has no excess and which foreigners cannot do without; on the productions of frivolous and overly lucrative arts; on the entry into towns of things that are pure amenities and in general on every object of luxury will all fulfill this double purpose. Such taxes, which help the poor and burden the rich, must be used to prevent the continual increase of inequality of fortunes, the subjection to the rich of a multitude of workers and useless servants, the multiplication of idle people in towns, and the desertion of the countryside.

It is important to establish a proportion between the price of things and the duty to be paid on them such that the greediness of private individuals is not too tempted to fraud by the size of profits. Ease of contraband must also be prevented by giving preference to merchandise that is the least easy to hide. Finally, it is appropriate for the tax to be paid by the consumer of the taxed article rather than by the seller, who would have more temptations and means to use fraud due to the number of duties charged to him. This is the normal practice in China, the country in the world where taxes are the heaviest and the best paid. The merchant pays nothing. The buyer alone pays the duty, without giving rise either to protest or sedition, because since the vital foodstuffs, such as rice and wheat, are absolutely exempt, the people is not downtrodden and the tax falls only on those who are well-to-do. Moreover, all these precautions should not be dictated so much by fear of contraband as by the attention the government should give to protecting private individuals from the seduction of illegitimate profits which, after creating bad citizens, would not be long in turning them into dishonest people.

Let high taxes be placed on liveries, on carriages, on mirrors, chandeliers, and furnishings, on cloth and gilding, on the courtyards and gardens of mansions, on theatrical performances of all kinds, on the idle professions such as those of buffoons, singers, or actors, and in short on that mass of objects of luxury, diversion, and idleness that are visible to all, and that can scarcely be hidden because their only use is display and they would be useless if they were not seen. There is no need to worry that the proceeds of such taxes would be unpredictable because they are only based on things that are not absolute necessities. It is a great misunderstanding of men to believe that once seduced by luxury, they can ever renounce it. They would a hundred times sooner renounce necessities, and would prefer to die of hunger rather than of shame. The increased expense will merely be a new reason to sustain it, when the vanity of displaying opulence will benefit from both the price of the object and the expense of taxation. As long as there are rich men, they will want to distinguish themselves from the poor; and the State could not create a less burdensome nor more secure revenue than one based on this distinction.

For the same reason, industry would not suffer in the least from an economic order that enriched public finances, revived agriculture by relieving the farmer, and gradually brought all fortunes closer to that moderation that creates the true force of a State. It could happen, I admit, that these taxes might contribute to making some fashions disappear more rapidly. But this would never occur without the substitution of others from which the worker would profit without any loss to the public treasury. In short, one of two things will happen if we suppose that the government's tendency is constantly to place all taxation on the surplus of wealth. Either the rich will renounce their superfluous expenses in favor of useful ones which will redound to the State's profit. In that case the tax base will have produced the effect of the best sumptuary laws, the expenses of the State will necessarily have diminished along with those of private individuals, and the public treasury could not thereby receive any less without having still less to pay out. Or, if the rich do not diminish their extravagances, the public treasury will have, in the proceeds from taxes, the resources it sought to provide for the real needs of the State. In the first case, the public treasury is enriched by all the reductions in its expenses; in the second, it is likewise enriched by the frivolous expenses of private individuals.

Let us add to all this an important distinction of political right, to which governments, anxious to do everything by themselves, should pay much attention. I have said that since personal taxation and taxes on absolute necessities directly attack the right of property, and consequently the true basis of political society, they are always subject to dangerous consequences if they are not established with the express consent of the people or its representatives.[30] The same does not hold true for duties on things whose use can be forbidden. For then, since the private individual is not absolutely constrained to pay, his contribution can be considered voluntary. So that the private consent of each of the taxpayers replaces the general consent, and even presupposes it in a way. For why would the people be opposed to the assessment of any tax that falls only on anyone who is willing to pay it? It appears certain to me that whatever is neither proscribed by the laws nor contrary to the mores, and that the government can forbid, it can permit subject to the payment of a duty. If, for example, the government can forbid the use of carriages, it can with all the more reason impose a tax on carriages, which is a wise and useful way to blame their use without ending it. Then the tax can be considered as a kind of fine, whose proceeds compensate for the abuse it punishes.

Someone may object that since those whom Bodin calls *imposers*,[31] that is those who impose or invent the forms of taxation, are in the class of the rich, they will not take care to spare others at their own expense and burden themselves in order to relieve the poor. But such ideas must be rejected. If in each nation those to whom the sovereign commits the government of the people were its enemies by definition, there would be no point in seeking what these men should do to make the people happy.

EDITOR'S NOTES

[1]Originally an article in the *Encyclopédie*, Vol. V, pp. 337–349 (which appeared in November 1755), this text was subsequently published—apparently without Rousseau's consent—as *Discourse on Political Economy* (Geneva; Emanuel Du-Villard, 1758). It is generally assumed that Rousseau wrote it after completing the *Second Discourse* in 1754. The notebook containing Rousseau's fragmentary first draft has been deciphered and published (Launay, II, 294–305). Both a citation in this manuscript (Ibid., p. 295, note 152) and explicit references in the final version (see editorial notes 9 and 12 below) indicate that Rousseau knew Diderot's article on *Natural Right;* Diderot's concept of a "general will of the human species" thus seems to have inspired both *Political Economy* and *Geneva Manuscript.* But whereas the latter text explicitly criticizes Diderot's use of the term "general will" (see *Geneva Ms,* I, ii, and editorial notes 8–11), here Rousseau merely accepts the idea of a "general will" and adapts it to his purpose. As Derathé has noted, this difference may result from the focus of *Political Economy,* which is devoted to the administration or execution of laws by the government rather than to the principle underlying sovereignty (Pléiade, III, lxxiv–lxxvii). But in 1754–1755, Diderot was both editor of the *Encyclopédie* and Rousseau's friend; hence, it may simply be that Rousseau sought to avoid an open criticism of Diderot's article in this context. While *Political Economy* is significant as Rousseau's first published exposition speaking of the "general will," it is probably even more important as a presentation of his distinction between the people as "sovereign" and the "government" as executor of the laws. As one editor concluded, "It would hardly be too much to say that the whole political theory of Rousseau, on its more abstract side, was already formed when he wrote the *Économie Politique*" (Vaughan, I, 230). Although there are several passages which appear both in this article and in the *Geneva Manuscript,* it does not follow that the latter was written first; see *Geneva Manuscript,* editorial note 20, and editorial note 3 below.

[2]A cross-reference to the article of this name in the *Encyclopédie.* As Derathé points out (Pléiade, III, 1390), Rousseau himself subsequently presented his own views on "domestic economy" in the novel *Julie, ou la Nouvelle Héloïse,* especially IV, x–xi and V, ii–iii (Pléiade, II, 440–488, 527–585).

³This paragraph, and the four that follow (to " . . . human wisdom has ever made ten men capable of governing their fellow men") also appear in *Geneva MS,* I, v (paragraphs three through seven). It is quite possible that the *Geneva Manuscript* borrowed the already published text of *Political Economy,* and not vice versa (consider Pléiade, III, 1390–1391—note 1 to p. 242). On Rousseau's rejection of paternal authority as a ground for political right, see also *Second Discourse,* Part 2 (ed. Masters, pp. 165–168).

⁴In the posthumous edition of Rousseau's works (1782), the following passage is added at this point: "The power of the father over his children, founded on their private advantage, cannot by its nature extend to the right of life and death; but the sovereign power, which has no other object than the common good, has no other limits than those of the public utility, properly understood: a distinction that I will explain in its proper place." (Pléiade, III, 1390). Rousseau doubtless refers to *Social Contract,* especially II, iv–v; see *Social Contract,* editorial note 50.

⁵On Rousseau's conception of inequality between males and females, compare "Sophie, ou la femme" in *Émile,* V (Pléiade, IV, 692–763), especially pp. 697–698: "When woman complains about the unjust inequality [of duties related to sex] imposed by man, she is wrong; this inequality is not a human institution, or at least it is not the work of prejudice, but of reason: it is appropriate for the one of the two [sexes] to which nature entrusted the deposit of bearing children to answer for it to the other. Without doubt no one is permitted to violate his word, and every unfaithful husband . . . is an unjust and barbarous man. But the unfaithful wife does more, she dissolves the family and breaks all the bonds of nature . . ." On the contrast between Plato's argument for the equality of the sexes and Rousseau's contrary view, see Masters, *Political Philosophy of Rousseau,* pp. 21–27, 98–105.

⁶In the edition of 1782, the last clause was changed to read: " . . . happy, their rights could not come from the same source nor could the same rules of conduct be suited to both" (Pléiade, III, 1391).

⁷In the edition of 1782, this sentence was changed to read: " . . . since Aristotle himself, who adopts it in certain places in his *Politics,* judges it appropriate to criticize it in others." (Pléiade, III, 1392). Compare *Politics,* I, i.1252a (ed. Barker, p. 1)—rejecting the analogy of statesman and father—with I.xii. 1259b (pp. 32–33), III, vi.1278b (pp. 111–113), III, xiv.1285b (pp. 139–140), and *Nicomachean Ethics,* VIII.x. 1160b–1161a (ed. Ostwald, pp. 234–235). The two critics of Filmer mentioned in the preceding sentence are John Locke (*First Treatise of Government*) and Algernon Sidney (*Discourse Concerning Government*).

⁸Rousseau refers to articles which were to appear in subsequent volumes of the *Encyclopédie.* But since Diderot did not complete the editorial work on this immense project until 1761, and the volumes at the end of the alphabet weren't published until 1765–1766, it is not clear whether Rousseau referred to manuscripts of the entries under *Politics* and *Sovereignty,* or simply anticipated their inclusion. On the importance of Rousseau's distinction between the government and the sovereign, see *Social Contract,* III, i, and editorial note 68, as well as Introduction, pp. 14–24. For the "common comparison" in the next paragraphs, compare *Social Contract,* III, xi; and Hobbes, *Leviathan,* Author's Introduction (ed. Oakeshott, p. 5).

⁹Rousseau here refers to Diderot's article on *Natural Right,* published along with his own article in Volume V of the *Encyclopédie,* as the "source" of his concept of the "general will." Rousseau, however, modifies Diderot's conception in a fundamental way: compare Introduction, pp. 15–17 and *Geneva Manuscript,* I, ii, especially editorial notes 8, 10, and 11 citing Diderot. For the full French text of *Natural Right,* see Vaughan, I, 429–433. Some commentators have questioned whether Rousseau was

238   *Political Economy*

actually inspired to use the term "general will" by Diderot (Pléiade, III, 1394–1395). It is, however, perfectly plausible—especially since this sentence was deleted from the editions of 1758 and 1782 (Vaughan, I, 242), presumably reflecting Rousseau's break with Diderot. On Rousseau's relations with Diderot, see the balanced account in Arthur M. Wilson's remarkable *Diderot* (New York: Oxford University Press, 1972).

[10]On the "group theory" of politics presented in the foregoing paragraph, see Introduction, pp. 21–23, and *Social Contract*, III, ii. Rousseau's conclusion that "the voice of the people is in fact the voice of God" (*vox populi vox dei*) is more than a restatement of the old Roman precept; it also reflects Rousseau's rejection of any revealed religion which presumes that God speaks to some individuals rather than to others. In effect, according to Rousseau's personal religion, "It is to be believed that particular events are nothing in the eyes of the master of the universe; that his providence is solely universal; that he contents himself with conserving genera and species and with presiding over the whole, without disquieting himself concerning the manner in which each individual uses this short life." Letter to Voltaire, August 18, 1756 (cited in Masters, *Political Philosophy of Rousseau*, pp. 68–69). See also the second part of the "Profession of Faith of the Savoyard Vicar," *Émile*, IV (Pléiade, IV, 607–635).

[11]Compare Cicero, *De Re Publica*, I.xxvii. 43–xxviii.44 (ed. Keyes, pp. 69–71); *Second Discourse*, Dedication (ed. Masters, p. 82); and *Social Contract*, III, iii, especially editorial note 79.

[12]Diderot had written: "Alas, virtue is so beautiful that thieves respect its image even deep within their hideouts." (Vaughan, I, 433). In the posthumous edition of 1782, the paranthetical reference to Diderot's article on *Natural Right* was deleted (Vaughan, I, 244); compare editorial note 9 above.

[13]For Rousseau's judgment of Machiavelli, see *Social Contract*, III, vi.

[14]The following passage, up to the words " . . . and not to be in contradiction with himself," appears in *Geneva Manuscript*, I, vii (pp. 177–178). Note especially the phrase "to force them to punish themselves when they do what they did not want" and compare *Social Contract*, I, vii and editorial note 37.

[15]Plato, *Laws*, IV.719e–724a. On the ineffectiveness of punishment, compare *Second Discourse*, Part 2 (ed. Masters, pp. 172–173); *Social Contract*, II, v; and the educational proposals in *Émile*, II (Pléiade, IV, 299–324, 335, et passim). Rousseau's critical remarks in this paragraph can also be read, however, as an attack on the legal procedures of the *ancien régime*. As an example of what Rousseau may have had in mind, consider the following account of the famous Calas case, which occurred a few years later: "Marc-Antoine Calas, a member of a devout Huguenot family in Toulouse, was a moody young man who met a violent death, almost certainly by his own hand. The authorities persisted in the attempt to prove that he had been a secret convert to Catholicism, for which, they alleged, he was murdered by his fanatical Calvinist family. As a result the father, Jean Calas, a man sixty-four years old, was adjudged guilty and on 9 March 1762 was broken on the wheel and then strangled by the public executioner. Research has now revealed that the outburst of fear and hysteria that led to the tragedy of Calas was really caused by apprehension in Toulouse lest the Calvinists take advantage of the Seven Years' War in order to revolt." Wilson, *Diderot*, p. 441.

[16]Compare *Social Contract*, II, vii–xi and III, viii. On the word "mores" (manners, morals, and customs), used to translate the French *moeurs*, see editorial note 128 to the *Social Contract*.

[17]Compare *Social Contract*, II, iii, and Introduction, pp. 19–20.

[18]Rousseau's emphasis on "virtue" in the *First Discourse* often seems to suffer from

the absence of any definition of the term beyond the remark that it is "the strength and vigor of the soul" (Part I [ed. Masters, p. 37]). The definition offered here could thus be seen as the link between Rousseau's attack on the moderns in the *Discourses* and the presentation of his own political principles in the *Social Contract*. Compare *Geneva Manuscript*, I, iv: "the habit that disposes us to practice these acts [that contribute to the greatest good], even to our own disadvantage, is what is called force or virtue."

[19]At this point, the edition of 1782 adds a quotation from St. Augustine's Letters: " 'Sicuti enim est aliquando misericordia puniens, ita est crudelita parcens' *Aug. Epist.* 54." (Pléiade, III, 1397). "Just as sometimes pity can punish, so cruelty can pardon."

[20]Rousseau here alludes to Cato's suicide (which had been criticized by some modern writers—including Montesquieu). The comparison between Socrates and Cato, developed in this paragraph, was apparently of considerable importance to Rousseau, as is shown by some recently published manuscripts in which he compares the two. See Claude Pichois and René Pintard, *Jean-Jacques entre Socrate et Caton* (Paris: José Corti, 1972), especially, pp. 97–99.

[21]So much for the charge that Rousseau was a totalitarian. On the role of patriotism, see *Considerations on the Government of Poland*, especially chap. III (ed. Watkins, pp. 167–176) and *Constitutional Project for Corsica*, Part 1 (ed. Watkins, pp. 280–281). These two works are very useful to compare to *Political Economy*, since they provide concrete instances of Rousseau's application of his own thought to what is today called "public policy."

[22]At this point, the text in the *Encyclopédie* adds: "See EDUCATION." However, an erratum to Volume V indicated that the cross-reference should be deleted, and it does not appear in the edition of 1758 (Pléiade, III, 1402). Rousseau's stress on public education is all the more remarkable, since such educational systems did not generally exist until the nineteenth century. On public education, see *Considerations on the Government of Poland*, chap. IV (ed. Watkins, pp. 176–181); *Émile*, I (Pléiade, IV, 250–251); and *First Discourse*, Part 2, note (ed. Masters, pp. 57–58).

[23]"Since the things that can become property are only useful to men while they are alive and since the dead have no more role in the affairs of this world, it was not necessary for the establishment of property to extend to giving the owner the right to choose whom he wants to succeed to the goods he leaves on dying. It was sufficient that each dispose of his goods during his life, leaving to those who survive him the care of doing what they would judge appropriate when he was no longer alive." Pufendorf, *Droit de la Nature et des Gens*, IV, x, § 4 (cited in Pléiade, III, 1403).

[24]"There are seven ways in general to get money for public finances, in which are included all that can be imagined . . . As to the first, which is public domain, it seems to be the most honest and most assured of all." Bodin, *Les six livres de la République* (cited in Pléiade, III, 1404). On the responsibility of the "founder of a republic" to establish public revenues, compare *Social Contract*, II, vii.

[25]"It nourishes and enriches." As Derathé points out, Rousseau's position is the opposite of the "physiocrats" like Quesnay, who favored free trade instead of public granaries (Pléiade, III, 1404–1405). On Rousseau's attitude toward Geneva, see *Social Contract*, editorial note 7.

[26]In the edition of 1758 and thereafter, Rousseau adds: "It was only at the seige of the Veii that the Roman infantry began to be paid." (Pléiade, III, 1405). On Rousseau's preference for a citizen army—and his hostility to mercenaries, compare Machiavelli, *The Prince*, chap. xiii (ed. Musa, pp. 111–117); *Social Contract*, III, xv; *Considerations on the Government of Poland*, Chapter XII (ed. Watkins, pp. 236–245); and especially *Dernière Réponse* (Pléiade, III, 82): "War is sometimes a duty and is not made to be a profession. Every man should be a soldier to defend his freedom, none should be

one to invade the freedom of others; and to die while serving one's homeland is too noble a function to confide to mercenaries."

[27]See Bodin, *Les six livres de la République,* VI, ii (cited Pléiade, III, 1406). The first draft of this passage reads: "This truth that taxes cannot be established—legitimately—except by the consent of the people or its representatives has been generally acknowledged by all the—philosophers and—legal theorists (such as Grotius—Locke—Pufendorf) who have acquired any reputation in matters of political right, (if there are any) *some like Bodin* have (given the prince the right to raise taxes on his authority . . .) established maxims that appear contrary . . . " (Launay, II, 304). Note that in both the draft and final text, Rousseau uses the phrase "the people or its representatives," and compare *Social Contract,* III, xv, and editorial note 105.

[28]"The tax by head is most natural to slavery; the tax on merchandise is most natural to freedom, because it is related in a less direct manner to the individual person." *L'Esprit des Lois,* XIII, xiv (ed. Caillois, p. 467). As Derathé points out (Pléiade, III, 1406–1407), Rousseau twists Montesquieu's preference for indirect taxation by substituting "property taxation *(la taxe réelle)*" for Montesquieu's "the tax on merchandise *(l'impôt sur les marchandises)*." More broadly, it is of interest to compare Montesquieu's argument throughout Book XIII with *Political Economy*—and especially with Rousseau's proposal for a progressive income tax in the following passage.

[29]Rousseau refers to Chardin's *Voyages en Perse* (4 vols.; Amsterdam, 1735)—a work which he cites at length in *Social Contract,* III, viii. On Herodotus, see *Histories,* III. 89: Darius, after becoming King, "divided his dominions into twenty governments, called by the Persians satrapies; and doing so and appointing governors, he ordained that each several nation should pay him tribute . . . In the reigns of Cyrus and Cambyses after him there was no fixed tribute, but payment was made in gifts. It is by reason of this fixing of tribute, and other like ordinances, that the Persians called Darius the huckster, Cambyses the master, and Cyrus the father; for Darius made a petty profit out of everything, Cambyses was harsh and arrogant, Cyrus was merciful and ever wrought for their well-being." Trans. A. D. Godley 4 vols. (London: Loeb Classical Library, 1921), II, 117. Rousseau's apparently innocent citation is thus an implicit criticism of monarchy and empire.

[30]Compare *Political Economy,* editorial note 27, and the references there cited.

[31]Rousseau again refers to Bodin, *Les six livres de la République,* VI, ii: "Thus most imposers and inventors of new taxes have lost their lives at it" (cited Pléiade, III, 1409). As one critic has put it, this last paragraph "is a finished piece of irony" (Vaughan, I, 273).

INDEX